Pass
Both Your
Driving Tests

D1428531

Pass
Both Your
Driving
Tests

by

A. Tom Topper

Contents

Introduction

PASS BOTH YOUR DRIVING TESTS draws together the complete picture needed to pass your car Driving Tests with ease. It goes well beyond the basic, simple Test syllabuses. My fervent hope is that by so doing it will also instil the advanced, safety thinking – the planned avoidance of danger (sometimes known as defensive driving) – that saves lives and should become your foundation for a lifelong, accident-free driving career.

Despite being able to drive becoming almost universally desirable, there exists no irrevocable "right" for anyone to keep their full licence once it has been awarded. It remains always a *privilege*; one continuously needing to be cherished and "earned" by safe, courteous and considerate conduct on the road, whatever the conditions, whatever your mood.

There is, incidentally, no such thing as "road rage". This media-bred term somehow implies a degree of self-justification. But you must discipline your mind; for there can be none. Drivers who neither tolerate reasonable give-and-take nor other (human) driver error, without "going ballistic", display uncontrolled savagery – no more, no less. If your teacher (or your mentor) shows any such symptoms – get a new one! If any rising anger is getting the better of *you*, stop driving until you have regained your composure.

Inexperienced drivers are the participants in a disproportionately high share of road accidents. It is not only the oft-blamed recklessness or exuberance of youth (especially male youth) that has been identified; it is simple lack of experience that seems to be the deciding factor. That being said, 17–25 year olds – perhaps because they are such a large proportion among learners anyway – are, statistically, way out in front in the accident league tables. Statistics *also* make conspicuous that it is those most often picked up for wild driving offences – such as reckless speeding or jumping red traffic lights – those who deliberately flaunt their bravado in breaking the rules within their first few, fully licenced, years, who, likewise, turn out to predominate in the severe accident records. If you have friends like that, you won't need enemies . . . don't drive with them!

I have written PASS BOTH YOUR DRIVING TESTS so as to complement the teaching of paid, professional Approved Driving Instructors (ADIs) as most learners will want to have at least some professional instruction. Nevertheless, my book starts you literally from scratch.

Because it maps out in logical order *everything* you are expected to know to pass both your two-part Theory and your Practical Tests, it makes it possible for you to do so solely with the help of amateur (i.e. unpaid) teaching, given by a parent or friend. (As I will reiterate in Chapter 1, however, such a person needs to have a considerable, and proven, aptitude for safe driving, and you will be wise to ensure his credentials also include a genuine knack for teaching.)

Whereas a professional instructor may, with dual controls, safely move you on to on-road driving earlier (and would probably expect so to do), with an amateur teacher it makes much more sense to crack absolute, safe handling of your car first – *long before heading near traffic*.

Therefore, my opening chapters make your initial target the achievement of first-class car control on an OPEN SPACE, rather than on public roads. Chapters 3 and 4 concentrate on sewing up the Multiple Choice Questions part of your Theory Test. From Chapter 5 you progress to open road driving but, before you do, you need to read all the remaining chapters. This is because you need first to absorb driving theory, both widely and in context. All the later chapters are written with that express purpose as well as being designed to tune your mentality perfectly for the Hazard Perception part of your Theory Test.

IN THEORY

You must reach the separate pass marks in both parts of the computer-screen-presented Theory Test in one sitting, in order to pass overall. You are given – *and should take* – every opportunity to familiarise yourself with what is required before doing each part; they are separated by a brief interval.

In the Multiple Choice (first) part you touch your screen to confirm the right answers; you can return to any answers for which you may want more time to think, by touching navigation "buttons" along the bottom of your screen. Pay attention to what each one does.

In the Hazard Perception (second) part you flag *developing* hazards on video clips by clicking your computer mouse directly you first see them. Use the headphones supplied to listen to the explanation of a sample clip which you can watch twice. Although some of your Test clips will have more than one hazard to flag, you can only have one go at each clip. Each hazard is scored out of 5 marks according to how quickly you respond. Every mouse click registers with a flag appearing at the bottom of the screen. Your score for a clip will be zeroed if you click absurdly often but don't be afraid to click again if a situation seems to worsen or you recognise another hazard.

Watch the screen from a comfortable distance, remembering that you are now the *cameraman's* driver. (Avoid trying to "drive" any vehicle ahead.) The shortcomings of film make it difficult to judge your own speed and distance, especially on a night-time clip; however, you can sense it better if you keep half an eye on the outer edges of the picture. This may give you a clue that the film crew driver is already losing speed.

Hazards which count are events that demand you react to avoid or at least to reduce the risk of any potential collision danger. Most usually this would be by slowing or stopping or changing your positioning. They develop from changing road conditions or weather, or through the movement, or a change of direction or the likelihood thereof, of *any other road user* – whether or not he may yet be in full view or driving or behaving correctly.

Thus, vehicles passing by in the opposite direction are not in themselves hazards but a deep puddle on his side which an approaching driver may wrongly swing out towards you to get round, *is* a developing hazard – unless/until you see he will wait for you instead; a bus pulling in to its stop across the road combined with a pedestrian hurrying on your nearside pavement, suggests that he may well try and dash over to catch it; walkers will typically step into the road outside parked cars just to avoid a deep snowdrift blocking their pavement; having noted in the far distance on a single carriageway an oncoming driver pulling out onto your side to overtake a slower vehicle among the approaching stream, you shortly realise he has left himself neither time nor room enough to get back to his own side – so you must slash your own speed to make them for him; animals, loose or otherwise, always add risk; and so on.

The earlier in their development that you perceive and flag *the need to react to the hazard(s) in each clip, the higher your total score will be.*

Other examples: with a minor road to your left shortly ahead, you notice an oncoming motorcyclist a little further away and whom you suspect has the sun in his eyes, snatch a glance over his shoulder – might this foretell his swinging across your bows to turn right? You need to edge out to confirm whether you can overtake a caravan before oncoming traffic denies the opportunity, when your mirrors fleetingly show a motorcyclist spurt out and move up to within two spaces behind you – be warned that any such move might coincide with his next burst of impatience; an innocent looking queue waiting to emerge from a side road often conceals on its far side the sort of pedal cyclist who habitually ignores Give Way markings, spinning out in front of your wheels; anyone cutting-in in front forces you to slacken speed to regain an adequate following distance; note the difference between a lone "lollipop" school crossing patrol and one with children milling around; you are about to pass to the left of a low-loader which is aligned to turn right, when you spot a "risk of grounding" symbol across that arm of the local direction sign – dare you risk being squeezed if he now abandons his turn . . .?

On sex it may be politically correct to convolute the English language but I prefer to believe that, rather than have me mutilate words like *man*hole cover the whole time, my readers, sensibly, will twig that for *he,* I also mean *she* and vice versa.

I salute Tim Barnard for his vision, patience and skill in producing the illustrations which so ably enhance my text.

Good luck with your Tests! After passing, I hope you will become enthused by your success and newly won freedom, to carry on improving your driving, mile-by-mile, for as long as you continue to drive. Do join me in this, if you wish, by reading my book **VERY ADVANCED DRIVING**, published inexpensively by Elliot Right Way Books in their *Right Way* series and available from good second-hand bookshops or on the Internet. The book will set you *thinking* anew [about your driving] as you seek to build [and cherish] the lifelong good, safe driving record for which we all must aim.   A. Tom Topper

Car Handling

1

Beginning In The Right Order

The priceless bonus for beginning your driving career in the right order as this book shows will be calm confidence and understanding of what to do in virtually all situations, tricky or otherwise, once you drive out further on our congested roads.

Meanwhile your first Practical Test task is to master control of the car. You can – and I am sure will want to – be preparing for your Theory Test (which has to be the first one passed) at the same time. I will return to this in a moment. If you are learning with an amateur teacher then, as explained in my Introduction, by far the best way so far as car control is concerned is for this to be complete *before* you head for the open road. If you are learning with a professional instructor, the detailed explanations here will nonetheless be immensely valuable in consolidating your understanding. You need at least to read them through so as not to miss out any vital information.

I divide this *beginning*, Practical stage into three. I urge you to be patient; wait until you have *all of the stages* mastered *before* you move on to **DRIVING IN PRACTICE**, from Chapter 5 onwards. There will be time enough for practical driving, then, once you have absorbed all you need to read, and this should avoid any danger, when you do venture out amongst traffic, of coming to grief through ignorance.

STAGE ONE is to familiarise yourself with the controls – not to try to drive.

STAGE TWO is OPEN SPACE PRACTICE. You need with your teacher to find a quiet open space and learn in safety to start smoothly, to stop (including being introduced to emergency stops), to steer, to change gear, to reverse and so on. Good places for this are worth seeking out; quiet empty car parks, disused air-strips, or dry fields (with farmer's permission) are examples. Failing these, choose a quiet area of side roads as do good driving schools. You don't want to inconvenience hordes of other traffic (also making your job harder) and you must avoid danger to children. Your teacher should drive there.

STAGE THREE is to learn proficiently to carry out the manoeuvring control tests, any two of which the examiner can be expected to give you on your Practical Driving Test: these are the **Three-Point-Turn**, the **Reverse Round A Corner** and **Reverse (Parallel) Parking**. It also includes becoming master of **Steep Hill** starts, both uphill and downhill. Your teacher should select suitable, quiet locations for gaining each of these essential skills. Again, initially, he should always drive there.

Beginning with the above three stages – in order – *is the safest way to learn to drive*. Believe me, when you move on to the open road, the knowledge that you have already reached the Practical Test standard in *car control* becomes very reassuring. It sets you free to concentrate on traffic situations, undistracted by worry about how to handle the car.

On the same score, one of the first things you should do then is to look again at Emergency Stops. Do some more, this time from faster speeds than before, to consolidate that work before any unexpected emergency can catch you unawares.

LEGALITIES (see also page 18 FOREIGN LICENCES AND RESIDENCY)

Before you can take the wheel of a car AT ALL *on any public road* you have to be at least 17 years old – or 16 if you are in receipt of a mobility allowance. You must have in your possession a current, Great Britain or Northern Ireland issued, provisional photocard driving licence. Application forms **D1** (or **DL1**) *and* **D750** can be obtained at most post offices. I repeat, you cannot drive on public roads until you have *received* your provisional licence. Understand, too, that a photocard provisional or full driving licence is defined in law as having two parts – the plastic photocard and the paper *counterpart*. When required to produce your licence you must have BOTH available. Study all the information sent to you with your licence. (**Note:** Full licences for certain other

12

categories of vehicle can be used as a substitute provisional car driving licence. If so, this fact should be clearly stated thereon.) You must display standard-size red **L** plates front and back (properly – not just stuck in the windows blocking your view). Within Wales you may use red **D** plates if you prefer. Your car must be insured for you, have an MOT test pass certificate if more than three years old and display a current, valid, tax disc, face-forward in the bottom left corner of its front windscreen (or a 'nil' licence if exempt from tax). You should also know whereabouts you could place your hands on the Registration Document (logbook); every car has to have one. You have to have a qualified driver, aged 21 or over, who has held a full EC/EEA car driving licence for at least the last three years, to supervise and guide you.

It is essential that the insurance Policy and Certificate are endorsed if that is necessary to cover you as a **L***earner; it may cost a lot extra, especially if you are young, but to drive without proper cover is illegal.* An in-date insurance Certificate (or a temporary Cover Note), specifying the vehicle concerned, is the legal document required before you can drive or tax that vehicle. Make sure a full annual Certificate arrives before any Cover Note expires.

You should also understand that your insurance policy could become invalidated if you knowingly (or, for that matter, *un*knowingly), or deliberately, drive an unroadworthy vehicle (for examples, one having a defective tyre, or one over three years old but without a valid, in-date, annual MOT certificate), or if you are unfit through drink or drug, etc. (In Northern Ireland, MOTs are required only after 4 years.) Alternatively, your insurance company may pay out for an accident and then sue you. Either way you could lose your all and be bankrupted – a horrifying prospect which could ruin your life for many years.

You *must* wear your glasses or contact lenses if you need them. (Your examiner will check whether you can read a car number plate having 50 mm characters, at a minimum of 20 metres away.) Some types of eye surgery have to be declared to the Driver and Vehicle Licensing Agency. Look into this if it may apply to you.

You must know the basic "rules of the road" from the Highway Code *before* you ever drive on public roads. That learning will need to be reinforced as your lessons progress –

to the degree that you become an "authority" on the Code generally, and on such subjects therein as signs and road markings, documents, vehicle maintenance, safety and security and First Aid, well before your Theory Test.

As a new driver – whatever your age – be warned that you can now lose your licence under the penalty points system for new drivers explained in the Highway Code. If six or more points are endorsed on your licence in your first two years as a fully fledged driver, you can be faced with going back to L plates and having both to re-pass your Theory Test and then take an extended, seventy-minute, much more expensive, Practical Test which allows the examiner a greater opportunity to assess accurately your attitude to driving and the degree, or lack thereof, of your ability to maintain full concentration.

Thereafter you can still be forced, by the Courts, into a return to L plates and to have to take both another Theory Test and an extended Practical Test. They can impose such a penalty if you are convicted of dangerous driving or any other disqualification-designated driving offence. For lesser, though endorsable, "crimes", they can also put you back through both hoops but demanding only a normal length Practical Test instead. Either way, of course, you cannot start driving on L plates again until any period of disqualification is up.

A GOOD TEACHER
Driving schools live by *local* reputation. In choosing a professional instructor it's best to seek out a *named individual* known to be good. Quite rightly, *any* experienced qualified driver (as above) may also teach you, though none may charge for Practical driving lessons who have not also passed the government ADI (Approved Driving Instructor) test. Thus friends and relatives are equally able to provide you with the necessary one-to-one instruction. Many of them, particularly those with long accident-free mileages to their credit, do so supremely well. Indeed, despite years of incessant bleating from those with a vested interest in paid driving instruction, there remains no evidence that the professionals achieve any better Practical Test pass rate. For most Learners, however, a combination of driving school lessons *and* practice with family or friends suits best. It makes gaining the necessary amount of experience behind the wheel for a pass more affordable.

WHEN TO TAKE YOUR THEORY TEST

My strongest advice would be wait until you have studied the whole of this book. By then you should have competent CAR HANDLING of my **STAGES ONE**, **TWO**, and **THREE** well in hand, know the Highway Code and your DRIVING THEORY "backwards", and be well advanced with your Hazard Perception. In all probability, your actual driving on the open road will already be progressing nicely, including having had some of your practical lessons after dark.

Theory Tests are set shortly to allow an ample 57 minutes to answer 50 multiple-choice questions, of which you must get 43 right. The Hazard Perception part follows. It takes about 20 minutes to view 14 separate video clips. These contain a total of 15 hazards, each to be flagged *as it develops*. (One of them has two.) From 5 marks allowed for each hazard the current pass mark is 44 out of a possible 75. The two-part Theory Test can usually be taken at a convenient time and in a nearby location across the country. To find out where there is one which would suit you, and to obtain an application form and/or book, contact your nearest Driving Standards Agency (DSA) driving Test centre. If that is not easily located via your local phone book, there is a nationwide telephone "help" and booking line on 0870 01 01 372. (In Northern Ireland call 0845 600 6700.) Alternatively, at **www.dsa.gov.uk**, you can book online or print off an application form for faxing or posting. If you already hold a Theory Test pass certificate in connection with some different category of vehicle driving/riding licence, you may not need to take another Theory Test. Check with the driving Test centre as above. If you are dyslexic or do not speak/read English, make enquiries via the "help" line. Arrangements can be made to cover most such difficulties; for example, a translation via a headset may be available.

Remember, when you go to sit your Theory Test, that you can be turned away and forfeit your fee if you forget to take with you

1) *your booking appointment number confirmation*

2) *your Plastic Photocard carrying your signature* **and** its original, signed *Paper Counterpart* Provisional Licence.

Note: you can neither book nor take your Theory Test until you have your valid, signed, in date, licence. If, unusually, yours is not of the photocard type (for example, it may be foreign and from outside the EC/EEA) you will need with you instead, your current, valid passport – which needn't be British. Photo-card licences (or the passport where necessary) provide your ID. No other identification will do, except in Northern Ireland – for which check on the phone number on the previous page.

WHEN TO TAKE YOUR PRACTICAL TEST
A Practical Driving Test failed, taken too early, is both expensive and disappointing. Wait until *you* feel confident and relaxed at the wheel, have the measure of all this book says and your teacher no longer needs to remind you of anything basic. That will be soon enough to book up. Continue your lessons whilst waiting, to hone the "edge" a pass demands.

You cannot book your Practical Driving Test until you have your Theory Test pass certificate. You need its number, and – for the test itself – YOU HAVE TO TAKE IT WITH YOU. (Assuming success, you are given your Theory Test pass certificate before you depart from the Theory exam centre.)

Book your Practical Test using application form **DL26**, which you can get from any DSA office or driving test centre. (See **Theory Test** section above.) Alternatively, if you are prepared to pay by credit or debit card, you can book by telephone on the DSA "help" and booking line 0870 01 01 372. You can also print off a Practical Test application form for faxing or posting, at **www.dsa.gov.uk**. You can request a Practical Test appointment outside normal working hours (at a higher fee). You may also sometimes be given an earlier date than otherwise, provided you are able to take your Practical Test at short notice. Incidentally, you must take your Practical Test within two years of your Theory Test pass or you have to take another Theory Test first.

DRIVER'S RECORD
The DSA encourages you and your teacher *voluntarily* to log your progress, particularly towards your Practical Test. Forms, guidance and checklists are available at **www.dsa.gov.uk** to print off. These summarise what you need to know and to be able to do, and enable your teacher to "grade" you and sign a declaration when you are "ready". The examiner may ask you for this and your log; however, not before deciding whether you pass. That would be immoral. They are no pass guarantee!

SEAT BELTS AND OTHER MATTERS

By Law you MUST wear your seat belt. Remind other adults. You, as driver, are also legally *liable* for any child passenger under 14.

An infant under 3 MUST travel instead in a **baby seat** – until about 9 months old, or heavy and strong enough to be restrained by a **child seat** of appropriate size – which, likewise, he MUST be in when driven. *Baby seats face the back. So the law PROHIBITS securing one in a vehicle front seat having air-bag protection in place* – a potentially fatal combination. Consult your vehicle handbook before deciding whether to put baby there. The **child seat**, like the baby one, has its own integral body harness but faces forward. Again, a front air-bag may threaten danger for a child; so do check. Assume nothing about safety risks.

Your legal liability for kids over 3, whether in the front or back of the car, continues right up through the **booster seat/cushion** stage(s) until they become 14. The rules, in the Highway Code (with some back-seat exceptions), vary according firstly to the height – *and weight* – and then the age of each child. Makers of **baby seats**, **child seats**, **child booster seats**, and **booster cushions** all advise on their body-weight limits and instruct how each has to be secured by the vehicle seat belt.

Once the **child seat** is outgrown he MUST use a **child booster seat** or **cushion**, and the vehicle seat belt MUST harness him correctly, as well as securing the unit properly, up until he is 12 – unless he is already over 4ft. 5ins. tall; from then he MUST use an adult seat belt, just as when grown up (here defined as 14 up). The Highway Code urges use of child safety door-locks and control of children.

Unrestrained rear-seat passengers, flung forward in an accident may, apart from severe injury to themselves, easily cause the death of their driver or a front seat passenger. In Court a vehicle occupant not wearing a seat belt may be judged to blame for some of the *consequences* and suffer a reduced injury claim.

Head restraints (they are NOT rests!) are to prevent or reduce whiplash injury in a "shunt". Re-set for each occupier with the topmost part at least at own-eye level. Examiners notice!

Apart from your own potential loss you carry responsibility in the fight against theft, and joy-riding and its very public danger. Conceal valuables; lock up; set any anti-theft or tracker device *whenever* you leave your car, as urged by the Highway Code.

An examiner will expect you to uphold the Highway Code s*pirit* of unfailing courtesy and consideration toward other road users.

Learners who pass their Practical Test with automatic gears are restricted to automatics. Their licence is valid as a *provisional* manual transmission licence but another Practical Test with a manual gearbox is needed to up-grade. (You don't have to retake your Theory Test but the opposite does not apply; so the more flexible, manual-gearbox option is the majority choice). Refer for automatics to page 80; BUT *you must still study all Chapter 2* first, to understand manual-gearbox control and absorb other essentials and techniques which space precludes repeating there.

The registered keeper, named in its Registration Document/ logbook, must inform the Driver Vehicle Licensing Agency, using a SORN (Statutory Off Road Notification) *every twelve months*, if that vehicle is kept, untaxed, off public roads. Check on a logbook for this and other law you have to know for your Theory Test. Learners need not (beyond a touch of Theory) go in for towing! Beyond the tiniest trailer further Tests/licences are required anyway; as there are to drive a minibus or medium-size goods vehicle, for example; so always check your licence allows for what you plan to drive.

FOREIGN LICENCES AND RESIDENCY

A full current/only recently expired EC/EEA licence or one from certain designated countries, should be exchangeable for a full British licence. Holders need not pass our Theory or Practical tests. You can check with our licence authority (DVLA) on 0870 240 0009. Full, valid, in date licences from all other countries allow you to drive in Britain for 12 months. After that you MUST take both our tests. You can apply for a provisional British licence *early* to facilitate this. Otherwise, from then on, you can only drive accompanied – as must any *learner* here – until you have passed them. (See LEGALITIES page 12.) New residents from EC/EEA countries (though not elsewhere) applying for a provisional photocard licence may not apply for either test until resident here more than 185 days.

2

Master Car Control

HOW TO SIT

HOLDING THE WHEEL
Figs. 1 and 9 show you how to hold the steering wheel. Keep
your thumbs towards being along the inside surface and grip
lightly around the wheel-rim with your fingers.

ADJUSTING and SECURING THE DRIVING SEAT
With the seat adjusted properly, your knees and elbows will be
roughly half bent. You will find that you can easily depress
any of the foot pedals to its *fullest extent*. The gear lever will
be comfortably to hand.

The clutch foot pedal is the lefthand one of the three. Perfect
clutch control is essential for a **Smooth Start From Standing**,
as will soon be explained. The art of gaining it is to make sure,
whilst you use the clutch pedal during this process, that your
left heel *remains on the floor*, where it can act as a pivot. Bear
that in mind as you adjust the seat. Otherwise **Smooth Start**
clutch control will have to come from your thigh muscles
which is much more difficult. Never drive in sling-back,
high-heeled shoes, flip-flops or loose-fitting, open-toed san-
dals, etc. Safety demands the positive feel of well-fitting
shoes.

It is dangerous to sit slumped in the seat with outstretched
legs. You lose forward vision, especially near the car. You
distort your impressions of distance. If you have to brake hard
you may lack the ability; your leg already being too straight.
Short people may need a fitted seat cushion or a properly made

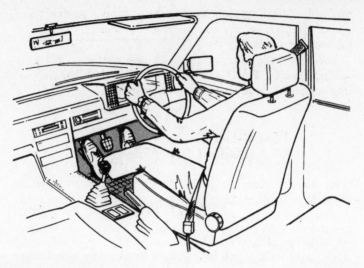

Fig 1 How to sit.

backrest in order to sit up properly. In some cars an adjustable steering wheel position helps solve any problems. Be *sure* to lock it after a change.

Make *certain* that your seat is secure after adjustment. Were it to slide back, spring up or drop down as you braked, your push on the footbrake could be ineffective – a potential killer.

Always wear loose-fitting clothing so that you are comfortable, at ease, and unrestricted.

HOW TO ADJUST THE MIRRORS

Fig. 2 shows proper mirrors' coverage. Sitting normally, with the car on level ground, your centre mirror should capture the view through the whole back window. Check how the anti-dazzle setting works if this mirror has one. Each door mirror adds to that view immediately alongside and behind the car, as shown. Aim them parallel with level ground to maximise distance seen. Note how the "blind" areas (shaded) cannot be covered. Vehicles often remain hidden almost alongside you (though slightly behind) during considerable distances of travel – even big lorries. To your front, substantial dangerous blind spots are caused by the roof pillars. Tall people may find that a similar problem, and one of which it is very important to be aware, is caused by the interior mirror.

There is little point in adjusting any mirror unless it is spotlessly clean. Treat them like the family silver. Let haze or fingerprints blot out your view at your peril.

FINDING THE CONTROLS BY TOUCH AND FEEL

With the car adjusted for *you*, your next task in **STAGE ONE** is to understand the *main* controls; then to practise working them *without running the engine* and WITHOUT LOOKING DOWN. To start with, your teacher should show you how. Then you can further practise this familiarisation on your own – but make sure that the car is parked in a safe place and that you never let the handbrake off unless you have the footbrake on and a gear engaged! Make no attempt actually to start the engine. You would be responsible for a runaway car. It is wise to chock one pair of wheels as an extra safety precaution.

This in-car preparation will be of tremendous benefit later,

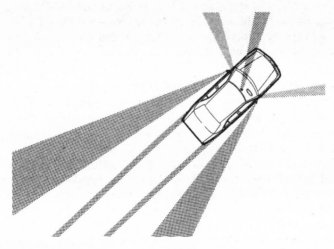

Fig 2 Adjusting the mirrors for maximum vision.

because muscles and reactions become experienced and get "into the groove".

As well as getting used to operating the foot pedals, gears, handbrake and sun visor, you must also become expert at quickly finding and working the important switches – all the lights, headlamp dipswitch, wipers, windscreen washers, horn, flashing indicators, heating/demisting controls, and so on – *by touch or feel*. You must also know what each dashboard warning light means so that you can recognise any of them on sight.

Many drivers would still have an unblemished driving record if they had learned to keep their eyes on the road. If a cyclist looks down at his front wheel he soon hits something. Pain and twisted front wheels teach him to take a longer view. Apart from an occasional (and quick!) instrument or warning lamp check you must *never look down*.

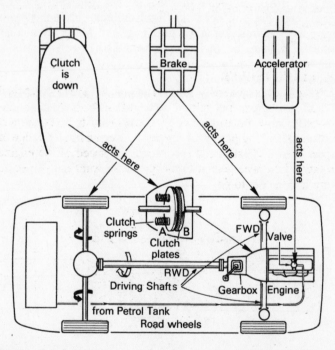

Fig 3 How the foot pedals control the car. The footbrake acts on all wheels at once.

THE FOOT PEDALS

They are, from your left: the clutch, brake (usually similar in appearance) and accelerator or gas pedal. The gas and brake pedals are used with the *right* foot, the clutch with the *left*.

Fig. 3 illustrates the use of each pedal. The clutch is further explained shortly.

WHAT THE ACCELERATOR DOES

To drive the car at varying speeds the engine must be fed accordingly with the right amount of fuel at all times. Extra power demands extra fuel and vice versa. A regulating "valve" between the petrol tank and the engine is therefore provided. This may be a carburettor, or fuel-injection may be used. Either way it is controlled by the accelerator (or gas) pedal. The pedal is spring-loaded so that it will return the engine to the lowest possible speed ("ticking over") whenever your foot is off it. The light spring-loading against your foot makes it easy to maintain any constant speed or to speed up or slow down, at will.

PULLING POWER

Engine speeds generally range from about 1,000 to around 6,500 revolutions per minute (rpm). Fig. 4 shows diagrammatically how the average engine only gives its best and most economic pulling power (or torque) between a limited range of rpm. In order best to use this range, the speed of the engine rotation has to be geared to the speed we want the wheels to turn and the car to go.

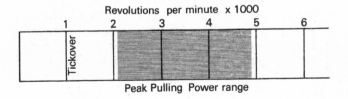

Fig 4 Engine pulling power.

23

THE GEARBOX

Most cars have four or five forward gears. First, or bottom, gear is for starting from standing and is used up to 10–15 mph (miles per hour); a 2nd and 3rd gear are necessary for increasing speed and/or to give extra power for climbing steep hills; and a 4th, or top, gear is required thereafter. Fifth is usually a fuel-saving, cruising-speed gear rather than for acceleration – as will be explained later, with fig. 16. Reverse gear is selected by the same lever; this reverses the direction of rotation of the driving shaft(s) and thus moves the car backwards.

A neutral position, where no gear is engaged, is provided so that you can use the gear lever to take the car out of gear. The engine can then be run without moving the car.

The lower gears have another use – that of adding control through "engine braking". I will return to this aspect with fig. 18, a few pages on.

WHAT THE CLUTCH DOES

Engaging gear to start off, or changing gear as you go along, would be difficult without disconnecting the engine whilst the different gear cogs are meshed together.

To enable this we have the clutch. It is designed to give a *smooth* transfer of the drive (or power) from the engine to the road wheels as you connect or reconnect that drive by using it.

Fig. 3 shows how the clutch consists of two circular plates facing each other. Here, they are shown separated by the clutch pedal being pressed down, so that the drive is disconnected – as if for the initial selection or subsequent changing of a gear.

The principle is simple. Plate **B** in fig. 3 spins with the engine at whatever speed it is running. Plate **A** is attached to the gearbox, and, if a gear were engaged, would, when turned, rotate the driving shaft(s) and the road wheels to move the car. (Fig. 3 shows a traditional, **R**ear-**W**heel-**D**rive "prop" shaft as well as more typical, stubby, **F**ront-**W**heel-**D**rive shafts.) This plate **A** only turns if you allow the clutch pedal to come up again, when the strong springs shown behind force it against plate **B**. Once it reaches plate **B** and locks against it the two turn as one, taking the drive from the engine. Unless you are in neutral that drive then passes on through the gearbox – geared according to the gear selected – to the wheels.

Plate **A** approaches plate **B** under pressure from the springs but controlled by the clutch pedal as you release it.

A smooth transfer of the drive for starting off depends upon *the period when the clutch is "slipping"; that is, when the two plates are only partially engaged.* This is the stage during your release of the clutch pedal which later on I will describe as the "biting point" – when plate **A**, beginning to bite against plate **B** which is already turning, starts to turn slowly itself, building up speed as it locks ever more tightly with plate **B**, until it, too, is turning at engine speed.

Careful control of your clutch pedal release at this stage is what makes sure the connection occurs gently and progressively, and that the car does not perform any "kangaroo" hops on the way. Thereafter, once your clutch pedal is fully released, the two simply go on turning together with no slip – the normal state when you are travelling along in gear.

A smooth reconnection of the drive, as you change up or down the gears once you are on the move, also depends on the way you release the clutch pedal. However, as will be explained when you come to **How To Change Gear**, it is then merely a smooth release passing through the biting point that is needed.

THE GEAR LEVER

Fig. 5 shows typical gear lever positions. The lever can only move in certain channels. A diagram of these is usually etched on the top of the gear lever knob or posted nearby.

You need to be able to visualise this "gate", as it is known, *without looking down.*

Then – *without the engine running* – you can, as suggested, with your handbrake securely on and a pair of wheels chocked, practise selecting different gears as well as finding neutral. (In neutral the lever should move freely from right to left and back.) Practise dozens of times until you have the feel of it all; and *don't look down*! Practise until you have no need to turn your eyes away from the front, whatever gear you wish to select.

Hold the clutch pedal down during this practice. This should ensure the lever can slip from gear to gear easily.

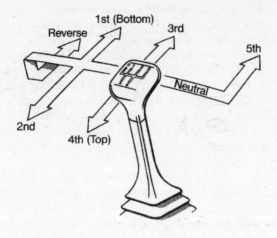

Fig 5 Gear box gate.

Your gearbox is made so that it should be impossible to select reverse in error. In most cars an extra push has to be made before the lever will slide along the neutral channel far enough to reach the reverse slot; sometimes a catch on the lever must be lifted, or else the lever knob has itself to be pressed down in line with the lever, before the reverse slot can be selected. Check with your teacher that you fully understand the design.

HANDLING THE GEAR LEVER
The knob on the gear lever should snug gently into the ball of your left hand, while the fingers and thumb drop lightly around the lever lower down; it should be just like holding a cricket ball lightly, with the palm of your hand facing down. Fig. 6 shows how changing the *angle* at which your hand takes hold of the gear lever knob enables you with precision to push, or pull, or move the lever sideways. Guide it gently. Persuade; never force. You will soon find you can change up or down the gearbox, find neutral, or select reverse – all with minimal effort as well as having your hand away from the steering wheel for the least possible time, all *without looking down*, and all with neat "fluid" movements.

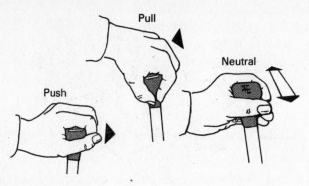

Fig 6 Gear lever grip.

THE FOOTBRAKE EXPLAINED

Look again at fig. 3. The footbrake acts via hydraulics (fluid pressure in pipes) on all four road wheel brake discs or drums at once, and is for stopping the car smoothly and progressively, or quickly in emergency.

Examine a bicycle brake and note how two pads squeeze the wheel rim, the friction created slowing the wheel. In a car the principle is similar; the brake disc (or drum with drum brakes), which turns with the wheel, is braked by lined pads being squeezed against it.

In fig. 7, **A** is the *off* position to which the spring-loaded, footbrake pedal returns automatically after use. Between **B** and **D** is the point where you can feel resistance, and the brakes begin to act when the foot pedal is pressed. The action is progressive. Light, continuous pressure slows the car straightaway. Gradually increasing this pressure stops the car more quickly.

At the first touch on the pedal your brakelights come on to warn drivers behind. They stay lit until you release the pedal fully.

THE HANDBRAKE EXPLAINED

This works mechanically (via rods or wires, and levers – entirely separately from the footbrake) and holds the car when standing. (You would only try to use it for stopping if your hydraulic brakes had failed. It has but a small fraction of the

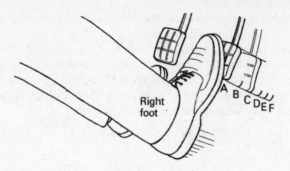

Fig 7 Brake pedal. If it goes below **D** your brakes need immediate repair.

power of the footbrake and normally only acts on one pair of wheels.)

Practise ''off'' and ''on'' with the handbrake while stationary, again, *without the engine running*, doing it by feel, and *not looking down*. So that there can be no danger of the car moving, again, chock one pair of wheels and remember to have your foot on the footbrake and a gear engaged. Your teacher must demonstrate first, just how much strength is correct to use so as to ensure the handbrake is fully on, but without overdoing it.

Normally a spring-loaded, button, locking-device is incorporated at the end of the handle of the handbrake lever. Fig. 8 shows the commonest type. The lever has to be lifted slightly

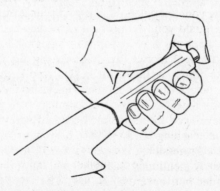

Fig 8 Handbrake application and release button.

and the button pressed in before the lever can be moved to the down, off position. Then you release the button again.

As you pull the handbrake back on, keep the button pressed in. Once the handle is fully up, you release it again to lock the brake on. Amateurs who pull on the handbrake without holding the button in cause a ''click-click-click'' which results in unnecessary wear to the ratchet mechanism.

OPEN SPACE PRACTICE

For **STAGE TWO** no substitute really matches a good-sized open space; that is, if you want to learn slow-speed car-handling to competition standard. And that – whether it is with manual or automatic gears – has to be your target if you want to become a first-class driver! Success with my personally devised (and much copied) training exercises is the golden key to worry-free car manoeuvring. So, do find a clear *level* open area, even if it means your teacher has to drive some way to it on several occasions. Having safe room to yourselves is paramount at this stage.

Beware! I'm afraid there are a few rogue, professional instructors. These chaps try to plunge you into heavy traffic practically before you have learned to move off and stop, never mind handle the car, or judge its length or width. By skimping the early teaching of clutch control and manoeuvring, they may hope to save wear and tear on their school car, or to prolong your lessons by slowing up your learning; I don't know. But, should you find yourself in the hands of a menace of this sort, look for a new instructor straightaway. There is little worse for your morale than to be driving along scared out of your wits whilst an instructor of this type keeps grabbing the steering wheel, or uses dual foot controls so much that you are constantly deprived of any real learning.

I have developed the following exercises specifically with parent/friend teaching in mind. So, as promised, they start from scratch. Professional instructors, aided by dual controls, may, as already mentioned, take you on a little quicker or in a different order but, nevertheless, read the next few sections which complete this chapter. They will instil the background understanding that will underpin your good, steady progress.

STEERING

I have not so far covered steering, because it strains the mechanism to steer while stationary. This applies whether or not you have power steering. Until the instant that a car is on the move, the forces that have to come into play at the steering joints, and the body attachment points thereof, would be excessive.

Remember you will have to be **LOOKING WHERE YOU ARE GOING** not at the steering wheel.

Relax! The steering wheel should always be held gently like you would hold an egg – although ready to grip harder in emergency. Steering is self-centering. That is, it tends always to keep the road wheels "straight ahead". It is thus bad to grip the wheel as if force were needed to keep straight. Indeed, such "conscious" steering results in a weaving, wiggly course. Keeping straight is more a matter of making occasional, minor corrections.

Fig. 9 shows how the steering wheel should be held between clock-face positions a "quarter to three" and "ten to two" during straight driving.

Both hands must be on the steering wheel all the time except when one is needed for changing gear, for an arm signal, or perhaps to use a switch. **NEVER** take both hands off at once!

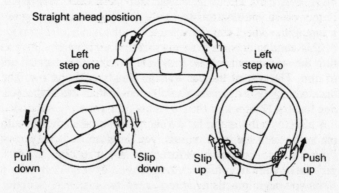

Fig 9 Steering hand-movements.

To alter course, very little steering wheel movement is needed, especially at higher speeds. It is only in turning at junctions, cornering acutely, reversing, and in "tight" manoeuvring that you have to turn the wheel much. Practice will soon show you how the car responds.

When you do need to turn the wheel substantially you must *never cross your hands*. You must also learn to do it quickly. The best way is to use two basic movements, repeating them alternately as needed. These are shown in fig. 9 as steps one and two.

Fig. 9 shows turning left. To turn right do the opposite. In step one the left hand pulls down, turning the wheel; at the same time the right hand moves down, allowing the wheel to slip through its fingers so that at the end of step one both hands are level, near to the bottom of the wheel, ready to start step two.

For step two the right hand pushes up and is turning the wheel, while the left one moves back up again, sliding up the wheel so as to keep level with the right hand, and ready to repeat step one.

Several movements may be necessary to put the steering into full lock (the wheel as far as it will go left or right).

To straighten up use the opposite hand movements. Again, speed in handling the steering wheel is often necessary. Learn to be vigorous and quick, for times such as during manoeuvring when you have to be. For *small amounts of steering* you may find the self-centering mechanism is sufficient but you *must not let go*, allowing the wheel to jerk back to straight. Rather must you control this self-centering action by lightly gripping the wheel as it slips back.

The steering acts on the front wheels; so, immediately you turn the steering wheel (with the car moving), the front starts to turn. The rest of the car and the back wheels follow. The back wheels thus describe a smaller circle than the front ones. See fig. 10. The back of the car "cuts" the corner. On the road this effect is only important if a sharp turn is taken too close to the kerb. Then the back wheels would mount it. Don't worry over this. Once you are used to it your mind will allow room to get round, without conscious thought.

As you begin practising starts and stops on your open space – in the next section below – also practise steering to the left

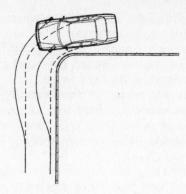

Fig 10 Broken lines show how the rear wheels cut corners.

and right. Do so *before* learning to change up out of 1st gear. Shortly thereafter, learn to hold a straight course with the right hand only. You will need to when changing gear. Do the same with the left hand only, so that it will be possible to give arm signals. Remember that, later, on the open road, all steering should be smoothly progressive – never jerky.

THE SMOOTH START FROM STANDING

In figs. 11 and 12 and the accompanying text I have set down all the steps in precise order but, *before that, and whenever you return to any driving seat,* you must run through the **cockpit drill** as follows:

1   Make sure your handbrake is securely on

2   Check that your seat and head restraint positions are right for you (see pages 17 and 19) and are locked in place

3   Likewise check with your teacher and any passenger(s) that theirs are too

4   Make sure everyone has their seat belt (or child restraint) fitted and buckled correctly

5   Adjust any mirror not correctly aligned

6   Check all doors are properly shut – the *driver* is responsible. (Once you know what a door ajar looks like in your wing mirrors you can check them there.)

For the first time you will start to drive the car on your *level* open space. Place your hands ready on the wheel as shown in figs. 1 and 9. After practising moving off and then stopping (which needs to be almost straightaway) a few times, your teacher may need to turn the car round using reverse, so that you can go back the other way but peek ahead to **Reversing,** page 49, now if you would prefer to do that yourself.

(Note: *moving off on the road, later on, will require a signal and additional safety steps such as a check behind over your right shoulder*. See Chapter 5, **MOVING OFF**, page 129.)

Meanwhile:

Key to Fig. 11
1 Check that the gear lever is in neutral. *Proof* of being out of gear is that the lever moves *freely* from side to side at least twice as far as it will if it is in a gear. To help you recognise the neutral channel, if ever you are uncertain, select (with your clutch pedal down) two odd- or two even-numbered gears, in turn. Try, say 1st and then 3rd. It then becomes easy to confirm that you have got back to neutral between them.

If you forget this check and start the engine in gear the car might jerk forward (or back . . .) and hit somebody.

Whenever the car is to be started, or re-started if it has stalled (stopped), this neutral check must be made. On your Practical Test the examiner will watch.

Key to Fig. 11
2 Switch on the ignition (but not the engine yet) with the key. Your teacher will show you how. Go through with him the meaning of all the warning lamps which light up, and thereby discover which ones should go out in a moment, when you start the engine. *Always check your fuel gauge*. (Also discuss, ready for your Theory Test, the purposes of all other gauges/dials on the instrument panel and how they are read.) If your engine is diesel wait for the pre-heat warning lamp to go out.

Then start the engine with a further turn of the key, now against a small but noticeable, spring pressure. Immediately it runs, release the switch. With practice, your ear will tell you the

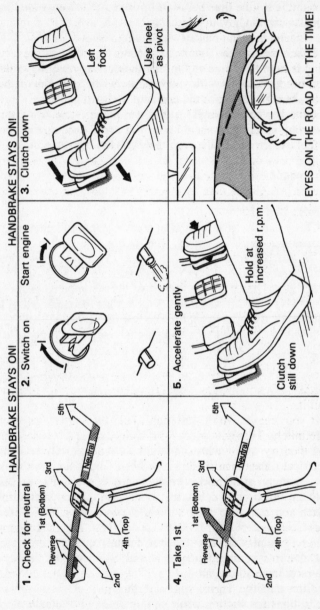

Fig 11 Starting from standing, first **5** moves.

HANDBRAKE STAYS ON!

HANDBRAKE STAYS ON!

1. Check for neutral

Reverse   1st (Bottom)   3rd   5th

Neutral

2nd   4th (Top)

2. Switch on   Start engine

3. Clutch down

Left foot

Use heel as pivot

4. Take 1st

Reverse   1st (Bottom)   3rd   5th

Neutral

2nd   4th (Top)

5. Accelerate gently

Hold at increased r.p.m.

Clutch still down

EYES ON THE ROAD ALL THE TIME!

34

instant the engine fires but at first your teacher can guide. (He can also explain how to release the steering lock by 'waggling' the wheel if the ignition key won't turn to begin with.)

Check through the warning lamps again to see that everything is in order and take a further look at the various gauges. You need to discuss with your teacher where each one of the latter should settle once the engine is warmed up. Assess now whether you have enough fuel for your planned trip. Make this a starting-up habit; it should help you avoid ever running out of fuel (which can easily cause a serious accident) because you will always then go straight to the first garage if necessary (and possible!). Familiarise yourself with reading the speedometer at a glance. If a rev-counter is fitted your teacher can explain its purpose.

THE CHOKE

Starting a cold engine may require the use of a choke control if an automatic choke is not fitted. This is usually a pull-knob on the dashboard, which is kept out until the *earliest moment the engine runs normally*. Then it is progressively pushed home, aiming to have it right off as soon as possible. The skill is to do so before lumpy, 'chug, chug' running occurs, but not before the engine can manage with less choke without stalling (stopping). Take great care not to leave the choke out by mistake. Eventually, this would flood the engine with fuel and stall it.

If your engine won't start, don't hold the starter-switch on indefinitely. That will wreck your battery. Rest a few seconds and then try again with short bursts. Make sure everything electrical (other than sidelights where the law says you must have them on at night) is switched off while you do so. Also hold the clutch pedal down; that saves turning over parts of the clutch and the gearbox. If the engine won't go after a dozen tries seek expert help. Otherwise, if you flog a flagging battery, you may never get the car started.

Delve into your particular car handbook and find out what the recommendations are for cold starting. Each make seems to differ slightly. There, you may also find necessary tips or precautions for starting when your engine is hot. Some older makes can be temperamental in this respect.

Key to Fig. 11

3 Return your starter hand to the steering wheel.
Put the clutch pedal fully down (left foot) *and hold it there*.

Key to Fig. 11

4 Slip the gear lever to 1st.
Return your hand to the steering wheel.

If you find difficulty in getting into 1st then, provided your open space is flat, 2nd gear will do for starting. (When facing downhill on a road, 2nd gear is correct anyway, as, helped by the decline, the engine gives sufficient power.)

Key to Fig. 11

5 Now in gear, and *with the clutch pedal still down*, gently increase the engine rpm. Press on the gas pedal (right foot). About a quarter of its movement will be sufficient. That will be just enough for the engine tone noticeably to increase. *Hold it there*. (If your car has a tachometer you will see the engine rpm rise from roughly 1000x to 1500x.)

The engine is now running at enough speed; *the clutch pedal is still down*; the gear is in 1st. Your hands are on the wheel in the correct position holding it lightly. **YOUR EYES ARE** *in front*. The handbrake has been on, holding the car, all the time.

Key to Fig. 12

1 and 2 The secret now is to allow the clutch pedal up *gently*, only until the biting point is *just reached, no further*. You then hold it there ready for **3** and **4**. You maintain your accelerator exactly where you set it in **5**, fig. 11, page 34.

Fig. 13 shows your clutch footwork in greater detail. The clutch begins to "bite" between **B** and **D**. The actual biting point, **C**, is not necessarily precisely mid-way between **B** and **D** as shown; its exact position will depend on how much the clutch plates are worn, and this naturally varies from car to car and with age.

The master key to raising the clutch pedal gently, to precisely where you want it, and then holding it there, is (as stated earlier) *to keep your heel on the floor, where it can pivot.*

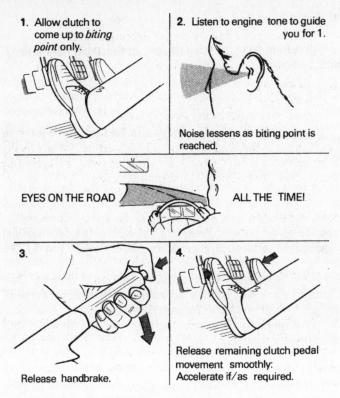

1. Allow clutch to come up to *biting point* only.

2. Listen to engine tone to guide you for 1.

Noise lessens as biting point is reached.

EYES ON THE ROAD ALL THE TIME!

3. Release handbrake.

4. Release remaining clutch pedal movement smoothly: Accelerate if/as required.

Fig 12 Starting from standing, next **4** moves.

You can recognise the biting point because the tone of the engine's purr will die down as this stage of clutch release is reached. You let the clutch pedal up *slowly, gently*, so that you can't overshoot the biting point.

Think of this point as your contact between standing and moving. To be brutal, between success and failure – it's that important.

The car is still held back by the handbrake, though it is now almost "straining" to go. The clutch plates, as depicted in fig. 3, are already skimming each other but only just.

Key to Fig. 12
3 (a) Let the handbrake off. (Check that the dashboard warning lamp has gone out, confirming full handbrake release.) Then

bring that hand back to the steering wheel.

(b) **Maintain your clutch and gas pedal positions as at 1 and 2 above**. The car should remain still.

If it creeps forward don't release your accelerator. Instead, dip the clutch pedal a tiny fraction. **One to two** millimetres should be enough to stop the car, without taking you back below the biting point. Again, hold your feet where they are now, with the car still. (You will know if you have dropped below the biting point because the engine tone will go up again to where you had originally set it. If that happens it is unwise then to see-saw with your foot. Instead, put the clutch pedal right down, pull your handbrake back on, and return the gear lever to neutral. Follow by releasing the foot pedals. Next, pause for breath! Then start again at **Key to Fig. 11, 3**.)

(c) Now, fractionally let the clutch pedal up, "slipping" the clutch to allow only enough engine power through for the road wheels to *begin* to move the car. The clutch plates as in fig. 3 are now partially engaged, carrying the car forward that ever-so-slow amount.

Key to Fig. 12
4 The more SMOOTHLY (not specially slowly) you now release the remaining movement in the clutch pedal the better.

If you jerk your foot off or raise it too quickly, the car can lurch forward and the engine may stall. Let it up steadily, in control, so that the car gathers speed without any "kangaroo" hops.

Further steady acceleration as the clutch pedal passes the biting point, **C**, in fig. 13 – clutch now fully engaged – increases speed as required until the maximum in 1st gear is reached.

As soon as your clutch pedal is fully up, remove your foot off it. There should be room to "park" your foot to the left of the pedal as shown shortly, in fig. 15. If not, draw your foot back towards you so that it can rest instead on the floor, well clear of the pedal.

Never travel along with your foot still touching the pedal; that will quickly cause undue and expensive wear on the clutch thrust bearing.

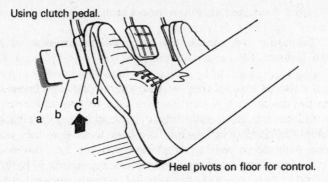

Using clutch pedal.

a b c d

Heel pivots on floor for control.

Fig 13 Clutch begins to engage between **B** and **D**.

LEARNING TO STOP

First gear is not normally used much beyond walking speed, then 2nd is engaged: but *before* you learn to change gear on the move, or accelerate strongly, *you must learn to stop*.

After a few metres, *not miles*, make your first stop. Practise on your open space, starting, going a few metres and stopping, not once, but dozens of times until the ''system'' for stopping becomes instinctive. *It will be the life-saver later*.

STOPPING FROM *SLOW* SPEEDS – BELOW 20–25 MPH

As you move your foot across from the accelerator and *gently* apply the footbrake the car will slow; just before stopping, the engine has to be disengaged from the road wheels or it will stall. To do so and prevent this, you need to put your clutch pedal down at the same time as you begin to apply pressure to your brake pedal. You must *both* keep your pressure on the footbrake, *and* hold your clutch pedal down, until you have *stopped, applied the handbrake, and slipped your gear lever into neutral* – IN THAT ORDER.

Then, and ONLY THEN, release the clutch pedal, followed by the footbrake, pending your next **Smooth Start**.

Your footbrake *must* remain on until all the other steps are complete. This ''fail-safe'' order ensures that you won't suffer a dangerous lurch forward if, inadvertently, the gear lever has not correctly reached its neutral position; and it allows you the opportunity instantly to hold the car again with your footbrake, if either your handbrake develops a fault or, perhaps, if you haven't applied it fully enough.

This strict – *handbrake on and return to neutral before taking first your clutch foot and then your brake foot off the pedals* – sequence, to be used *every* time you come to a stop, must also be applied prior to switching off the engine having parked the car.

(Switch off, incidentally, when you want to stop the engine, simply by turning the ignition key back to its insertion position, from which you can withdraw it.)

The rule then, for stopping from any *slow* speed, is BOTH FEET DOWN. *Gentle* braking should be quite enough; gradually increasing the pressure on the footbrake progressively stops the car.

EARLY EMERGENCY STOPPING FROM *SLOW* SPEEDS

As soon as you get used to using the clutch and brake pedals, and you feel comfortable starting off in 1st gear and then stopping again, try an emergency stop on your teacher's unexpected, snap command. (He should give it in the style an examiner would use. See page 127.) This tunes up your reactions. It ensures that your emergency drill begins to be ingrained before you ever change gear.

Make sure, even during this initial open space practice, that your teacher gives you plenty of periodic, snap emergency stops. You should soon be able to get BOTH FEET DOWN very, very quickly and without a sniff of panic. Later, as you learn to use 2nd and 3rd gears, reverse, etc., you must continue to practise stops, and controlled emergency stops, in each gear, before going on.

NORMAL STOPPING FROM *FASTER* SPEEDS

When stopping from anything over 20–25 mph your technique must change. Use *gentle*, progressive pressure on your brake pedal as before; however, you no longer depress the clutch pedal immediately your other foot goes on the footbrake.

Wait until speed has dropped to about 10 mph, before disengaging the engine from the road wheels by depressing the clutch pedal. You will comfortably avoid stalling, provided

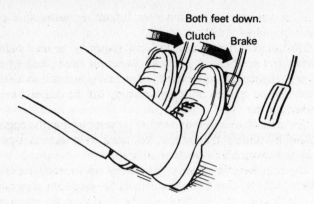

Both feet down.
Clutch
Brake

Fig 14 Early days' emergency stopping.

that you always have it down by the time the gear lever starts to "waggle" – indicating that a stall is imminent – and certainly by the time you reach the final car length before you stop. You delay because, with your foot off the gas (it's on the brake!), engine braking (see page 46) secures additional control and helps slow you down.

Another refinement to your stopping, one which makes for a smoother ride, is to ease your foot off the brake again for the last half-metre or metre. The car then stops without any jerk, before you hold it again with the footbrake and, subsequently, the handbrake.

Practise stopping at a pre-determined place, for example, beside an old tree stump or whatever. You need to become expert at coming to a stop both evenly AND precisely where you decide so to do.

EMERGENCY STOPS FROM *SLIGHTLY* FASTER SPEEDS

In *EMERGENCY*, stopping from any moderate speed up to about 40 mph, you can forget the "wait until 10 mph clutch pedal down technique" given above. *In these early days of learning* you need only remember BOTH FEET FIRMLY DOWN TOGETHER, as quickly as humanly possible.

There is no time to think separately of when to press the clutch, so you press both brake and clutch pedals at once. Fig. 14 shows you.

41

Every emergency stop, however, has to be controlled, especially in skiddy conditions. It's useless stamping on the pedal, "locking" your brakes and skidding. (Braking too hard causes "locking", a condition where a road wheel stops turning and, instead, *slides*. Often several, or all, wheels slide at once. Even worse, the car can also swing off course.) In later chapters I will investigate for you in depth the proper control of such skidding, and explain further refinements of your emergency stopping technique which you must learn to incorporate from all higher speeds. Meanwhile, during your open space emergency stop practice, avoid wet, skiddy weather or loose surfaces, and, always, *always*, keep both hands on the wheel during stops.

THE FEET POSITIONS

Fig. 15 shows where your feet should normally be placed once you are going along, after the initial start. The right foot pivots on the floor and is on the gas pedal with – most of the time – only a light touch; the left lies beside the clutch ready to return to it either during the next stop, or, as will be required later, when you come to change gear.

NEVER drive in *heavy boots, "wellies", or muddy or greasy shoes*. Clean off mud or anything slippery – especially, for example, spilt forecourt diesel. There *must never be any possibility* of one foot hitting two pedals, or of a shoe slipping off the brake or the clutch (or onto the accelerator). *In emergency, split-seconds matter*. For the same reasons never allow either foot to find its way under the pedals; and keep the footwell clear of all loose articles and rubbish.

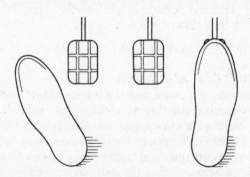

Fig 15 Position of the feet driving along.

42

MILE-AN-HOUR DRIVING

A superb exercise for your initial, live practice in **STAGE TWO** is, having made normal preparations up to that point, to hold the clutch and accelerator pedals as at **Key to Fig. 12, 1 and 2**. Next, let the handbrake off and drive ten or fifteen metres at "one-mile-an-hour", controlling speed for this by fractional up or down movements of the clutch pedal as required – up to begin – but holding the accelerator steady. Practise in 1st gear – until you can go so slowly that it would take an observer at least a couple of seconds to be sure you were moving at all – and you will have become master of the clutch. *This clutch work is the bread and butter of car control.*

MINIMUM SPEED – CLUTCH PEDAL UP

An extension of the above exercise is to see how slowly the car will move with the clutch fully engaged (clutch pedal right up) without stalling. Return to the **Smooth Start From Standing**, figs. 11, 12 and 13. This time, at **Key to Fig. 12, 4**, instead of steadily increasing acceleration after the clutch pedal is fully up, reduce it. Do so *very* gently. In 1st gear it should be possible to make the car drop back down to a crawl without stalling. Thereafter, it should be equally easy (provided your right foot pivots on the floor properly, as explained earlier under **The Feet Positions**) to squeeze the accelerator down ever-so-gently and progressively, in order to pick up speed again without any "kangaroo" hopping. This is known as "feathering in" your accelerator.

When, shortly, you come to reversing, remember to practise the same essential techniques in reverse gear. It's worth discovering how slowly you can operate in *2nd* gear without clutch slip, too.

CLUTCH WEAR AND TEAR

Learning to slip the clutch during a **Smooth Start**, and to gain ultra-slow-moving control for manoeuvring, naturally wears out your clutch plates faster than normal. This is a small price to pay – for 100% competence here is essential.

However, within quite a short time, you will become able to merge the **4** steps of fig. 12 into one smooth operation – subject only to constraints from other traffic. You will learn, in the same way that all good, qualified drivers do, to minimise the time that you need to hold the clutch at its biting point. Thereafter, noisy over-revving of the engine and/or jumpy starts will, for you, be consigned to history.

Keep **Mile-an-Hour** driving practice down to 2–3 minutes at each occasion. This will limit any undue wear. (Going on too long *at one session* may overheat the plates, which can increase the wear dramatically.) You shouldn't need very many practice goes to achieve success.

Incidentally, now you are familiar with the biting point, you no longer need to press your clutch pedal "right to the floor" at every **Key to Fig. 11, 3** stage of your Smooth Start; comfortably below the biting point will do nicely.

GEAR SPEEDS
Fig. 16 shows the speed range in which each gear is normally used. Use 1st gear for starting on the level or uphill; and keep in 1st up to 10 or 15 mph. However, when facing downhill the decline helps anyway, and you should therefore start in 2nd.

Use 2nd up to about 25 mph. Use 3rd to accelerate between

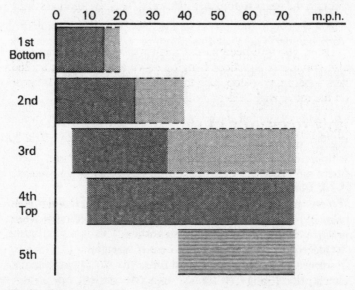

Fig 16 Gear speeds.

44

20–25 and about 35 mph. Take top thereafter for ordinary driving, until you begin learning to use 5th gear – for which see below – and refer, also, to **Gears On The Open Road** in Chapter 5, page 151.

You would only push up toward the top speed available in each gear (broken outlines) when you want maximum acceleration, for example for overtaking.

Notice from fig. 16 that, at times when best acceleration is not needed, you can also pull away in 3rd (or even top) from as low a speed as 10 mph.

On most cars there is a 5th gear. It is shown in fig. 16 with a different shading because it is not normally used for building up speed. That would take too long and hold up traffic behind. It is intended as a fuel-saving, cruising-speed gear which, in addition, reduces noise and wear because the engine does not need to turn so fast.

Once you understand **How To Change Gear** which follows next, you can begin to practise changing up the gears on your open space. Since the engine will go on pulling perfectly adequately in 3rd and top gears from remarkably low speeds, a clear flat run of 250 metres will be ample to work your way up through the gears to top, and then stop. Travel a short distance with just a little acceleration in each gear. *You need never exceed 20 mph.*

Later, you will need an extended run so that you can then also commence practice changing down again – as far as 2nd gear – before you stop each time. (Changing down to 1st gear on the move will be dealt with later; see page 141.)

HOW TO CHANGE GEAR
Fig. 17 tracks the **3** steps of changing up the gears, starting with pressing your clutch pedal down to below the biting point (there's no need for the pedal to hit the floor) as you release the accelerator.

You should already be **Handling The Gear Lever** (see page 25) fluidly, WITHOUT LOOKING DOWN, after your practice earlier, without the engine running.

Once you have persuaded the gear lever home confidently to select your next gear up the gearbox (fig. 17, 2), release the clutch pedal (fig. 17, 3), in one *smooth* (not slow), continuous movement. Simultaneously, *gently* re-accelerate.

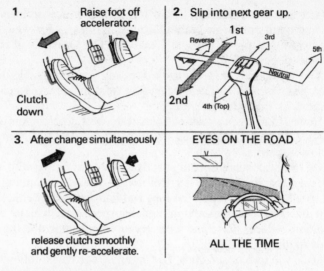

1. Raise foot off accelerator.

Clutch down

2. Slip into next gear up.

Reverse 1st 3rd 5th

Neutral

2nd 4th (Top)

3. After change simultaneously

release clutch smoothly and gently re-accelerate.

EYES ON THE ROAD

ALL THE TIME

Fig 17 Changing up the gears.

Changing from gear to gear you do not pause while the clutch bites; nor do you need to use your heel as a pivot unless preferred. You can, instead, lift your foot entirely off the clutch pedal using your *thigh* muscles. Either way the time it takes to say "zero" is enough.

Always re-accelerate promptly after an upward change (though progressively and not too much); don't dawdle or speed is lost.

Fig. 18 tracks changing down the gears. The **3** steps are similar to those for changing up *except that no immediate acceleration follows the change* – unless the lower gear is required for extra power for climbing a hill, or for quicker acceleration to overtake someone.

A change down the gears will, in most circumstances, be being made in the course of slowing down. With no acceleration the lower gear will help reduce your speed through "engine braking". Instead of the engine powering the road wheels to go along, or to go faster, the momentum of the car causes those wheels to try to turn the engine faster than it is set (by the accelerator position) to go. Engine compression

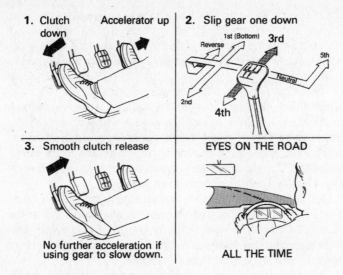

1. Clutch down   Accelerator up

2. Slip gear one down

1st (Bottom)   3rd
Reverse
5th
Neutral
2nd
4th

3. Smooth clutch release

No further acceleration if using gear to slow down.

EYES ON THE ROAD

ALL THE TIME

Fig 18   Changing down the gears.

resistance (or "engine braking") then starts to hold speed in check and slow the car.

The addition of "engine braking" helps avoid skidding and makes using your brakes safer. Going down a steep hill – especially a long one – it is a vital safety addition in case your brakes fail, or overheat and then fade.

Apart from the essential, greater control afforded by the lower gears as you slow down, another reason for changing down is so that you will be in the appropriate gear, ready for speeding up again, just as soon as any opportunity arises.

ALMOST STOPPING ... BUT NOT QUITE

A further open space exercise is to practise slowing down in 2nd gear to the point when the engine begins to falter; then, when it is about to stall, recovering – by means of neat footwork – so as to move on again without ever stopping completely.

You often have to do this at times when dropping instead into 1st gear would be inappropriate. An example might be when turning left into a side road at a level junction, one where there would be no need for the extra power of 1st. For

47

this you may well require almost to stop just before you enter the new road, in order to avoid any danger of swinging into it too fast. However, equally probably, you may not want actually to stop at any stage; nor, indeed, should you so do if there is no need.

The technique is, whilst you are still just on the move, to insert clutch-slipping, start-off control. With the car almost stopped – just a little before the engine will stall – push the clutch pedal down a touch below the biting point. Simultaneously, raise the engine rpm as if for a **Smooth Start From Standing**. Then instantly raise the clutch to stage (c) of **Key to Fig. 12, 3** and follow directly to stage **4**.

Deft footwork should come within a very few practice tries. You will soon find that with this simple, neat, quick dip of the clutch you can slow right down at any place you select, and then have the car moving forward under controlled power again, at exactly the moment you require.

This may only be done without "coasting" (in effect out of gear – see page 79) so make sure your feet get the message!

CHANGING VEHICLES
Should you change cars at any time (before *or* after your Practical Test) make sure that you know *before you set off* where all the important controls and switches are, and how they work. An overtaking driver may not expect you to turn right when he sees your rear-wash-wiper come on . . . unless he is as astute as you must aim to become when you have read this book.

MORE, HELPFUL OPEN SPACE TRAINING

Figs. 22–28, a few pages on, show the next few exercises to master. The ideas given create perfect conditions for learning how to place your car – to the centimetre – exactly where you want it during manoeuvring, all with zero risk of damage to your car. Obtain the necessary, second-hand, cardboard boxes illustrated, from grocers, etc. They can be flattened for transporting and then re-sticky-taped together.

REVERSING

Apart from the steering (and the gear), all controls are used in the same way as for driving forwards.

In reverse:

* You NEVER *exceed a brisk walking pace*.
* YOU LOOK mainly **BACKWARDS**, directly through your rear window (adding necessary glances forwards and all around).
* It is ILLEGAL to reverse more than necessary.
* You always GIVE WAY to anyone else.
* FIND someone who can guide you if you cannot see properly.
* You NEVER back out of a driveway or from a side road into a main road.

STOPPING IN REVERSE

Remember the SLOW SPEED stopping rule (page 39): BOTH FEET DOWN, *for stopping when reversing*. Beware! Brakes are often less efficient while reversing. Allow for the difference.

YOUR EYES WHEN REVERSING

Turn well round and look out of the back window over your inside (left) shoulder. In this position you can see a little out of the windows each side as well. Get your shoulders right round as far as you can but retaining control of the foot pedals. Bend/extend your neck so that you can reduce the blind spots created by the roof supports either side of the back window. Never reverse with your head out of your side window or looking out with your door open.

Fig. 19 projects the *vital* need for developing fishy eyes, for you *must* see all around.

For example, when reversing straight, as well as **LOOK-ING BACKWARDS** over your inside shoulder **WHERE YOU ARE GOING**, you must move your head and switch your eyes rapidly about. You need to include frequent glances forwards as well as to both sides – with an occasional "snapshot" right back over your right shoulder. You have to be *sure*, not just that you are not going to hit anything, but also

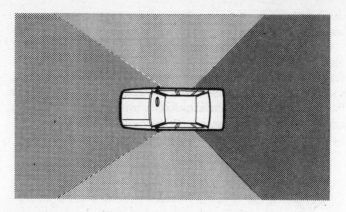

Fig 19 Where to look when reversing. Concentrate where the shading is heaviest – you must look where you are going – but never neglect the lighter-shaded areas.

that you are not causing trouble to other road users *from any direction*.

Accidents happen remarkably easily while reversing. You might be "lucky" and just hit a kerb or a low pillar but what if it were a child? *So take care*.

Most pedestrians, believe me, assume that you *have* seen them. Always be ready to let them pass. Especially watch for children running, perhaps crouched low after a ball . . . Should you have the slightest question as to what might be behind (e.g. at night) seek help. At the least, if help is not to hand, get out first and look. Never reverse "blind".

STEERING IN REVERSE

Keep both hands on the wheel. During straight reversing it may help – and it is acceptable – to hold your respective hands on the wheel a little to the right of the top and a little to the left of the bottom, instead of the normal, straight ahead, forwards position of fig. 9. However, you still use the same basic steering movements described with fig. 9.

Re-study fig. 10; imagine that, rather than being about to go forwards, you are now reversing back to that position. The path of your *road wheels* will be identical but reversed.

In this direction it is the back of the car, now leading, which tends to "cut" the corner – and the wheels at the new "back" of the car that take a wider arc. Thus the steering (or new "back") wheels are going to swing wide, and you must remember it.

To help you visualise which way to turn the steering wheel for the direction you want to go, I have created fig. 20. The correct way to turn it can seem unnatural at first; however, you soon get used to it. The secret is always to start off *very slowly*; then your eyes can almost at once confirm you have got it right, and you can switch instantly to the other way if necessary – before you have gone too far or anyone need notice.

Fig 20 How to visualise steering in reverse. Picture this figure in your mind's eye to remind you which direction on the steering wheel takes the car which way.

In fig. 21 you are taking your position in a car park, later on, when you feel competent so to do. **A** will be an obvious front-wing danger point. So might be **B**, or even **C**, during straightening up in the final stages of entering your "slot". Look out for pedestrians throughout the manoeuvre, especially for kids wandering or leaping from areas **D**, **E** and **F**.

Fig. 22 shows parallel lengths of thick rope, wide cloth, or tape to represent kerbsides, held down by a few large stones so as to create your own straight *level* "road", 7–8 metres wide and 70 metres or so long, on your open space.

It is far better to be off-road; however, if you cannot find an open space big enough and have to use a very, very quiet *level* road instead, find a straight one where there are no parked cars and without any high kerbstones on which you might damage your tyres or wheels.

51

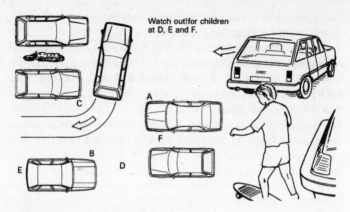

Watch out!for children
at D, E and F.

Fig 21 Danger in a car park.

Reversing in a straight line is the first thing to learn. Nobody ever succeeds in going backwards dead straight for more than a few metres on the first attempt. You soon wander. This is because you actually learn to go straight by making mistakes and then putting them right. These errors quickly diminish as you acquire the knack of keeping straight through

Fig 22 Your own "road" set out on an open space.

tiny steering corrections made only when needed.

Aim to back down the full length of your "road" at a set distance out from your nearside (left) "kerb". Judge it by eye at between 1 to 2 metres out. The idea is to keep straight all the way. GO VERY SLOWLY. (Remember, in reverse you NEVER *exceed a brisk walk anyway* but, to begin with, this *must* be **Mile-An-Hour** stuff.)

On your first try use clutch slip, if necessary, for most of the distance, so that you are going slowly enough to have time to concentrate on exactly how your car is responding to you moving the steering wheel.

By your second or third go you should be ready to raise speed to a modest stroll, with your clutch pedal right up. (See earlier, **Minimum Speed – Clutch Pedal Up**, page 43.) You shouldn't now need clutch slip in this exercise, except for starting off and for when you need to **Almost Stop ... But Not Quite** (the footwork technique you learned at page 47), while you rectify any steering error before it can spoil your manoeuvre.

You must slow right down whilst you sort out a steering mistake. It may sound silly to slow down from a stroll to a clutch-slip speed but, if you don't, you'll quickly find yourself in the "ditch".

Another exercise I offer here will impress on your mind which is the right way, while reversing, to turn the steering wheel to go the way you want. It is gently to weave your way back down your "road" from one side to t'other.

Again, use clutch slip control most of the way on your first try. (N.B. If you are on a real road you have to be able to see, in *both* directions, a *very, very long way* – to be sure that you could pull in and stop before any traffic might come unexpectedly. Otherwise, use an empty cul-de-sac for the exercise, backing down towards the closed end.)

A lesson or two of practice between these two exercises, combined with pulling in to the kerb backwards, as part of the next exercise, will resolve any worries you may have about controlling your steering during reversing. As you improve at reversing NEVER go faster than my stated maximum of a brisk walk, even on the straight; this disciplined restraint should ensure that you never scare yourself or others. Remember, all the time, even on your open space, that children pop up from "nowhere". And that they're liable to assume you have seen them . . .

Your "road" in fig. 22 is now the place to learn to pull in and stop (forwards and backwards) close in to the kerb. Practise mainly with the passenger's side (the nearside) of the car next the kerb. But become skilled for your side (the offside) too. An expert is able consistently to pull in parallel to and well within a couple of tyre-widths from the kerb, forwards or backwards, either side of the road – without ever bashing the kerb! An advanced driver, such as I hope you will become, always gets it down to one tyre-width or less. His car is then, whenever parked, less likely to get hit, or to have a wing mirror "wiped", or to inconvenience passing traffic in any way.

Each time you pull in and stop to begin with, get out and look how close and how parallel you are to your "kerb" – with both the front and back wheels. You may be surprised to find that things are not as you thought . . . but looking for yourself is the quickest way to learn. This way, you quickly imprint on your mind what you should be able to see from the driving seat whenever you've got it right.

For the 4th exercise see fig. 23. Here you need at least four

Fig 23 Build cartons one half metre wider apart than your car.

54

large cardboard cartons. On a windy day you may need a brick or two placed inside each one to stop them blowing away. Because you cannot block a public road you will *have* to find some such place as a private yard (with permission) for this and the remaining few exercises, if you can find no handy, open space.

Build the cartons as shown a total of one half-metre wider apart than your car. Practise driving slowly between them under clutch-slipping control, forwards and then backwards. As your gap-judgement improves you will be able to go a little quicker. Reduce the gap and test your skill at going through dead centre.

Keep the cartons where they are. Now, as shown in fig. 24, approach them from an angle before passing through. Do it forwards first, then in reverse. Your starting position should be as shown, parallel with an imaginary line joining the boxes, with the front wheels pointing straight ahead. Keep starting from positions closer to the boxes – e.g. dotted lines fig. 24 – and see how good you can get.

As you work towards an ever-smaller angle you'll find you need to be progressively more adept at handling the steering. Remember not to turn the steering wheel until you have the car moving; as mentioned earlier that requires undue effort from the steering gear. However, really tight manoeuvres are impossible unless you "bustle" your steering wheel rapidly round – *always using the correct basic movements learnt earlier* – from the instant you move.

Fig 24 Discovering at just how acute an angle you can approach a narrow entrance, e.g. to a private garage.

A lock-to-lock turn should easily be accomplished at **Mile-An-Hour** speed *before* you have travelled one metre.

The essential success factor with this exercise is moving the car really slowly, especially when you are putting lock on or taking it off to straighten up. Loads of practice here will instil a "natural instinct" for knowing precisely the best moment to start turning into your "garage" (or whatever you choose your boxes to represent), and for appreciating exactly when to begin to straighten up and how quickly that steering change needs to be done.

As with learning correctly to pull in to a pavement, be ready to stop the car and get out and look. That is the finest way YOU can learn how the picture YOU see from the driving seat relates to the facts.

It is always better to pull forwards again (but never further than necessary), and then make a correction, than to try to "get away with" a poorly executed entry, and (in a real garage) possibly scraped paintwork.

The next exercise is simpler. See fig. 25. Stand some boxes up to represent a wall. Drive slowly up to your "wall" and see how close you can get without hitting it. Use **Mile-An-Hour** clutch slip just before you finally stop, regaining that control (if you started from a long way back) as in **Almost Stopping ... But Not Quite**, a few pages ago. Do this forwards then backwards. Get out each time after you stop and see if your clenched fist will go through the gap you have left. When it won't more often than it will, you're on the way to becoming good!

Fig 25 Getting to know the length of your bonnet and your boot.

Fig 26 Mock-up of a space in a multi-storey car park.

If you have enough boxes or perhaps if you can procure some chest-high wooden poles and bunting as well, you can now recreate the problem of reversing into a single space in a multi-storey car park. See fig. 26. Because of the bunting (or boxes) representing the front bumpers of cars parked opposite your space, you are forced to back in at a tight angle. There are plenty of "solid objects" (like concrete pillars) at close quarters to worry about. You soon learn to choose your starting position

Fig 27 Open space exercise to teach how to stop with your bumper exactly at the kerb. Learner has here got out to double-check her skill.

with skill so that the rest becomes easy! This exercise also prepares you for backing in to an individual, outdoor parking bay which you may be asked to do on your Practical Test. Fig. 21 and its text warn you of dangers to consider. An indicator signal may be appropriate. You may need to pull forward and back, finally, so as to occupy the middle of the bay – allowing doors to be opened on either side. (Next door spaces might be full before you leave.) Make up other difficult exercises too; for example, mock up parking between cars at the kerb, known as reverse (parallel) parking, and dealt with in the next section. You'll never regret becoming expert at parking. And you'll avoid all fear of city-centre parking that haunts many so-called drivers.

Figs. 27–28 show an exercise to help with the **Three-Point-Turn**, which I come to next. Your length of rope or tape is shown representing the line of the gutter at the edge of a road. Practise driving up slowly at right angles and stopping with your front (or back) bumper vertically above this edge.

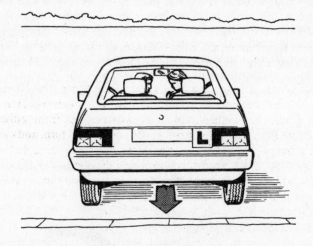

Fig 28 Same exercise as fig. 27, in reverse.

CAR CONTROL TESTS ON YOUR PRACTICAL TEST

I now come to **STAGE THREE**, the main manoeuvring requirements of your Practical Driving Test.

1. THE THREE-POINT-TURN
2. THE REVERSE ROUND A CORNER
3. STEEP (up)HILL STARTS
4. REVERSE (PARALLEL) PARKING

Remember, get your teacher to drive to very quiet, suitable places for each exercise. If you are learning with amateur instruction and, as I very much hope, you have been able to stay with me and keep off-road so far, remind yourself that, from now on, you will have to contend with other traffic. You are permitted to remove your seat belt for those manoeuvres which require reversing; however, you would be at fault if you forgot to re-buckle it afterwards and, unless your belt is of an ancient, non inertia-reel type, it is unnecessary; so I recommend that you keep yours on.

1. THE THREE-POINT-TURN
(Turning your car round between the pavements of a quiet road.)

Your teacher should find a level road 7–8 metres wide with pavements both sides, and as quiet as a cul-de-sac. Pick a spot well away from any junction, and where there are no tree trunks or lamp-posts, etc., to bump!

No signals are expected of you during the Three-Point-Turn so you must be especially careful about other drivers. Don't start a turn if another vehicle is approaching from either direction. Let it pass. If you are in the middle of a turn, and can wait at the point you have reached to let anyone coming go by, do so. You must expect not only children but thoughtless adults, too, to step in front of or behind your car in the middle of your progress. Mad or irresponsible, that is their whim. You stop – unless you wish to appear in Court. See PEDESTRIANS CROSSING in Chapter 5, page 159.

The three-point, or three-move, turn is only possible if the road is wide enough. On your Practical Test, if the examiner picks too narrow a road and you need five moves, don't worry. This won't be held against you. All you are expected to do is turn the car in the least possible number of forward and backward moves, without overhanging unduly, or biffing, the kerb either side, and without, as far as possible, inconveniencing others.

At the start, the car should be next to the kerb on your side of the road. At the finish, it should be facing the other way, parked next to the kerb on the other side – unless the examiner directs you to drive on as you reach the end of the final move.

Stop Properly At The Kerb

Whenever you pull in, do so correctly. Your nearside wheels should always be well within 2 tyre-widths from, and parallel to, the kerb. Set your handbrake and return to neutral. Then release the clutch and, lastly, your footbrake. Adopting these good habits from the outset will – I remind you – make certain you cannot slip up when it comes to your Practical Test or, for that matter, in years to come.

Whilst you are out on test, not only will your examiner then be impressed by your ability to pull in neatly, close to the kerb, you will be ready to begin whatever he asks you to do next. So far as he is concerned, keep your engine running; you can relax while you listen to what that is. (The only time you switch off the engine on your Practical Test is when you finish, back at the Test Centre.) If it is to "turn the vehicle in the road to face the opposite way using the forward and reverse gears", as examiner parlance would rather have you refer to the Three-Point-Turn, here follows what you must do:

Sequence For Three-Point-Turn

In fig. 29, **1** you are correctly pulled in next to the kerb.

Check *both* ways that all is clear. *Turn round and look*. Do not just rely on mirrors.

When all is clear make a **Smooth Start** forwards in 1st gear at **Mile-An-Hour** speed.

Immediately the car is in motion swing the steering into full, righthand lock to take you towards the other side.

Whilst doing this make a double-check for traffic behind by looking over your right shoulder. (You can still safely stop and wait if anyone is coming.)

As fig. 29, **2** shows, you should be *on full lock* well *before* the car has moved one metre.

Once full lock is on, you can go a little quicker by releasing the clutch pedal a fraction more but you must still move *slowly* towards the other side. This is to make sure you continue to

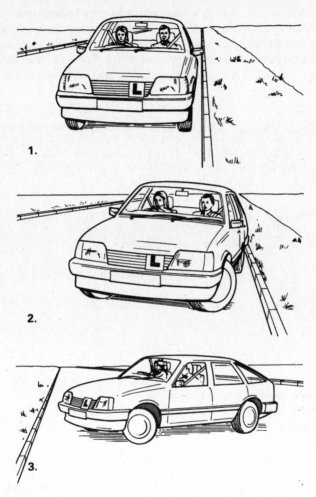

Fig 29 Three-Point-Turn sequence **1, 2, 3.**

have time to keep an eye both ways for traffic, as you progress.

You must slow down again, by dropping the clutch pedal back down that same fraction, for the last one to one-and-a-half metres towards the opposite kerb. Or, if the road banks steeply down into the gutter (which it often does), and the car starts to run on into the gutter under its own momentum, you will instead have to put your clutch pedal further down and use your footbrake to prevent your car going too fast or too far.

Fig. 29, **3** shows this stage, still on the first lock, still under way, but where you have again slowed down to barely moving.

You are about to switch your steering fully over to the other lock (ready for the reverse back) *before* you stop.

During that final metre-and-a-half, *not before*, you rapidly make your lock-change. You stop – using your footbrake (and putting your clutch pedal down if it is not there already) – with your front bumper at the kerb, as in fig. 30, **4**.

Your steering is already on the opposite lock (you have just put it there). The car can overhang the kerb slightly – though not to the danger or inconvenience of pedestrians – but your tyres must not biff the kerb. (Should you fail to get the full opposite lock on before you stop, this can be completed when you start the reverse. However, you will not achieve such a neat turn.)

Next, handbrake on, gear into neutral and look both ways, as the lady driver is doing in fig. 30, **4** – to be sure all is still clear. Wait until it is. If you need to wait more than a few seconds, for example for unexpected traffic to pass, release your clutch and footbrake pedals. This saves wear on the clutch mechanism and gives a moment for your leg muscles to relax!

You now do a **Smooth Start** reverse backwards, remembering to get the whole upper part of your body, head and neck round, so that you can see over your inside shoulder exactly where you are aiming. All the time be alert as well for traffic coming along; if you are moving slowly enough under clutch-slipping control as suggested, you should easily be able to manage quick glances up and down the road during the period between leaving one kerb and approaching the other.

Having said that, I should add that you mustn't dawdle across, possibly as a result holding up traffic unnecessarily; however, no examiner will want to see you attempting this, or any other manoeuvre, at any speed above one at which *you* can remain calm, comfortable and in absolute control of your car.

Provided you learned your **Smooth Start From Standing** properly, there should be no danger of slipping forwards into

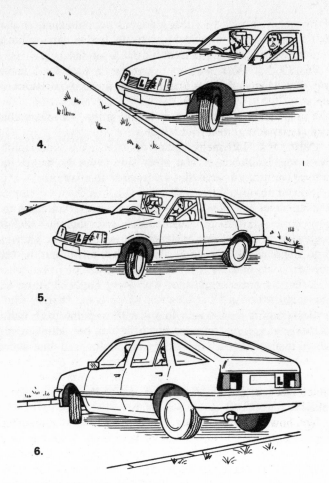

Fig 30 Three-Point-Turn sequence **4, 5, 6**..

the gutter before you can get on the move backwards. If a steeply banked gutter causes trouble, see **Steep (up)Hill Starts** a few pages on.

Keep *fully* on this second lock until your back bumper is one to one-and-a-half metres off the original kerb. See **5**, fig. 30. The driver is *yet* to start changing back to the first lock.

Once again, it is only in the last metre-and-a-half, *not before*, that you swing back to the original lock, *ready to go forwards.* Stop with your rear bumper level with the kerb as in **6**, fig. 30. Put your handbrake on again and, as ever, return to neutral before taking your feet off the footpedals.

(*Don't be afraid to work "furiously" with the steering wheel* to achieve the lock changes. The *slower* you control the speed of the car whilst you do them, the *easier* they are. Use the proper, basic steering movements, given with fig. 9, and watch you don't cross your hands.)

Next look both ways again. As soon as it's safe, drive forwards, pulling in on the other side correctly, as you did before the turn was started, unless asked to drive on.

Sometimes on a fairly wide road you will, from experience, realise about half way across during the backward move that you *could* go forwards and round from there. If so, do. Likewise do so on Test; however, you are more likely then to find you need all the road available to make your turn in three moves, so do practise on "difficult" roads.

After you are accomplished with **Steep (up)Hill Starts** and *Downhill* Mile-An-Hour Control, which come shortly, find a really steep hill on which to try a three-point-turn. You're unlikely to get that on your Practical Test but, knowing you could manage if you did, works wonders for your confidence!

2. THE REVERSE ROUND A CORNER

Most Practical Test candidates are asked to reverse to the left – being the more difficult side – as in fig. 31. You can be asked to use a turning to your right as in fig. 32, so you need to practise both. (The latter is the one most usually requested of Learners taking their Practical Test in a light van. The fact of it being slightly easier to see down into the road, the one into which you are backing, compensates a little for the van's lack of rear, side windows.)

The examiner normally asks you on some relatively *minor* road to pull in shortly before a side-turning he has chosen, and then explains what it is he will want you to do. (The first thing, before you begin the manoeuvre, will be to move on *safely* to a correctly judged "starting position", about 10 metres beyond the turning.) He may give explicit instructions about how far you are to back down the turning having entered it, or he may leave it that you are to keep going until he says stop. Do ask if you are not clear on this point. As you continue backing you should judge by eye to keep less than one metre from, and parallel to, the kerb on your own side (whichever that may be). Stick to that until you are ready to pull in and stop. However, unless given insufficient warning, aim to edge in to within 1–2 tyre-widths off the kerb by the time you reach the point requested.

Find suitable quiet places to begin learning this manoeuvre, again, with your teacher driving there. HE should park or re-park the car safely in the ''starting position'' (**A**, figs. 31–32) each time. (Quite soon later on, after a reasonable amount of on-road experience, first of **Moving Off** and then of **Pulling In On The Left** – for which see Chapter 5 – you will be able to do that yourself. For example, you have to be careful not to signal too early and have people think you are going directly into the turning; and you must be able yourself to select the safest point to stop.)

You must pick a perfectly flat street corner for your first attempts. As will become clear, extra skills are needed if the opening or the road it leads off are on a slope. Move on to sloping terrain in due course once **Steep (up)Hill Starts**, the **Smooth Start Downhill**, and *Downhill* **Mile-An-Hour**

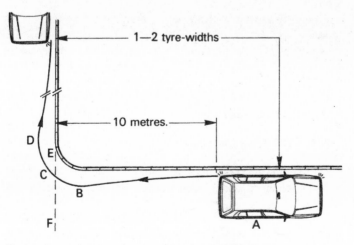

Fig 31 Reversing round a corner on the nearside (passenger's side).

Control (in reverse for this exercise), no longer cause you any problems. All of these are explained in the next few pages.

Although you are not officially expected to give a signal during this reverse, it is a better practice. So do it; set your lefthand indicator signal before you begin the lefthand reverse, a righthand one before you reverse to the right. Remember to cancel the signal at the end of the manoeuvre.

Sequence For Reverse Round A Corner

Assume you have pulled up correctly by the kerb at **A** – say 10 metres beyond the opening (figs. 31–32). Check for traffic from all directions.

(*Throughout this manoeuvre you must* maintain eye-flashing spot checks at likely moments toward every avenue from which danger could come.)

Then, when all is clear – including from *ahead* of you AND from *down the turning you will enter* – reverse towards **B** under superb clutch and accelerator control.

Whether doing a reverse to the left or right side, look backwards over your *left* shoulder. This makes sure you will always be able to see as much as possible of the road you are leaving.

Ease your car away from the kerb straightaway but not so suddenly or acutely that one of the front (steering) wheels, *swinging wide in the first metre or so*, mounts it or rasps along it. (The latter is one of the worst treatments you can give a tyre or wheel.)

Between **B** and **D** the whole side of the car next to the kerb will need to be a maximum of 4 tyre-widths from it as you go round.

If you are doing the ''easier'' reverse (fig. 32, to the right side) then, as you approach and go round **B–D**, you will have the advantage of being able to glance *temporarily* over your right shoulder to check how closely you are rounding the pavement.

Maintain clutch-slipping **Mile-An-Hour** control of your speed between **A** and **B**. About half way to **B** drop your clutch pedal below the biting point briefly. You will feel at once whether the car will simply stop until you move it on again by

66

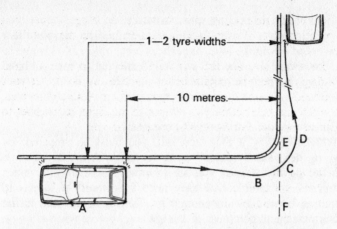

Fig 32 Reversing round a corner on the offside (driver's side).

raising the clutch pedal, or whether there is, in fact, a downward slope, one which will cause the car to carry on *too quickly* into the turn. If the former happens you immediately know that, provided you don't over-shoot, you will be able to **Almost Stop ... But Not Quite,** at **B**, and then continue to use your **Mile-An-Hour** technique to take you round **B–D**, and on into the turning under total control. If the latter occurs – with the instant feeling the car will run away too fast into the turn – then you know you will need a *Downhill* **Mile-An-Hour** technique.

Downhill **Mile-An-Hour** *Control*

This simply means you are going to have to control your speed further, slow as it already is, with the footbrake (and the clutch pedal down to prevent stalling), during the critical stage from just before **B**, at least until just after **D**.

You take charge with the footbrake for the minimum distance necessary because, during that time, the car is not strictly speaking being "driven". It is freewheeling (coasting). However, that is unavoidable. You use a fine touch on your brake pedal during this critical period so you never quite stop (unless you have to, e.g. for a pedestrian) but are enabled to control speed exactly as you want it. Easing the brake a smidgen lets you go faster. Restoring your pressure on the pedal checks increasing speed instantly.

Anticipation of overshooting the turn in error, despite there being no downhill slope, or perhaps recognition of a change to a downward slope on the way round, may mean you will have to combine both techniques.

Reverse Round A Corner – Continued

Whichever way it may turn out, you must be prepared, by going dead slowly when you arrive at **B**. You will soon see better down the road you are to enter. There may be snags there. For example, you may need temporarily to stop, and then to move forward enough to allow someone safe vision and passage to come out of the opening, before you can go on again.

(A reversing driver should always give way.)

Or you may misjudge and need to pull out again a little before you can correct your mistake. (You would move forward the minimum distance necessary before continuing; your examiner would be better pleased that way, than if you carried on, foolishly, backwards, and then mounted the kerb or made a very wide entry.)

If you do have to move forward at any stage, always remember to look both ways along your original road *first*!

Another reason for stopping might be for pedestrians, especially tiny tots, anywhere in the close vicinity. Wait until you know what they want to do.

The line of the opening's kerbstones – if extended in your mind's eye into the road you are leaving – will, just after **B**, pass through both of your rear wheels (dotted lines **E–F** in figs. 31–32).

Check again at this juncture, for traffic. Glance all ways; especially watch the road you are *leaving*. If you are forced to stop, *no harm done*. As your outer front wing will shortly *swing wide*, out towards the road you are exiting, it is best to wait while traffic from *either* direction along that road passes.

From **B** onwards, still *barely moving*, you keep the car parallel to the kerb as it rounds away from you.

Swing the steering wheel into lock (as much as required – probably immediate full lock) as you move incredibly slowly between **B** and **C**. Towards **D**, you start to straighten up again, so that you will be able to continue your reverse, running parallel to the kerb just under one metre off it. Don't be afraid to work really fast with the steering wheel – *at your barely moving speed* – both to get your car round neatly and then to get it squared up again at the correct stage.

Now carry on at a gentle reverse pace until instructed by the examiner to pull in and stop parked by the kerbside. Ease in to within 2 tyre-widths of the kerb as you so do.

It is usual to be asked to reverse several car lengths after straightening up, both to show that you can time your straightening up correctly and not overdo it, and to show that you can then back the car straight and in control. Your continued vigilance, looking all around for other traffic during the extended reverse, is also being watched. See **Your Eyes When Reversing**, page 49.

Unless you have been asked to pull in and stop less than three or four car lengths down the turning, your foot needs to come right off the clutch pedal during this extended reverse. Aim to have it right off immediately after you have straightened up. You must bring your foot off the gas at the same time, or off the footbrake if you have been restraining speed with that. Then you can see at once how fast your car will continue going on this **Minimum Speed – Clutch Pedal Up** basis (see page 43). If you now need any additional acceleration, which you may well do, "feather" it in with a very gentle squeeze of your foot. But remember, a brisk walking pace is the maximum for safety for going backwards. If you are now going downhill and beginning to go too fast despite the effect – on zero acceleration – of "engine braking" (see page 46), slow up again by braking lightly as required.

With practice you will come to recognise whether you need more acceleration (or braking), with no measurable pause before you do whichever it is – indeed, almost without thinking.

If your judgement of *when* to swing into lock for these reverses is poor, the answer is practice. During early attempts stop at different stages, and get out and look each time at how your car is placed. Once you get it right this will cement in your mind how things *should* look from the driving seat. Unless you *really* are *barely moving* between **B** and **D** (figs. 31

and 32) there is little chance that you will get your steering right.

Note: After a righthand reverse you are parked on the "wrong" side of the road facing on-coming traffic. Before you can come out again on to the road you reversed off, you first have to cross to your own side of your side-turning. You have to do this immediately you move off, using a proper left indicator signal and suitable care in the course of so doing. It is a case of adapting the full moving off procedure of fig. 41, page 129. However, your teacher should do this for you at this early stage. Once you are well into Chapters 5 and 6 of this book you will be able to tackle it yourself.

I mentioned earlier that extra skills are needed if your chosen side-turning is not on level ground. If the first stage of reversing towards the turn is uphill to any marked degree, then ability to make a **Steep (up)Hill Start** (for which see below) will be essential. If going into the turning itself will still be considerably uphill, then between **B** and **D**, barely moving and under clutch slip control, you will, in addition, need rather more engine rpm than would be needed on the level. (This is akin to the extra rpm that would be needed for a **Steep (up)Hill Start** at the same place.) If, on the other hand, the slope is very much downhill to reach the turning, and goes on steeply down as you enter it, you will need to have had a reasonable amount of practice both with the **Smooth Start Downhill** which follows a few pages on, and with the *Down-hill* **Mile-An-Hour** *Control* mentioned a few paragraphs back. Hence my hints to leave more tricky reverses until you have all the control skills well "taped". Practise harder ones later on, as you progress through the rest of this book.

Finally, have you worked out why you must learn the three-point-turn and these reverses – apart, that is, than for your Practical Test? It is so that you can stick to the final principle listed on page 49. Look there (don't be lazy). And never be a lazy driver by ignoring that principle. When you are on a busy main road and need to turn back to go the other way, ideally, you should turn left down a minor road first; then find a side turning off that. Either a three-point-turn in it, or reversing round into the side turning, then enable you to make your way back to the major road and turn right. An alternative might be a **U**-turn – preferably carried out in the minor road – unless it is a one-way street or signs ban it anyway. Position close to the kerb. Once traffic is clear *in both directions* swing onto full righthand lock to get round and away in one. Leave time for a three-point-turn lest you misjudge the width.

3. STEEP (up)HILL STARTS
Before you can (up)hill start, understand this:

PROVIDED ACCELERATION IS SUFFICIENT TO MOVE YOUR CAR UP THE HILL, there is one point at which the clutch pedal can be held, at which the slipping clutch stops your car rolling back downhill (handbrake off) but at which the gear is yet insufficiently engaged to move the weight of your car up the hill. With your clutch held at this point your car is "suspended" between going and rolling back.

For the level-road **Smooth Start** you already know about waiting until this biting point is reached before releasing the handbrake.

The only difference in the **Steep (up)Hill Start** is in the amount of gas required. More fuel is needed to hold the car against the hill and, after, to make it climb. You press the accelerator perhaps half as much again to start with (**Key to Fig. 11, 5**), as you would on level road. However, there is no need to overdo it, and have the engine "scream".

Then, as your clutch comes up to the biting point and this (raised) engine rpm begins to die away (**Key to Fig. 12, 1** and **2**), you hold the clutch pedal there – exactly as normally. Next, you squeeze your accelerator pedal down a tiny bit more so as to restore the higher rpm you had earlier set. This brings you to the point that you are ready to let your handbrake off, as in **Key to Fig. 12, 3,** (a) and (b).

Do so, and you will find the car "suspended", standing still on your uphill slope. It will be ready to complete your **Smooth Start** in the normal way – **Key to Fig. 12, 3** (c) onwards.

Let your teacher find a quiet, gentle hill. Make sure there is no one standing behind you into whom you could roll back, and that no one is coming along from either direction. Then experiment until you can consistently hold the car *still*, in 1st gear – neither going forward nor rolling back – when you let the handbrake off. A few attempts should be enough. There's no need to wear yourself (or your clutch) out in the process.

Don't attempt to move up the hill yet. This ''initiation'' practice proves that *you* (too) can ''suspend'' the car. (Try the same in reverse to prove you can do it that way as well!)

Once you achieve this correct ''balance'' between the accelerator and clutch pedals *every time*, your task is all but done. You are ready to graduate to moving off on a **Steep (up)Hill Start** as confidently and competently as you do on the level. Simply continue from **Key to Fig. 12, 3** (c).

The first time you practise a **Steep (up)Hill Start** the car probably will run back. For this reason see fig. 33! *Stop dead with your footbrake* (and your clutch down); pull on your handbrake and return to neutral; you can now release your clutch, then brake pedals, and prepare to begin again. Don't accelerate wildly or jump off the clutch. *Stop and re-start*.

When proficient try the **Almost Stopping ... But Not Quite** routine (page 47) *uphill* in 1st gear. Then see if you can slow to a *stop* using your skill with the clutch biting point alone. When you can do that – and hold it there for a few

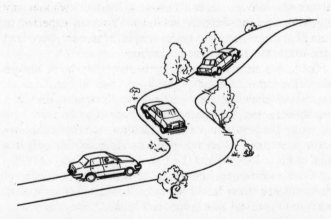

Fig 33 Hill Start. Practise first on slight inclines then progress to steeper hills.

seconds until *you* decide to move on – without touching your handbrake or footbrake in the meantime, you can tell yourself you have truly cracked the challenge of steep (up)hill starts! Now try in reverse!

Unless an obviously, seriously **Steep (up)Hill Start** occurs anyway during your Practical Test, perhaps due to an uphill queue or because of having to stop at a junction on a steep incline, you may well be asked to pull in at the left on a steep uphill, so that the examiner can check your skill. After the stop he will say words such as "drive on when you are ready". You must now use the full moving off procedure, shown by fig. 41 and described by text there, and demonstrate that you can move off again smoothly, in control, without any running back.

Smooth Downhill Starts are easier, you will be glad to hear! I will go into detail in the next main section of this chapter. First, however, I must deal with the final, essential manoeuvring skill you must be able to accomplish for your Practical Test – **Reverse (Parallel) Parking**.

4. REVERSE (PARALLEL) PARKING

This term is examiner-speak for parking alongside and parallel to the kerb, between two other vehicles. On your Practical Test he should point out in advance where he intends you to carry out the manoeuvre. He will choose a "space" without any vehicle parked immediately behind it. You are expected to estimate where such a vehicle might reasonably be, and demonstrate this manoeuvre accordingly.

First let me mention some fundamentals: you should always face in the same direction as traffic on your side of the road. Figs. 34–38 show the steps in sequence. Unless a space is a clear three car lengths longer than your car, it never pays to try and go in forwards. The exercise therefore deals with shorter spaces which are, of course, the problem ones. Judging if a short space is long enough will come with experience. One-and-a-half metres longer than your car is probably a minimum.

Judgement of the whole manoeuvre, when you later come to do it "live", will be transformed into "child's play" if you do proper open space trials now, using the same cardboard boxes and tape that were suggested for earlier manoeuvring exercises.

Otherwise, you may find that hitting parked cars is costly! Hence the partly dummy "space" used on the Practical Test.

(**Note:** For first "live" attempts of your own betwixt real cars – when that time comes – choose a road and a space at a point in the day when little other traffic is likely. You don't want to entertain any risk of unnecessarily holding up or annoying queues of people in a hurry! Meanwhile, I shall assume for the purposes of the rest of this explanation that you will, by the time you first go "live", have gained, through your reading further in this book, an innate safety-conscience; one which will cause you to make, as you progress with the manoeuvre, all necessary safety checks. These must include, for examples, for danger to other traffic from your front wing swinging wide as you progress, and for those idiotic pedestrians who invariably amble across the very space you are backing into, whilst you are so doing!)

In order to make the sequence of instructions in figs. 34–38 easier to follow I have drawn real cars into the scene. Although at this stage you will be substituting props for other vehicles and a kerb, I will, for the same reason, take you – in my text here – through the method as if it were already "for real":

Signalling left in advance with your indicator, arrive to a gentle stop beyond the space, parallel to and with the back of your car slightly ahead of the back of the vehicle next forward of the space. As you need to pull up for your "Start Position" with slightly less than a full door's opening width between your car and the other vehicle, keep a wary eye that no one inside it is about to swing open his door.

Select reverse gear straightaway, rather than moving to neutral once you have applied the handbrake. This necessitates continuing to keep your clutch pedal **DOWN** thereafter, until you are ready; however, the advantage is that your reversing light(s) – activated via the gear lever – come on, which helps warn people behind what you are planning to do. (**Note:** In a traffic-ridden street, your gentle stop just beyond the space, which can be observed in conjunction with your indicator being quite quickly followed by your reversing light(s) coming on, should be enough to make your intentions clear to anyone behind. Should such a driver pull up too close, it's best to drive on and find another parking place. Hopefully, he will

Fig 34 Kerbside parking between cars: start position.

stop short, to leave you room. On your Practical Test, however, there should be no need to move up to this beginning point other than when traffic from behind has ceased.)

You are now ready to reverse into the space, taking almost immediate, full lefthand lock to get you in. Do not begin, however, until you are sure: (a) that there are no pedestrians (from *either* side of the road) about to wander behind you; (b) that no oncoming traffic from in front of you can be compromised as your front wing – inevitably – swings outward to begin with (a bash would undoubtedly be judged your fault); and (c) that any driver, now waiting behind you, will continue so to do until you are sufficiently "in" to your space. (The trend, I must warn you, is for him to try to rush on with indecent haste, squeezing past as soon as possible. Again, if you touch him with your front wing, you will be hard pressed to avoid all the blame.)

Very slowly does it for this "Step Two" once you do start. The nearside back corner of your car needs to head for the kerb at the mid-point of the length of the space.

Before your back *wheels* are within three-quarters of a metre of that mid-point along the kerb, and as soon as you think your front wing will clear the car in front, you change

Fig 35 Kerbside parking between cars: step two – full lefthand lock to get you in.

back to the other lock (fully). During this lock changeover of "Step Three", your car speed must be so slow as to be barely observable. Only that minuscule pace will give you the chance

Fig 36 Kerbside parking between cars: step three – lock change-over to (full) righthand lock.

Fig 37 Kerbside parking between cars: step four – a little further to go on full righthand lock before you are "in", ready to straighten up.

to avoid a biff on your nearside front wing, and time to observe fully all around – especially for pedestrians trying to slip in front of or behind you – as you progress. For "Step Four", with that wing now clear, stay (or get) on full righthand lock to bring your car fully parallel to the kerb and "in". Once parallel to it, speed still being hardly discernable to the onlooker, use any more backing room you have, to straighten up. "Step Five" – continuing to straighten up if necessary – is

Fig 38 Kerbside parking between cars: final step – leave your car in the middle of the available space.

now a matter of making sure you leave the car in the middle of the space. Then, if either the car ahead or the car behind needs room to manoeuvre, it is there for them.

No more than two, back-and-forth, "shunts" may be regarded as normal in order to make sure you leave your car tucked in correctly within 1–2 tyre widths of the kerb. If it ever looks as if you will need to "shuffle" more than that, the chances are that you would be better to pull right out, and start again fresh. The same applies if, at "Step Three", you are already too near the kerb – but it has become obvious that your front wing has no chance of clearing the back of the car in front were you to make the lock change on time. (In that event, it is probable that your initial "aim" was adrift of the mid-point of the space, or that the space is actually too small for your car.)

FURTHER MATTERS OF CONTROL

To complete your grasp of basic car control you need to know about two more, important aspects of making use of engine compression resistance – i.e. *engine braking*. These concern moving off, and parking:

SMOOTH START DOWNHILL

In **Key to Fig. 11, 4**, and later, I said 2nd gear is correct for moving off downhill. I can now add that, on any reasonable downhill slope, you omit from your **Smooth Start** procedure the raising of your engine rpm. As the decline is going to cause the car to roll forward on its way anyway, directly you release the handbrake, the process from **Key to Fig. 11, 4** onwards also changes. It becomes more like the latter part of changing gear. (See fig. 17 and **How To Change Gear**.)

Assume you have selected 2nd gear, your foot holds the clutch down and you are ready to release the handbrake. Leaving aside, for the moment, safety procedures when moving off (to be dealt with by fig. 41 in Chapter 5), all you now need to do, when you decide to go, is to let your handbrake off and then release your clutch in one smooth movement, no more than an instant later – directly the car is gathering pace.

Depending on how steep the decline is, you can then follow up straightaway with gentle, initial acceleration, or you can allow the engine braking of being in 2nd gear to hold the car back from increasing speed more than you want.

On a *very* steep hill you might soon need to add your footbrake so as to control speed to a safe level.

The above technique helps avoid the car ever *freewheeling*; that is, running forward with your clutch pedal still down and therefore "coasting", having no gear engaged. Apart from the very short distances when such coasting sometimes cannot be avoided in reverse (see page 67) or momentarily, during gear changes, it is unacceptable. It equates to letting your car run on the open road, in neutral, under its own momentum and with your clutch pedal up; which is more wrong still. Either error can lead to increased speed, particularly on a steep decline, and put unsafe reliance on your brakes; you can run into danger just trying to get back into gear, too; and, when your steering wheels are neither driven nor engine-braked, your steering becomes less positive.

An examiner would, were you to coast without good cause, rightly conclude that you were not maintaining full control of your vehicle.

HILL PARKING

When you park on a hill you need first to be parallel to the kerb with your back and front, nearside wheels about one tyre-width out from it. Then you can gently run the steering wheels in, on lock, to touch the kerb (but not to press it hard), before you firmly set the handbrake.

Turn the steering wheels as shown in fig. 39 so that, if the

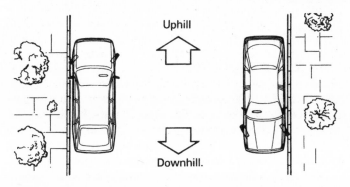

Fig 39 Parking on a hill.

79

handbrake were to fail, the car should quickly be stopped, "chocked" by the kerb. On your open space you can get into practice by "wedging" your front tyre against your taped out, substitute kerb.

Note the difference in what you do – when you park on real roads later on – depending upon whether you are facing uphill, or pointing downhill.

Then, in addition, when facing uphill, leave the car in 1st gear after you switch off; this adds engine compression hold. Similarly, on a downhill slope, leave the gear in reverse. Leave automatic transmission in the **Park** position whether facing uphill or down (this locks engine and transmission together to give the same effect). Engine compression hold then becomes your second-line defence against handbrake failure.

Always lock doors so that children cannot tamper. See also page 17.

AUTOMATIC TRANSMISSION

I remind you that a Practical Test pass with automatic transmission restricts you to this type of vehicle only (see page 17). Below, I bring together for those readers concerned *all* you need to know about how an automatic-geared car should be driven. I have so done to avoid unnecessary, detailed references to automatic gears elsewhere. Whilst my explanations therefore include some matters which will only become relevant later, on the open road, I sincerely hope you will *not*, as a result, be tempted to cut back on your OPEN SPACE, initial mastery of car control, the secret of safe, successful learning that is the cornerstone of this book!

ONLY THE RIGHT FOOT
To drive an automatic USE ONLY YOUR RIGHT FOOT, NEVER THE LEFT. There are only two pedals with which to cope. You move your right foot from the accelerator, on the right, to the brake, on the left, and back, as required.

Don't listen to those who claim you can brake with the left foot. This technique can only lead to muddle and the danger, in emergency, of finding yourself accelerating against your own brakes.

THE SELECTOR LEVER

At the time of writing, there are, with the majority of automatic transmissions, four basic positions of the selector lever. One, or more, numbered, gear *Lock* position(s) is/are also usually provided.

The lever itself generally incorporates a button (or other device, the precise method of operation of which your teacher must explain) which is there to prevent inadvertent selection of positions which, mechanically, cannot be allowed to follow each other directly in sequence. You must find out – and remember (!) – exactly for which selections of the lever this button/device must be employed. The easiest way to do that is to ask your teacher to demonstrate precisely how the lever is shifted to each separate position, as well as any other model-specific niceties about which you need to know.

I will deal with the four basic positions first. They are: *Park, Neutral, Drive* and *Reverse*:

Park This provides a safety hold on the transmission, preventing the car running away should the handbrake fail when parked. Use it only when parked. Never even contemplate engaging it during driving. So doing could cause severe damage.

Neutral The *Neutral* position is usually next to *Drive*. In *Neutral* the gears are disengaged.

For safety, on most makes, it is only possible to start the engine with the lever in *Neutral* or in *Park*. Otherwise the car could shoot off on the starter.

So the procedure to ingrain clearly in your mind – for the inevitable times when your engine *stalls* – is at once to hold the car on your footbrake while you get the lever back into *Neutral* FAST. That then enables you quickly to re-start the engine and re-select *Drive* (or *Reverse*) to get you moving again. *It is a process you must practise many times, so that you can do it almost without conscious thought should you ever need it in a hurry.*

Drive In *Drive* (the normal driving position) gear changes *look after themselves*. When you select *Drive* before moving off, the gearbox automatically selects 1st (but doesn't, yet, engage it); then, as you come to accelerate for moving off, the viscous fluid (or otherwise variable) coupling of the engine to the selected gear becomes made, and an ultra-smooth transmission of power to the driving wheels is achieved progressively – just as it would be with a correctly used, ordinary clutch; after that, the gearbox changes itself to 2nd directly the proper speed is reached, and so on. It takes account of other factors too, such as extra loading being carried or whether you are driving uphill or downhill. Likewise, downward changes are automatically made as you slow down.

All you need to grasp initially, therefore, are the correct procedures for moving off, and for stopping again subsequently, whenever you need so to do. Here they are. I presume, as I write this particular piece, that your car will be standing – as I urged at the start of this automatic-gears section – on a *level*, OPEN SPACE, well away from public roads; that you are already at the wheel; that your handbrake is on securely and your engine is ticking over in *Park* or *Neutral*; and that, last but not least, you are now only waiting for your teacher to give you the go ahead command for the first time.

(Moving off *downhill* or, for that matter, *uphill*, incidentally, causes few additional problems. Downhill, gentler than usual acceleration or, possibly, the retention of a little footbrake control, easily solve any that occur; moving away steeply uphill demands a little further refinement of technique, needing more explanation but, I promise, nothing that is at all difficult. I will return to the latter in just a few moments, under **Hints And Pitfalls**.)

MOVING OFF

You are ready to begin, so here goes:

(1) Apply the footbrake *using your right foot*.
(2) Select *Drive*. (Move the lever as your teacher has already shown you. If you were originally in *Park*, simply pass, gently, through *Neutral* to *Drive*. You will need to pass through *Reverse* too, if, as is normal, that is so positioned within the selector "gate".)
(3) Release the handbrake but keep your footbrake applied.
(4) Check your mirrors and, accordingly, signal when the moment to go appears ripe. (See **Moving Off**, in Chapter 5, page 129.)
(5) Continue holding the car with the footbrake while you make your final checks that it is safe to move.

(6) If/when they confirm that you are still clear to go, move your right foot from the brake to the accelerator, and *gently* squeeze it.

That will deliver you a **Smooth Start**.

Then you can add acceleration at will, until you build up the speed you require.

A **Smooth Start From Standing** is almost guaranteed with automatic transmission: for one thing because you can wait in *Drive* (still holding the car on your footbrake) for as long as you need so to do; secondly because, unless your foot lands on the accelerator like might that of a stampeding elephant, the system is, as already explained, designed to transfer the take-up of power from the engine to the wheels in an entirely even, jerk-free progression. Even quite a clumsy jab at that pedal should only result in a modest surge of power, at once controllable by taking your foot off again and putting it back onto the footbrake pedal if necessary. The characteristic "kangaroo" hops associated with manual gears and clutch are surprisingly difficult to achieve automatically!

Make it your rule, in the above moving-off sequence, never to select *Drive* or release your handbrake until you *first* have the car secure on the footbrake. On a hill it could run forward (or even back) before you are ready. Equally important, *Drive* and *Reverse* are quite capable of taking your car forward against the handbrake, especially if the choke on a cold engine is causing a high tick-over speed.

SLOWING OR STOPPING

To slow down or when stopping, you simply, to begin with, release your accelerator. Add braking as required, *using your right foot on the footbrake*. (Using that foot, remember, is what stops you from ever hitting the accelerator whilst trying to brake.) Note that, when stopping, you must always finally halt on your footbrake, never your handbrake.

To cut speed or stop *more quickly*, simply go directly onto the footbrake with that right foot, and squeeze it accordingly. Your gears, of course, change down automatically, however rapidly you slow or stop.

In stop-start traffic you can just hold the car on the

footbrake at most stops. Stay in *Drive*. Simply switch your foot to the accelerator when ready to go. (You might need to add your handbrake on a very steep uphill – see **Hints and Pitfalls** below.)

However, there is more to consider. When stopped for any long period, it is better driving to *use your handbrake* AND then return to *Neutral*. You are thus enabled to take your foot off the footbrake and relax. As a bonus your brakelights are thereby extinguished, which saves eye-strain for people behind, particularly when it is wet or dark. It doesn't take a moment to prepare to go again once you can move on.

It is also safer driving to use your handbrake AND come back to *Neutral*, whenever you stop for long *at the front* of any queue; at traffic lights, other junctions, Zebra crossings, and wherever pedestrians may wander across in front of you, are example places. The habit safeguards you against mistakes and calamities. Form it from the outset.

(Suppose you are the first to stop, say, at a Pelican crossing. Dreaming for a moment, your foot crosses to the accelerator and revs up the engine. If you were still in *Drive* . . . Equally, suppose a spasm of cramp suddenly caused you to straighten your leg, unintentionally ramming on the accelerator . . . In either instance or in any similar one, then where might you be?)

MANOEUVRING

Manoeuvring becomes a joy with automatic transmission. For the equivalent of the **Mile-An-Hour** OPEN SPACE exercise on page 43, all you need normally do at number (6) in the moving off routine above is partially release your footbrake. This allows you to move your car, still under control of the footbrake, however little, or slowly, you want. The **Minimum Speed** exercise, which follows that one, becomes equally simple. You just gently fine-tune the snail's pace you require, by feel, here using a featherlight touch on your footbrake pedal. If, at any stage, you should require a smidgeon of additional speed, you merely transfer that featherlight right foot across to the gas pedal as appropriate.

Reverse Delicate, manoeuvring control can also be achieved in reverse by using your right foot (and your brain!) in exactly the same way as just described for going forwards. Generally, if you are having to alternate forward and backward moves, you can hold the car on your footbrake*while you move the selector, gently, from *Drive* via *Neutral* to *Reverse*, or vice versa. You won't necessarily need your handbrake at each stop unless you are on a steep slope, or other factors, such as safety, demand its use.

Now *Lock 1, 2, etc.* These selector lever positions enable you to override the automatic, upward gear changes and keep in a low gear. This may, as an alternative to **Kickdown** (for which see below), be important for overtaking (it will prevent the gearbox from changing up before you want it to, for example, if, temporarily, you were to slow down at any stage of the overtake). Another important use of *Lock* positions is for keeping in a low gear to achieve engine braking.

Your vehicle may well have more gears and additional options. Discuss with your teacher, before you start, the precise details of the set-up. A glance at the vehicle handbook could be useful too. Improvements to automatic transmissions are being developed all the time, and new types are being introduced which work on entirely different principles. However, space here precludes discussing all the variations.

KICKDOWN

For rapid acceleration a "kickdown" gear change facility is usually provided. Flooring the accelerator fully *and holding it there* makes the gears change down immediately. Depending on speed this will be to 1st (if not already in 1st) or to 2nd if speed is too high for 1st anyway (unless already in 2nd). The gearbox, thereafter, only changes up as the maximum in each gear is reached (but only as far as any *Lock* gear above 1 which you may have selected at the time), thus providing – whilst you continue to floor your accelerator – the quickest possible acceleration. Release your accelerator pedal pressure *at any time* and your speed will level off instantly, with the gears immediately changing up (unless still in a *Lock*). Top kickdown speed varies but in some cars is as high as 70 mph.

Avoid using kickdown on skiddy surfaces. The sudden onslaught of power of such a forceful, automatic-gear change can be enough to trigger a skid.

HINTS AND PITFALLS

For moving off uphill use the normal, Smooth Start **Moving Off** procedure explained on page 82. *For steep hills only* (more than say 15%), you may need to alter that technique slightly and, instead of holding the car only on the footbrake from (3), keep the handbrake on until (5). While you are checking that all is safe during (5), switch your right foot to giving *slight* acceleration – until you feel the car straining to go. For (6) you simply release the handbrake, increase your acceleration and away you go! If, for some reason, you can't go straightaway, remove that acceleration earlier set, until you are ready to begin this version of (5) again.

Never allow your handbrake operating mechanism to get slack. Otherwise, as you may by now have guessed, steep uphill starts *can* cause plenty of problems!

If you get stuck in mud or on ice or snow, you can often manage to extract your car by selecting *Reverse* and then, gently, via *Neutral, Drive*, alternately – whilst using very little or no accelerator at all (vital to avoid both spinning wheels and/or transmission damage). A second or two held in each gear, in reasonably quick succession, "rocks" the car to a stage where (hopefully) you climb away from the sticking point.

Driving Theory

3

Getting To Grips With All The Theory And Hazard Perception Requirements

Homework! Your own safety and that of the public, demand you study both the written and unwritten Rules of the Road in the rest of this book and your Highway Code before driving on the open road. Then, at the wheel, you will be quick to understand any crucial prompt from your teacher. Acute Hazard Perception, for that part of the Theory Test, will come naturally as you learn to prioritise your focus on potential hazards – to all of which you must react safely without fail.

SIGN "LANGUAGE"

Signs have both a *colour* and a *shape* language – making them easier to learn. Signs giving orders come in a red circle almost always on a white background, with one exception – the stop sign which is octagonal with a red background. On any of these "order" signs (and the same applies to other signs), if something is depicted in red that will be the negative message. Thus, the outside (righthand) car on the no overtaking sign is in red; on the sign for giving priority to oncoming vehicles, the upwards arrow is red – which means it is YOU who must wait; whereas the sign giving *you* priority over oncoming vehicles (a rectangular one with a blue background) has the red arrow pointing downwards – again, red denotes who must wait.

Signs with a blue background and which are also circular give positive instructions, giving them similar strength to "order" signs. For example, the mini-roundabout sign makes you circulate clockwise. Just two, rectangular, blue-background signs have a similar strength of meaning: the sign indicating one-way traffic, and the sign stopping you from using a contraflow bus lane. Look carefully at the latter in your Highway Code. It won't be any use misunderstanding it when you first see one!

Signs on a white background inside a red triangle give warnings of what you are about to meet. Compare, for example, the red triangle sign showing a bicycle in it with the red circle, "order" sign carrying a similar picture. Then look at the blue-background circular sign with a white bicycle on it and, finally, at the rectangular blue-background sign, again depicting a bicycle. Getting to grips with what is essentially the same picture, and what it denotes as differentiated by the use of different colours or shapes, gives you the best method of grasping their correct meanings. See how many other signs in your Highway Code share a picture but, because of their colour/shape features, mean totally different things.

Notice with red triangular signs that the all-important **GIVE WAY**, and the Distance To Give Way or Stop signs, all use inverted triangles; thus you can "read" even snow-covered ones – the same reason that the stop sign is octagonal. On red triangular signs depicting the shape of a junction in black, the thickest line denotes the road having priority.

The centre line along the road also has a language of its own. Once you understand it you will find this "language" being "spoken" on all types of road. You will find that centre lines vary between a straightforward one, which does no more than identify the centre, to one with long dashes and short gaps, which is a *hazard warning* line, to double white lines, which are there to allow or disallow overtaking. The *hazard warning* lines are probably the least observed but possibly the most important. You will always discover, where the centre line turns into a *hazard warning* one, that there is a reason; perhaps it is a bend, a brow, or a junction that will be adjacent to it. As you drive, see if you can fathom the reason, each time and every time. Where the line also has cats' eyes, you will notice that the frequency with which they are installed increases wherever the *hazard warning* line is also being used – quite a helpful pointer at night.

Other signs of special interest to which I draw your attention include: The school bus sign – for which look in the front or rear window of all buses. Series of red-and-white-banded low posts, each with a reflective patch at the top which are found alongside some roads mostly in the country – these tell you where the road narrows or takes a bend, or both; seen on your left the reflective patch is red; seen on your right the reflective patch is white. There is a "Slow Lorries" sign *NOT* depicted in the Highway Code. A black lorry climbs a black, steep gradient on a white background within a red triangular border. If you see this on a dual carriageway or a motorway, you can (and should) safely predict that you will run into bunching shortly – as left- and middle-laners shift outwards to pass lorries. On dual carriageways, lanes sometimes carry overhead on a gantry a red cross, a white diagonal arrow, or a green downward arrow. **Pay attention**! The red crossed lanes are designed so that the authorities can *reverse* the traffic flow at peak, 'tidal' hours. If one of them is above your lane, it is closed to traffic from your direction; move to a green arrowed lane if you value your life, something which a white diagonal arrow may well be telling you to do. A clearway sign (I will leave you to find one in the Highway Code) denotes a piece of road, possibly several miles in length, where you must not stop except in emergency or breakdown or because of a queue; you are not even allowed to drop off passengers. Marchers at night, apart from having reflective clothes, should have a look-out at the front carrying a white light, and someone at the back carrying a bright red one. If you see such a lantern swinging in the darkness ahead, pick up the clue at once; you are probably about to come upon a whole column of people. A ford sign is important; if the flood water you pass through is at all deep you must dry your brakes afterwards. They can lose all power. Wait until a gap in traffic allows you to drive slowly, gently holding the brakes on with your left foot until efficiency returns, as it will quite quickly. Unlit skips are deadly at night. Make sure you would recognise at once in the dark the reflective strips mounted vertically on them.

Finally, did you know that if a blind person's white stick has a red reflective band this means he is also deaf? His guide dog has a yellow harness. (A hearing dog for the deaf sports a black lead and collar, and a special, slip-on, burgundy jacket.) Would you recognise signs for holiday routes, ring roads or contra-flow systems? If not, get back to your Highway Code!

PARKING MATTERS

See **Hill Parking**, page 79, and **Pulling In On The Left**, page 133. Always attend to vehicle security as set out in the Highway Code. Make sure your handbrake is securely on and always lock your vehicle. You must face the correct way: i.e. other than in a one-way street, you park on the left. Observe all parking, waiting or loading restrictions denoted primarily by yellow gutter lines or kerb dashes (discover the differences from your Highway Code). Only park on a pavement where local, blue background, signs, showing a white car on a raised pavement, suggest and allow it.

You must not park near a tram lane in such a way others are then forced to drive onto it to get round you. Be very careful not to park where you will obstruct a driveway, a lowered kerb for the wheelchair-bound, or adjacent to tactile paving (it has a bobbled surface) where the blind will want to cross the road. At night dowse your headlamps. There are complex rules about where you may park *without* sidelights; these relate to street lamps and speed limits; you will need to learn them from your Highway Code. Otherwise, always leave sidelights on.

You must not sound your horn when stationary except when a moving vehicle is likely, otherwise, to hit you (or someone else).

On exiting your vehicle, *you and your passengers* must *each* check that no passer-by can ram your door(s). On the offside cyclists are the most vulnerable but, if a car had to swerve, it could hit oncoming traffic. On the pavement side, a pedestrian could be badly hurt. Look round; don't just rely on mirrors.

SPEED LIMITS

Your Highway Code tabulates National speed limits you must know *both* by type of road *and* by vehicle. The presence or absence of street lamps may be your only clue as to a prevailing limit where none is signed. Notice how a low mph zone entry sign warns you also to expect traffic-calming features, to allow motor-and pedal-cycles extra leeway and not to overtake other moving vehicles there. Road humps are *meant* to slow you! They can be very fierce and may not be individually signposted. A pair of white triangle markings on the leading edge will sometimes alert the observant – most usefully by reflection in your headlights at night.

STOPPING DISTANCES

Learn these from your Highway Code. You are likely to get a Theory question on them. Be sure that you grasp how distances given are split between thinking and stopping distances; all figures are based on good, dry conditions on level road.

MECHANICAL APTITUDE

Highway Code breakdown advice is extensive; study it well – space precludes including it all here. Pay special note to vehicle maintenance, safety and security – especially to fire, which can engulf a vehicle murderously fast. If you see flames or smoke – even if you smell petrol strongly – STOP, hazard warning lights on, engine off, keep everyone well clear, ban smoking; seek help. Inside a long tunnel, as well as fire itself, smoke suffocation is a major threat to everybody. Driving on until out of the other end, instead of stopping at once, may be your safest, bravest choice. Forced to stop, FIRST take precautions as above; then use a fire extinguisher, if possible, but never open the bonnet, which risks air fanning the flames into an explosive fireball.

Mechanical faults compromising safety can make driving illegal or your insurance invalid. Less obvious faults command equal attention: "play" is movement at the steering wheel that does not transfer directly to the front wheels; play measurable by eye, or clunking noises on the move, demand expert advice; exhaust emissions (**20%** of UK totals) must be within MOT-acceptable limits (also minimizing fuel wastage) – so, if you see clouds of blue smoke in your mirror or sooty deposits around the exhaust tailpipe, get your engine tuning checked. Likewise, excessive exhaust noise is outlawed. If your vehicle is too noisy, sort it! A third "silent" fault is headlights' maladjustment. Should they seem to dazzle others even when dipped, check the alignment.

Good tyres are vital. See *The Mechanics* on page 282. Rapid or unusual tyre wear can reveal suspension, steering alignment or brake faults overdue for repair. Reputable tyre suppliers know tyre law and can advise on types of tyre that mustn't be mixed on one "axle" or (sometimes) on one vehicle. Tyres must all be suitable for the vehicle *and* its use. Maintain the correct air pressures – soft tyres waste fuel (check them visually every trip and weekly, when cold, at the air pump), and break the law if any tyre tread is worn down to less than 1.6 mm in depth. More than this must show across at least three quarters of the tread width all round the tyre. Bald patches are illegal. No bulges or cuts in either of the side walls (including those facing inwards) are allowed if they are deep enough to affect the body cords; nor is any severe cut across the tread area if it amounts to more than 10% of the tread width. When your car is loaded, e.g. on holiday, your tyre pressures must be raised. See the car handbook. Lower them when you return or you will suffer undue wear in the centre of your treads.

Keep an eye on your brake power. See pages 148 and 283. Remember brake linings easily wear through *between* long service intervals and that brake hydraulics can spring a leak at any time (see fig. 7, for a vital warning symptom). Check your brake fluid level every time you open your bonnet.

The latter you should do at least every third time you fill up with fuel – when a check on the engine oil, coolant and other levels (see page 314) also needs to be made. Such stops are a good time to check round that all your lights/indicators work too – which they must by law. Act if your charge warning light ever lights on the move. You don't want a flat battery shortly! (Also top up battery electrolyte with distilled water between major services, if needed, just covering the plates in each cell.)

Your vehicle's handbook is a "must read" for your Theory Test as regards regular checks a driver must make, including: use and care of all controls and instruments, seat belts and airbags; maintenance service intervals; safe towing; secure loading and weight distribution; and so on. Add this to what you will find on the subject at the back of the Highway Code.

A "CHAPTER" OF ACCIDENTS

Some 90% of accidents result from road user *mistakes*. If you are involved in an accident which causes damage or injury to any other person, or other vehicle, or any animal (horse, cattle, ass, mule, sheep, pig, goat or dog) not in your vehicle, *or roadside property*, you **MUST** attend to certain documentation procedures *by Law* as so highlighted in the Highway Code.

No matter how slight the accident you **MUST STOP**.

First, calmly organise – if you are still able-bodied or can delegate to someone practical and quick-witted – to prevent further carnage from fire, and to WARN other traffic not to run into the crashed vehicle(s). Hazard warning lights on, engine(s) off, NO SMOKING, help being called, First Aid begun, uninjured parties, children and animals rounded up to a safe place, are the major priorities. Warn people not to stand where they obscure hazard warning lights from traffic. Put out warning triangles if you can but NOT on any motorway lane.

Make sure, whoever calls help, that they can describe where you are, state how many may be hurt and ask for police, fire brigade and ambulance, as appropriate. If anyone has been injured it is wise to include the ambulance; for example, whiplash neck injury may not be immediately obvious but could require a hospital visit. If hazardous chemicals may be leaking or at risk of catching fire, that needs to be reported accurately, so that the appropriate resources can be summoned to cope with it. Look at the hazardous chemicals warning plates, depicted in the Highway Code, so that you understand the system. These plates always appear on the side and at the rear of the vehicles concerned. Just as at a petrol station never use a mobile phone anywhere close to a flammable product.

It is wise to carry a fire extinguisher and a First Aid Kit in your car and to keep a Highway Code permanently there so that its Accidents section and First Aid advice are to hand to remind you of everything else to be done. For your Theory Test these sections contain the minimum advice you must know. Absorb it all carefully during your studies. (Better still, on First Aid, attend a proper training course.)

The law's demands about obtaining and giving information are all reprinted in the Highway Code too, so that you can follow them through properly once everything else is under control.

As well as your driving licence, you may wish voluntarily to carry your insurance certificate and MOT certificate (if applicable). The police or others may need to see them and this can save problems later. However, keep these latter documents well hidden. They might make it easier for a car thief to sell it! (Police only accept sight of original documents, not photocopies.) Your Theory Test may question how many days you otherwise have to produce them at your nearest police station or, perhaps, about who else is entitled to see them at the time of the accident, so you need to study these matters assiduously in the Highway Code among the annexes at the back.

Make sure you get the other driver(s) name(s), address(es) and insurance details, plus the registration numbers of all vehicles involved and who owns them if the driver(s) do(es) not. If any pedestrians are hurt, you need their names and addresses too. Get addresses of any friendly witnesses if you can as a legal case might turn on their evidence. Sketch at the time what happened, together with road names, and who was, or came from, where, and take measurements – especially of the position and length of skid marks. It is worth taking photos if you have a camera.

Do not admit blame. That may be a condition of your insurance. Fault may not be yours or wholly yours anyway. But do note down material comments made and by whom, especially, for example, estimated vehicle speeds, whether or not signals were given or the lights were faulty on any vehicle involved, etc.

Finally, if you decide to return and tow your vehicle home, remember to release the steering lock, and do not do so with your hazard warning lights flashing! How would others know when you are signalling for a turn? Use appropriate lights; check first whether you need your ignition on so that your brake lights/indicators work.

TRAMS

You may not have local tramways but your Theory Test might! Tram drivers, bound by normal Highway Code Rules, are also specifically instructed by the white "slit" shaded light signals incorporated at traffic lights, and by the small, diamond-shape signs, black-edged with black lettering on a white background, found along their routes. Trams are often very long, come fast and *silently*, only follow their own tracks and need large distances to stop. Always Give Way to trams! Their tracks may be slippery and can trap thin bicycle wheels; so beware cyclists near them.

LEVEL CROSSINGS

The Code devotes much space to these. Learn it well including the array of different signs. When the steady, amber light, followed rapidly by the twin flashing red lights and gongs come on, a train is coming. *The train triggers them.* You STOP! The train cannot. You are likely to die if there is an accident. See also page 278. Never drive nose-to-tail across a level crossing. Never go onto one until there are **TWO** (or more) spaces clear beyond it. Then you won't get stuck on the crossing in mortal danger, and nor can the chap behind who may follow you absentmindedly.

MISCELLANEOUS

Multi-storey car parks tend to be dark, even in daytime. Little children scamper. So do big "children"! Therefore, my advice is always put your headlamps on while your car is on the move inside. Other drivers might just see you better, too.

NEVER wave another road user to act be he on wheels or afoot. Wait by all means but *always let him* make his own decisions. Your signal might be "accepted" wrongly by someone else. There may be danger you cannot see.

You may carry spare fuel *only* in a purpose made container.

Don't just watch for pedestrians appearing from behind buses; watch for them jumping off moving ones!

A driver has to be medically fit. The law requires that you report any illness/disability likely to affect your driving ability to the Driver and Vehicle Licensing Authority. You must check whether medicines you take could make you drowsy or affect your reaction times. Examine the label and any notes. If in doubt ask your doctor or chemist before driving. Don't drive when you are ill, preferably not even with a bad cold.

A route order helps on longer journeys. Plan regular rest and refreshment stops with fresh air and exercise. Keep your car well ventilated and avoid too much heat or food; either can make you sleepy. Drive no more than 2 hours at a stretch.

Should you ever tow a caravan, boat or trailer (see page 18), snaking or losing the trailer are serious risks. Have a stabiliser fitted to the towbar; always hook up the [last resort] break-away cable. Excessive speed invariably leads to snaking, especially downhill. Ease off at once to stop it. Never overload what you tow. Keep most weight evenly across the axle(s) and so as to press downwards on the towball.

Note that authority dislikes any U-turns but especially at dangerous, dual carriageway junctions where signs ban them.

You must know roof- or cycle-rack loads remain secure.

4

Official Theory Test Multiple Choice Questions

Answers begin on page 116.

All these questions are from the latest DSA question bank. *Some answers provide fresh material about which you must know*; most, however, are backed up in my text. My selection focuses where there are hard-to-remember facts and where intelligent guesswork will not suffice. So, if you *really* know your Highway Code *and* you know these, you will pass. Avoid learning by heart. Go for *understanding*. Test friends too!

A few questions concern recent initiatives not yet embodied within existing Highway Code Rules; e.g. **Active Traffic Management** (ATM) pilot schemes and **Highways Agency Traffic Officers'** motorway and trunk road patrols. The latter have no law enforcement role; however, they have the same traffic-direction powers – with which it is an *offence* not to comply – as the police. They carry IDs and wear 'luminous' orange/yellow jackets. Their vehicles are distinguished by large-checked, black/yellow livery and use amber (with red) – as distinct from blue – flashing emergency lights.

Q1
Your vehicle is fitted with a hand-held telephone. To use the telephone you should
Mark one answer
- reduce your speed
- find a safe place to stop
- steer the vehicle with one hand
- be particularly careful at junctions

Q2

To help keep your car secure you could join a
Mark one answer
- vehicle breakdown organisation
- vehicle watch scheme
- advanced driver's scheme
- car maintenance class

Q3

You are waiting in a traffic queue at night. To avoid dazzling following drivers you should
Mark one answer
- apply the handbrake only
- apply the footbrake only
- switch off your headlights
- use both the handbrake and footbrake

Q4

You are in a line of traffic. The driver behind you is following very closely. What action should you take?
Mark one answer
- Ignore the following driver and continue to travel within the speed limit
- Slow down, gradually increasing the gap between you and the vehicle in front
- Signal left and wave the following driver past
- Move over to a position just left of the centre line of the road

Q5

You are driving a slow-moving vehicle on a narrow winding road. You should
Mark one answer
- keep well out to stop vehicles overtaking dangerously
- wave following vehicles past you if you think they can overtake quickly
- pull in safely when you can, to let following vehicles overtake
- give a left signal when it is safe for vehicles to overtake you

Q6

Which THREE of these emergency services might have blue flashing beacons?
Mark three answers
- Coastguard   (continued overleaf)

97

- Bomb disposal
- Gritting lorries
- Animal ambulances
- Mountain rescue
- Doctors' cars

Q7
Rear facing baby seats should NEVER be used on a seat protected with
Mark one answer
- an airbag
- seat belts
- head restraints
- seat covers

Q8
New petrol-engined cars must be fitted with catalytic converters. The reason for this is to
Mark one answer
- control exhaust noise levels
- prolong the life of the exhaust system
- allow the exhaust system to be recycled
- reduce harmful exhaust emissions

Q9
A cycle lane is marked by a solid white line. You must not drive or park in it
Mark one answer
- at any time
- during the rush hour
- if a cyclist is using it
- during its period of operation

Q10
Before entering a tunnel it is good advice to
Mark one answer
- put on your sunglasses
- check tyre pressures
- change to a lower gear
- tune your radio to a local channel

Q11

As a driver, you can help reduce pollution levels in town centres by
Mark one answer
- driving more quickly
- over-revving in low gear
- walking or cycling
- driving short journeys

Q12

You must NOT sound your horn
Mark one answer
- between 10 pm and 6 am in a built-up area
- at any time in a built-up area
- between 11.30 pm and 7 am in a built-up area
- between 11.30 pm and 6 am on any road

Q13

Congestion Charges apply in the London area. Who of these will NOT have to pay?
Mark one answer
- A person who lives in the area
- A driver making deliveries
- A person who is just driving through the area
- A driver with no other passengers in the vehicle

Q14

Driving at 70 mph uses more fuel than driving at 50 mph by up to
Mark one answer
- 10%
- 30%
- 75%
- 100%

Q15

'Red routes' in major cities have been introduced to
Mark one answer
- raise the speed limits
- help the traffic flow
- provide better parking
- allow lorries to load more freely

Q16

Motorway emergency telephones are usually linked to the police. In some areas they are now linked to
Mark one answer
- the Highways Agency Control centre
- the Driver Vehicle Licensing Agency
- the Driving Standards Agency
- the local Vehicle Registration Office

Q17

You are driving on an urban clearway. You may stop only to
Mark one answer
- set down and pick up passengers
- use a mobile telephone
- ask for directions
- load or unload goods

Q18

You are going through a congested tunnel and have to stop. What should you do?
Mark one answer
- Pull up very close to the vehicle in front to save space
- Ignore any message signs as they are never up to date
- Keep a safe distance from the vehicle in front
- Make a U-turn and find another route

Q19

You are going through a tunnel. What should you look out for that warns of accidents or congestion?
Mark one answer
- Hazard warning lines
- Other drivers flashing their lights
- Variable message signs
- Areas marked with hatch markings

Q20

You are turning left into a side road. Pedestrians are crossing the road near the junction. You must

Mark one answer
- wave them on
- sound your horn
- switch on your hazard lights
- wait for them to cross

Q21

Areas reserved for trams may have
Mark three answers
- metal studs around them
- white line markings
- zig zag markings
- a different coloured surface
- yellow hatch markings
- a different surface texture

Q22

A horse rider is in the left-hand lane approaching a roundabout. You should expect the rider to
Mark one answer
- go in any direction
- turn right
- turn left
- go ahead

Q23

What is the maximum specified fine for driving without insurance?

Mark one answer

- £50
- £500
- £1000
- £5000

Q24

You have just passed your test. How can you decrease your risk of accidents on the motorway?

Mark one answer

- By keeping up with the car in front
- By never going over 40 mph
- By staying only in the left-hand lane
- By taking further training

Q25

Your vehicle needs a current MOT certificate. You do not have one. Until you do have one you will not be able to renew your

Mark one answer

- driving licence
- vehicle insurance
- road tax disc
- vehicle registration document

Q26

At a junction you see this signal [bottom left traffic light green; bottom right traffic light with white horizontal]. It means

– cars must stop
– trams must stop
– both trams and cars must stop
– both trams and cars can continue

Q27

You are travelling behind a bus that pulls up at a bus stop. What should you do?
Mark two answers
– Accelerate past the bus sounding your horn
– Watch carefully for pedestrians
– Be ready to give way to the bus
– Pull in closely behind the bus

Q28

At the scene of an accident you should
Mark one answer
– not put yourself at risk
– go to those casualties who are screaming
– pull everybody out of their vehicles
– leave vehicle engines switched on

Q29

You are at the scene of an accident. Someone is suffering from shock. You should
Mark four answers
– reassure them constantly
– offer them a cigarette
– keep them warm
– avoid moving them if possible
– avoid leaving them alone
– give them a warm drink

Q30

You have to park on the road in fog. You should
Mark one answer
– leave sidelights on
– leave dipped headlights and fog lights on (cont'd overleaf)

– leave dipped headlights on
– leave main beam headlights on

Q31

You are on a motorway in fog. The left-hand edge of the motorway can be identified by reflective studs. What colour are they?

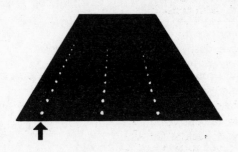

Mark one answer
– Green
– Amber
– Red
– White

Q32

The cost of your insurance may reduce if you
Mark one answer
– are under 25 years old
– do not wear glasses
– pass the driving test first time
– take the Pass Plus scheme

Q33

Which of these IS NOT allowed to travel in the right-hand lane of a three-lane motorway?
Mark one answer
– A small delivery van
– A motorcycle
– A vehicle towing a trailer
– A motorcycle and side-car

Q34

You arrive at the scene of an accident. There has been an engine fire and someone's hands and arms have been burnt. You should NOT

Mark one answer

- douse the burn thoroughly with cool liquid
- lay the casualty down
- remove anything sticking to the burn
- reassure them constantly

Q35

How should you use the emergency telephone on a motorway?

Mark one answer

- Stay close to the carriageway
- Face the oncoming traffic
- Keep your back to the traffic
- Stand on the hard shoulder

Q36

As a car driver which THREE lanes are you NOT normally allowed to use?

Mark three answers

- Crawler lane
- Bus lane
- Overtaking lane
- Acceleration lane
- Cycle lane
- Tram lane

Q37

Your vehicle has broken down on a motorway. You are not able to stop on the hard shoulder. What should you do?

Mark one answer

- Switch on your hazard warning lights
- Stop following traffic and ask for help
- Attempt to repair your vehicle quickly
- Stand behind your vehicle to warn others

Q38

You arrive at an accident where someone is suffering from severe burns. You should

Mark one answer

- apply lotions to the injury
- burst any blisters
- remove anything stuck to the burns
- douse the burns with cool liquid

Q39

You are on a three lane motorway towing a trailer. You may use the right hand lane when

Mark one answer

- there are lane closures
- there is slow moving traffic
- you can maintain a high speed
- large vehicles are in the left and centre lanes

Q40

You are on a three-lane motorway. There are red reflective studs on your left and white ones to your right. Where are you?

Red   White

Mark one answer

- In the right-hand lane
- In the middle lane
- On the hard shoulder
- In the left-hand lane

Q41

A single carriageway road has this sign [black diagonal, white background]. What is the maximum permitted speed for a car towing a trailer?

Mark one answer
- 30 mph
- 40 mph
- 50 mph
- 60 mph

Active Traffic Management schemes hope to reduce motorway congestion. In operation, gantries above all lanes *and the hard shoulder* carry variable, mandatory, speed limits within a red circle: a steady, large red cross signal displayed instead above the hard shoulder limits that to normal, emergency use; whereas a limit posted above the hard shoulder changes its use to that of an extra running lane up to that speed. Plenty Emergency Refuge Areas – located beyond the hard shoulder – populate these sections for emergency/breakdown use; however, never forget that an unlucky driver may still have to stop and block the hard shoulder. To rejoin running-lane-mode hard shoulder traffic, select an extra long gap.

Q42

You are in an Active Traffic Management area on a motorway. When the Actively Managed mode is operating
Mark one answer
- speed limits are only advisory
- the national speed limit will apply
- the speed limit is always 30 mph
- all speed limit signals are set

Q43

Why can it be an advantage for traffic speed to stay constant over a longer distance?

Mark one answer
- You will do more stop-start driving
- You will use far more fuel
- You will be able to use more direct routes
- Your overall journey time will normally improve

Q44

You are leaving your vehicle parked on a road. When may you leave the engine running?

Mark one answer
- If you will be parking for less than five minutes
- If the battery is flat
- When in a 20 mph zone
- Never on any occasion

Q45

You will see these markers [red on white background] when approaching

Mark one answer
- the end of a motorway
- a concealed level crossing
- a concealed speed limit sign
- the end of a dual carriageway

Q46

You are waiting at a level crossing. A train has passed but the lights keep flashing. You must

Mark one answer
- carry on waiting
- phone the signal operator
- edge over the stop line and look for trains
- park and investigate

Q47

At an accident it is important to look after the casualty. When the area is safe, you should
Mark one answer
- get them out of the vehicle
- give them a drink
- give them something to eat
- keep them in the vehicle

Q48

You see a car on the hard shoulder of a motorway with a HELP pennant displayed. This means the driver is most likely to be
Mark one answer
- a disabled person
- first aid trained
- a foreign visitor
- a rescue patrol person

Q49

What does this sign [red triangle, black symbol, white background] mean?

Mark one answer
- Turn left ahead
- T-junction
- No through road
- Give way

Q50

When traffic lights are out of order, who has priority?
Mark one answer
- Traffic going straight on
- Traffic turning right
- Nobody
- Traffic turning left

Q51

What does this sign [red triangle, black arrows, white background] mean?

Mark one answer
- Two-way traffic straight ahead
- Two-way traffic crosses a one-way road
- Two-way traffic over a bridge
- Two-way traffic crosses a two-way road

Q52

How will a police officer in a patrol vehicle normally get you to stop?
Mark one answer
- Flash the headlights, indicate left and point to the left
- Wait until you stop, then approach you
- Use the siren, overtake, cut in front and stop
- Pull alongside you, use the siren and wave you to stop

Q53

Where would you see these road markings?

Mark one answer
- At a level crossing
- On a motorway slip road
- At a pedestrian crossing
- On a single-track road

Q54

What is most likely to cause high fuel consumption?
Mark one answer
- Poor steering control
- Accelerating around bends
- Staying in high gears
- Harsh braking and accelerating

Q55

Before driving anyone else's motor vehicle you should make sure that
Mark one answer
- the vehicle owner has third party insurance cover
- your own vehicle has insurance cover
- the vehicle is insured for your use
- the owner has left the insurance documents in the vehicle

Q56

What is the legal minimum insurance cover you must have to drive on public roads?
Mark one answer
- Third party, fire and theft
- Fully comprehensive
- Third party only
- Personal injury cover

Q57

You have third party insurance. What does this cover?
Mark three answers
- Damage to your own vehicle
- Damage to your vehicle by fire
- Injury to another person
- Damage to someone's property   (continued overleaf)

- Damage to other vehicles
- Injury to yourself

Q58

When is it legal to drive a car over three years old without an MOT certificate?
Mark one answer
- Up to seven days after the old certificate has run out
- When driving to an MOT centre to arrange an appointment
- Just after buying a secondhand car with no MOT
- When driving to an appointment at an MOT centre

Q59

When you are giving mouth to mouth you should only stop when
Mark one answer
- you think the casualty is dead
- the casualty can breathe without help
- the casualty has turned blue
- you think the ambulance is coming

Q60

Which THREE pieces of information are found on a vehicle registration document?
Mark three answers
- Registered keeper
- Make of the vehicle
- Service history details
- Date of the MOT
- Type of insurance cover
- Engine size

Q61

You have stopped at the scene of an accident to give help. Which THREE things should you do?
Mark three answers
- Keep injured people warm and comfortable
- Keep injured people calm by talking to them reassuringly
- Keep injured people on the move by walking them around
- Give injured people a warm drink
- Make sure that injured people are not left alone

Q62

How should you dispose of a used battery?
Mark two answers
- Take it to a local authority site
- Put it in the dustbin
- Break it up into pieces
- Leave it on waste land
- Take it to a garage
- Burn it on a fire

Q63

You arrive at the scene of a motorcycle accident. No other vehicle is involved. The rider is unconscious, lying in the middle of the road. The first thing you should do is
Mark one answer
- move the rider out of the road
- warn other traffic
- clear the road of debris
- give the rider reassurance

Q64

You are involved in an accident with another vehicle. Someone is injured. Your vehicle is damaged. Which FOUR of the following should you find out?
Mark four answers
- Whether the driver owns the other vehicle involved
- The other driver's name, address and telephone number
- The make and registration number of the other vehicle
- The occupation of the other driver
- The details of the other driver's vehicle insurance
- Whether the other driver is licensed to drive

Q65

When parking and leaving your car you should
Mark one answer
- park under a shady tree
- remove the tax disc
- park in a quiet road
- engage the steering lock

Q66

You have broken down on a motorway. When you use the emergency telephone you will be asked
Mark three answers
- for the number on the telephone that you are using
- for your driving licence details
- for the name of your vehicle insurance company
- for details of yourself and your vehicle
- whether you belong to a motoring organisation

Q67

You have just passed your practical driving test. You do not hold a full licence in another category. Within two years you get six penalty points on your licence. What will you have to do? You will have to
Mark two answers
- Retake only your theory test
- Retake your theory and practical tests
- Retake only your practical test
- Reapply for your full licence immediately
- Reapply for your provisional licence

Q68

At an accident a small child is not breathing. When giving mouth to mouth you should breathe
Mark one answer
- sharply
- gently
- heavily
- rapidly

Q69

When a roof rack is not in use it should be removed. Why is this?
Mark one answer
- It will affect the suspension
- It is illegal
- It will affect your braking
- It will waste fuel

Q70
Are passengers allowed to ride in a caravan that is being towed?
Mark one answer
- Yes if they are over fourteen
- No not at any time
- Only if all the seats in the towing vehicle are full
- Only if a stabilizer is fitted

Q71
Which FOUR of the following may apply when dealing with this hazard?

Mark four answers
- It could be more difficult in winter
- Use a low gear and drive slowly
- Use a high gear to prevent wheelspin
- Test your brakes afterwards
- Always switch on fog lamps
- There may be a depth gauge

Q72
You forget to switch off your rear fog lights when the fog has cleared. This may
Mark three answers
- dazzle other road users
- reduce battery life
- cause brake lights to be less clear
- be breaking the law
- seriously affect engine power

Q73
You have a duty to contact the licensing authority when
Mark three answers
- you go abroad on holiday
- you change your vehicle   (continued overleaf)

- you change your name
- your job status is changed
- your permanent address changes
- your job involves travelling abroad

Q74

You service your own vehicle. How should you get rid of the old engine oil?
Mark one answer
- Take it to a local authority site
- Pour it down a drain
- Tip it into a hole in the ground
- Put it into your dustbin

ANSWERS

A1
- find a safe place to stop

A2
- vehicle watch scheme

A3
- apply the handbrake only

A4
- Slow down, gradually increasing the gap between you and the vehicle in front

A5
- pull in safely when you can, to let following vehicles overtake

A6
- Coastguard
- Bomb disposal
- Mountain rescue

Author's Note: Blood transfusion service vehicles may also use blue flashing lights

A7
– an airbag

A8
– reduce harmful exhaust emissions

A9
– during its period of operation

A10
– tune your radio to a local channel

A11
– walking or cycling

A12
– between 11.30 pm and 7 am in a built-up area

A13
– A person who lives in the area

A14
– 30%

A15
– help the traffic flow

A16
– the Highways Agency Control Centre

A17
– set down and pick up passengers

A18
– Keep a safe distance from the vehicle in front

A19
– Variable message signs

A20
– wait for them to cross

A21
– white line markings
– a different coloured surface
– a different surface texture

A22
– go in any direction

A23
– £5000

A24
– By taking further training

A25
– road tax disc

A26
– trams must stop

A27
– Watch carefully for pedestrians
– Be ready to give way to the bus

A28
– not put yourself at risk

A29
– reassure them constantly
– keep them warm
– avoid moving them if possible
– avoid leaving them alone

A30
– leave sidelights on

A31
– Red

A32
– take the Pass Plus scheme

A33
– A vehicle towing a trailer

A34
– remove anything sticking to the burn

A35
– Face the oncoming traffic

A36
– Bus lane
– Cycle lane
– Tram lane

A37
– Switch on your hazard warning lights

A38
– douse the burns with cool liquid

A39
– there are lane closures

A40
– In the left-hand lane

A41
– 50 mph

A42
– all speed limit signals are set

A43
– Your overall journey time will normally improve

A44
– Never on any occasion

A45
– a concealed level crossing

A46
– carry on waiting

A47
– keep them in the vehicle

A48
– a disabled person

A49
– T-junction

A50
– Nobody

A51
– Two-way traffic crosses a one-way road

A52
– Flash the headlights, indicate left and point to the left

A53
– On a motorway slip road

A54
– Harsh braking and accelerating

A55
– the vehicle is insured for your use

A56
– Third party only

A57
– Injury to another person
– Damage to someone's property
– Damage to other vehicles

A58
– When driving to an appointment at an MOT centre
Note: consult your insurance provider first. You dare not risk
not being covered even for this short journey.

A59
– the casualty can breathe without help

A60
– Registered keeper
– Make of the vehicle
– Engine size

A61
– Keep injured people warm and comfortable
– Keep injured people calm by talking to them reassuringly
– Make sure that injured people are not left alone

A62
– Take it to a local authority site
– Take it to a garage

A63
– warn other traffic

A64
– Whether the driver owns the other vehicle involved
– The other driver's name, address and telephone number
– The make and registration number of the other vehicle
– The details of the other driver's vehicle insurance

A65
– engage the steering lock

A66
- for the number on the telephone that you are using
- for details of yourself and your vehicle
- whether you belong to a motoring organisation

A67
- Retake your theory and practical tests
- Reapply for your provisional licence

A68
- gently

A69
- It will waste fuel

A70
- No not at any time

A71
- It could be more difficult in winter
- Use a low gear and drive slowly
- Test your brakes afterwards
- There may be a depth gauge

A72
- dazzle other road users
- cause brake lights to be less clear
- be breaking the law

A73
- you change your vehicle
- you change your name
- your permanent address changes

A74
- Take it to a local authority site

Driving In Practice

5

Onto The Open Road

BEGINNING ON THE ROAD

To pass your Practical Test there can be no substitute for thousands of miles of experience. Seize every opportunity but never overdo it; a little over an hour at a time is enough.

Tiredness kills. If only we could measure it like blood alcohol, its true role in road accidents would be revealed. Never, never drive or continue to drive if sleepy or exhausted. Rest awhile – take a nap; walk or jog; restore your zip with a refreshing, non-alcoholic drink or a coffee.

Research from Loughborough University showed that, even after one alcoholic drink, your driving concentration over the next several hours will lapse momentarily by up to 10 times as often as it might otherwise. Lapses which, boosted by that drink's soporific effect, could risk blundering into a senseless, fatal crash. Fatigue often peaks during the post-party/early-riser hours around 4 – 6 am. If ever you can't recall the road just driven or your eyelids droop, STOP! Before it's too late.

RUNNING COMMENTARY

Ask your teacher, and friends/family, to explain as they drive, why they do what they do. Learn how they anticipate their own and others' actions. When is danger abroad? Why? How fast is safe? When? How soon do you position for turns? How often do you check your mirrors, change gear, start braking, give signals? Which road signs/markings demand a direct response? How must you react to traffic lights' changes, to signals from others (or, perhaps, just to their positioning and speed) or from anyone controlling traffic? Grasp the need to think ahead *all the time and never dare invite catastrophe by gazing at scenery.*

CONCENTRATION

Tiredness increases tension. So start fresh. Aim for relaxed, attentive concentration. If you feel distracted, stop driving!

At the wheel "rubbernecking" at an accident or trying to read, eat, drink, smoke, retune or listen to a radio/loud music **risk distraction becoming *manslaughter* in a split-second**. STOP such evil habits. Using any *hand-held* mobile phone, whilst driving *or instructing*, is illegal. Any thought that a hands-free mobile is safe is rubbish! All phones engage your mind away from the road. Accident risks multiply FOUR **X**. Fumbling at a small screen spells real danger; lacking proper control, you can be had up for careless or dangerous driving. A driver should ignore all incoming calls and make none. The law, as interpreted by the Highway Code, goes further: "**Do not operate, adjust or view**" any electronic or other aid, such as a navigation system, PCs, multi-media, etc., "**if it will distract your attention while ... driving.**" *Arguing at the wheel is off limits whoever provokes you.*

NOTES FOR TEACHERS

Within *some* families any attempt to teach can be a disaster. So be honest if it's not working; let an outsider take over.

Try to explain the right technique for first tackling any new experience, *beforehand*; draw in, traffic permitting, so that you can discuss it in safety. Do this soon after any incident with which you are not entirely happy. Then ask your trainee to explain it back to you so that you are sure he fully understands.

Before each new traffic complication you must assess where your pupil's reactions may be slow or his judgment *wrong*. Prompt early if needed; too late could be just that! Extend his experience gradually. Plan easy routes that won't unnerve him early on. Avoid practice in areas or ways conducive to queues forming behind you. The frustration caused leads to accidents.

Demonstrate mirror blind spots *on the move* on a safe dual carriageway; your pupil front-passenger watching how traffic passing or falling behind "disappears" both in the door and instructor mirrors (see page 314). He'll truly believe [you] only when *he* can't see!

MIRRORS

Review **How To Adjust The Mirrors** in Chapter 2. First class mirrors' watching is an art to develop. You aim to keep a "running picture" of what is behind; however – **LOOKING WHERE YOU ARE GOING** must always take precedence. This keeping tabs on what is going on behind is what enables you to position and adjust speed accordingly, so that traffic following will always know your intention in extra good time.

You have to learn to flick your eyes to each mirror to gather the whole position, with your *eyes back on the road* betwixt every glance; see fig. 40.

Never gaze at a mirror. You'll soon hit something (other

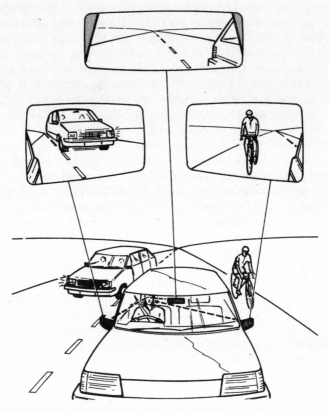

Fig 40 Split-second mirror glances behind.

125

than the mirror!) if you do. There's no need to know how romantic-looking the driver following is, only if a vehicle is there, how close and whether he is intent on passing.

A good teacher will ask you from time to time what is behind. If you cannot answer without another look, you are below standard. Equally, he will warn you at once if he senses that you are becoming over-preoccupied by the mirrors.

The Highway Code rightly emphasises **Mirrors – Signal – Manoeuvre**. I go further than this "**M-S-M**" routine. I say **Mirrors – Mirrors – Mirrors**, manoeuvring or not. My running picture is what should save you from being caught out overtaken by people hidden in your mirrors' blind spots (see fig. 2), for they can remain hidden for a surprisingly long time – even for miles; it should also alert you whenever someone wants to overtake or pass to your inside; another advantage is that you are forewarned whenever it will be wise to position, alter speed, and/or signal, earlier than usual – for example, before moving out to pass a parked car; and, last but not least, in emergency, when there may be no time to look again, you already have the rear view in mind!

Beyond this running mirrors' picture are specific actions which *must* or OUGHT to trigger from you a specific double-check in your mirrors. These are *before*: signalling; moving off (from the kerb *or* after halting in traffic); stopping; slowing down *or* speeding up; turning left or right; overtaking (even a cyclist); changing lane *either way* (including for passing any sort of obstruction); reaching any type of junction at which – whether or not you may have priority – it would be possible to come into conflict with turning or crossing traffic; passing through any place (including their own crossings) where there are pedestrians about, who may step out in your path; passing a *warning* sign or any sign demanding a positive action from you – for example, a red, octagonal STOP sign or a blue, circular "turn left" sign; and *before* you or any passenger open(s) any door to get out (though, whoever it is, a direct look must be mandatory too).

Mirrors blocked by swinging dollies, stickers on the back window, and a back shelf piled high with gubbins, are unforgivable except to demonstrate how little you know about driving . . .

Road traffic Law demands that you do not brake sharply *except* in emergency [you **must** apply "reasonable consideration" for others].

But suppose you *have* to stop suddenly and are then hit from behind? Or you stop gently but still get bumped at the back?

In Law that driver has to be to blame.

A basic Code dictum enshrines that Law: *NEVER* **DRIVE SO FAST THAT YOU CANNOT STOP** *WELL* **WITHIN THE DISTANCE YOU CAN SEE TO BE CLEAR**.

The rule is sacrosanct.

If the driver behind is any good such a bash ought never to happen. But what if it is all set to do so, and the potential whiplash could break your neck? Then my **Mirrors – Mirrors – Mirrors** drivestyle should make sure you know the imminent danger: you might be able to drive clear to reach the safety of a grass verge . . . you might manage to warn passengers to tuck heads below seat-back level . . .

EMERGENCY STOP ON (YOUR PRACTICAL) TEST

The examiner will pre-arrange with you a signal for when/if he wants you to demonstrate a SAFE emergency stop. For example, the instruction arranged may be slapping the dashboard at the same time as saying STOP! You need plenty of practice, using a similar signal, so that you learn to react as fast to a contrived emergency as to a real one. Your teacher must make a point of giving you at least one emergency stop on every lesson (although only in dry weather to begin with) until satisfied you are always on the ball. He must select carefully places to do this; places where the forward picture is free of pedestrians, street furniture, etc., or of oncoming traffic. Indeed, they must be clear of anything which might become a hazard were you to panic or make an error.

He must – as you can be certain the examiner will – also always have checked physically (not just in the mirror) that you are clear behind.

Your mirrors' running picture should mean that *you*, also, know it is clear but even if you do not, you don't check the mirrors again; on the signal – instantly get *both feet down firmly and stop*. Keep your steering straight and maintain a controlled grip on it with both hands until you have stopped completely. Once stopped, handbrake on, gear out, clutch pedal up and footbrake off. But be ready. The examiner will be telling you almost straightaway to drive on. (He can't have you sitting there obstructing the road!) Then follow **Moving**

Off which I come to next, except that you don't need to signal or move out (item **6**, fig. 41) as you should already be a normal distance out from the kerb.

Under **Emergency Stops From Faster Speeds** in Chapter 2 and until now, I have taught you **both feet down** for any emergency stop from moderate speed. As it is normal for the **Emergency Stop On Test** to be carried out in a built-up area subject to a low speed limit, this is fine. Your reaction speed, one keynote of what is being tested, is the first essential thing that needs to become ingrained. Once it is and you have greater confidence, then is time enough to learn to leave putting the clutch down until you have almost stopped, as in a normal pull up. This shows greater skill. It needs learning for real emergencies from higher speeds because engine braking can then be a marginal extra help to you in stopping. However, if, in the excitement of the **Emergency Stop On Test**, your clutch goes down a little early in relation to the stopping, it shouldn't count against you, provided your stop is carried out as quickly as any average person would be able to do it.

To be SAFE and *in control* are the two other, major keynotes the examiner looks for. Your car mustn't just skid all the way to a halt! In Chapter 2 I promised to return to the problem of skidding because of "locking" your brakes. Keeping your steering straight (*with both hands on the wheel*) is as much part of this as it is to hold you on course. This is because your front wheels are more likely to lock easily if they are on the turn.

If your wheel(s) lock and skid, your brakes must be freed off at once, momentarily; then they must instantly be reapplied as hard as possible without re-locking them. In practice, unless you have anti-lock brakes – for which see below – they tend swiftly to lock again; so this becomes virtually an on-off-on process as fast as your brain can switch the instructions to your feet. A technical description for it is cadence braking.

The right technique must be learned in *dry weather* first. In Chapter 7, **Skids When Braking Hard**, page 284, I suggest an exercise to help you master it. On dry you can tell at once when a wheel is locking. The tyre screeches. Thus you know instantaneously when you must ease your brake for a split-second. Later on, when you come to practise on the wet, you will hear the tyre "hiss", instead, as it slides. Again, this warns you to ease your foot off within a trice, before resuming as much braking as you reckon you can, and so on.

Open your window. Then you can hear exactly both when skidding starts and when – in response to your quick reaction – it ceases.

In cars with anti-lock brakes (ABS) none of this brake-foot skill is normally needed. The system does it all. It senses whenever a wheel locks, and temporarily releases the brake pressure to that wheel accordingly; all you have to do for an emergency stop is **pounce HARD** on your footbrake and hold that pressure there until stopped. You may feel the ABS "kick in" (reverberating through the brake pedal) once you hit maximum braking. This can herald a surprise if you are not aware it is normal. It might lead you instinctively to relax your foot pressure on the brake – which you must NOT do with ABS because its effective working depends on that hard pressure! When learning with anti-lock brakes you must still know what drivers without them have to do. For one thing, they may not be so efficient on snow, etc.; for another, you might also need to drive a car without them. And you may be asked about locked-brake skidding in your Theory Test. ABS brakes have another plus; this time in respect of steering. As it bears more relation to SKIDS I return to it – and to the specific need to practise with ABS – there, from page 294.

MOVING OFF
Key to Fig. 41

For your *first* attempts, now that you are on the open road, do make sure you begin in an area where traffic is very quiet indeed. Follow the sequence of fig. 41. Define "clear" on that figure as when you can safely go without *anyone* else having to take evasive action of any kind, no matter how slight. You should not, for example, be the cause of any traffic, coming along from behind, having to slow down.

Once checks **1** and **2** confirm you are in the clear, signal. However, the presence of any traffic in close proximity, and about to pass you by, means that you *must not signal yet*. Wait. In this event, only begin your right indicator signal, as your final step during **3**. Otherwise, there is the risk that your signal may distract a passing driver and lead to an accident. Thus you are really only using it to let traffic much further behind (or ahead)

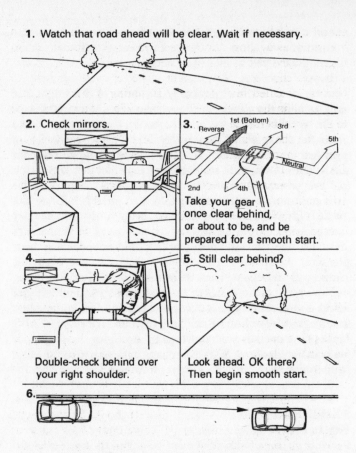

1. Watch that road ahead will be clear. Wait if necessary.

2. Check mirrors.

3. Take your gear once clear behind, or about to be, and be prepared for a smooth start.

1st (Bottom)
Reverse
3rd
5th
Neutral
2nd
4th

4. Double-check behind over your right shoulder.

5. Still clear behind?

Look ahead. OK there? Then begin smooth start.

6.

Aim to reach normal distance from kerb gradually, not sharply.

Fig 41 Moving off from the kerbside. Use a right indicator signal, timing carefully when you begin it. Remember to cancel the signal as soon as you are off.

know what you are up to – even though you do not expect to cause them any difficulty – and in order to warn any *other* traffic.

As ''other traffic'' must include *every* vehicle (ahead or behind) – especially cyclists – *and* pedestrians, it is best always to signal in case there is anyone you haven't noticed. It is safer that way unless you are *certain* there is no one about. Keep your signal on as you complete **4** and **5**; you need to remember to

130

cancel it by hand during **6** because the shallow angle at which you draw away from the kerbside is usually insufficient to trigger the indicator's own self-cancelling device.

If you choose to use an arm signal as well (or have to because of failed indicators), do so during **4**. The right-turn arm signal is the correct one. See page 225. Return your hand to the wheel before **5**.

As the above signal may be the first "live" one you have ever had to give (apart from at my suggestion for some of the CAR CONTROL Practical Test reverses), I must now stress *the most essential fact* about *any* signal you make. It is that your indicator or arm signal IS ONLY A WARNING of your **INTENTION**. It does not bless you with *permission* to carry out the manoeuvre. Whether you can now do what you want to do, once you have signalled, will depend upon all the other *Rules of the Road* which apply in that particular situation. These will all become clear as you read on.

Never let your car move forwards during **4**. You will see idiots do this while still looking backwards . . . Wait until you *can* go, at **6**, *after* you have double-checked ahead, at **5**. At **5**, look out especially for pedestrians who may have stepped immediately in front of you by then. Believe me or not; they will! And beware of traffic having now pulled up just ahead of you, either next to the kerb or because a queue has formed!

At **6**, whilst your *moving out from the kerb* (in conjunction, I trust, with a perfectly **Smooth Start**!) should be at a gentle angle (and you must remember we drive on the LEFT!), your *picking up speed* should be smart – though not ferocious! (There is little more frustrating to the natural flow of traffic than the driver who dawdles below its general speed whilst joining the stream. Causing the bout of "indigestion" that can result for all concerned is thoroughly selfish.)

You must acquire one more moving-off *habit*: this is to begin that **Mirrors – Mirrors – Mirrors** drivestyle of a few pages back straightaway. It's a favourite, unexpected moment to find someone on your back bumper for whom, perhaps, to make allowances.

If, after your road checks at **4** and **5**, something has cropped up making you have to wait for more than a moment or two, pull on your handbrake, return your gear lever to neutral and release your accelerator and clutch pedals. Sitting at-the-ready for too long may cause undue wear on the clutch thrust bearing. Also, cancel your signal for the time being so that it cannot worry passing drivers. Renew the signal and take up **Smooth Start** preparedness again (from **3**, fig. 41), only when a fresh opportunity arises.

MOVING OFF FROM BEHIND A PARKED VEHICLE
When starting from behind another parked car you have to pull out more sharply (and therefore slowly, too) than in **6**. Depending on how sharp the angle is, you may *also* need to wait because of *oncoming* traffic. Because the manoeuvre is more difficult the examiner will be sure to test you on it. If you have any problems being certain that you won't bump the back corner of the car you are pulling out round, go back to the cardboard box practice of Chapter 2. But remember that hitting an oncoming car with your offside front wing is by far the more dangerous possibility! Allow, too, for the extra time that going slowly, and having to straighten up once you are out, will take. Remember that, downhill, it is harder for drivers arriving behind to stop, and, uphill, you won't be able to pick up speed very quickly even when you are out.

DISTANCE OUT
In the UK – I remind you – the basic rule for going along any road is that we *drive on the left*. Where exceptions apply – e.g., in one-way streets – the change of status is always marked.

On ordinary, single-carriageway, two-way roads keep well within your own, lefthand side of the road. Other than where a road is quite narrow, between a half and one metre out from the kerb is, as a rough guide, about right for most situations.

Avoid staying too close to the edge, so that your tyres pick up stones and debris. Once embedded, a flint or a nail can cause a puncture thousands of miles later. Stupidly close there is danger to pedestrians, and of hitting the verge or kerb and losing control – even of being flipped over onto your roof – as well as risk of bursting a tyre or damaging your steering. Neither, in wet weather, do you wish to be accused of soaking unlucky pedestrians near roadside puddles.

Equally, it is wrong to hog just left of the centre line of the road, risking a bash with oncoming traffic and making it difficult or even dangerous for anyone to overtake you. Help overtakers by travelling no further out than you need.

The crucial consideration at ALL TIMES, however, is to *relate your distance out to your speed* AND to the general conditions. E.g., on a wide urban road, even though going slowly because of them, you might sneak a little more out where pavements are crowded with jostling people; on a country, major road, a little further out would certainly be wise over 40–50 mph. If you lack room on your own side to add safety by driving with an extra margin of distance out, YOU CAN BET THAT YOUR SPEED OUGHT, INSTEAD, TO BE LOWER:

* *Should any emergency arise, the fact of having been further out – even by a few centimetres – can promise critical, earlier vision, warning and – hence – priceless, extra reaction time.*

* *Equally, the alternative – religiously lifting your foot off the accelerator whenever space is tight – can mark the difference between life and death if you need to stop.*

Your examiner will look for prompt action (or lack thereof) whenever your available road space/width contracts.

On dual carriageways (or other roads with more than one lane in your direction) a middle-of-the-(left)-lane position is where you would expect normally to drive. Using another lane for overtaking or, perhaps, when turning right, a middle-of-the-lane position is, again, usually the most appropriate.

PULLING IN ON THE LEFT
As this manoeuvre is a certainty after **Moving Off** – and probably quite soon thereafter – you have to do your Theory homework beforehand! It will always be up to you not only to select a *safe position* close in to the kerb but to pick a safe length of road in the first place! Never pull in by the roadside just after the brow of a hill or just round a bend, *in a dip* or anywhere else concealed from fast traffic from either direction which may not expect this or have room to stop if it cannot pass by at once. The Highway Code also has a comprehensive list of places where you *must not* stop, wait or park. Be sure that you know every one. They are backed by the law. You are

forbidden to park (or even stand) where you might cause danger or obstruct other road users unnecessarily. Think about sight lines; your car can create a hazard simply by blocking the view at a critical point, e.g. within 10 metres of *any* junction. Never pull up or park opposite a vehicle waiting or parked on the opposite side of the road if that combination could pose added danger for passing traffic – never even for one second . . . At first confirm with your teacher that the spot you are choosing is safe.

In Chapter 2 you practised the mechanics of stopping your car closely adjacent to a kerbside. Now, you must also follow the correct pulling-in sequence.

First, check in your mirrors. Then select your safe pull-in position. How far ahead that has to be will depend on your speed as well as on what may already be behind you. At 20–25 mph, in the quiet road I hope you chose on which to begin, that could be as close ahead as 50 metres. At 50 mph several hundred metres would be necessary. (However, at that speed, you would probably be on too busy a road for casual stopping or parking to be safe anyway. You should consider turning off to somewhere quieter first.)

Wherever you are, you must rule out any wild "dive" for the edge – such as you will sometimes witness. That sort of driving is dangerous.

Second, signal your intention with your left indicator, so that everyone around (not just those behind) will know what you are up to. Double-check whether traffic *has* come up behind, and that anyone who has so appeared – especially if he is close – has noticed your signal! (You can always postpone your pull-in if necessary.)

Then slow down gradually, timing it so that you can be/are down into 2nd gear for final control as you draw in to the edge.

Once stopped, and having followed your routine, hand-brake, gear, footpedals, safety sequence, remember to cancel your left indicator.

A left-turn, arm signal – *the correct one for pulling in* – can sometimes make your intended stop more obvious to others. Should you decide to give it, do so just after putting on your left indicator. (This is well worth practising, too – in case your indicators ever fail. See page 225.)

HOW FAST SHOULD I GO?

On your Practical Test, keep up to a reasonable speed that takes account of all important, changing conditions. You can be failed for undue dawdling. You must also take care not to be erratic about your speed in ways other road users couldn't expect to fathom; for example, "dreaming along" and then practically pulling up for a traffic light whilst it is, and remains, at green!

So, generally, keep up with the traffic stream. (Unless, that is, it is going too fast ... something, I must warn you, it frequently *does*. The added dangers of pavements that are overcrowded with shoppers are often, for example, utterly selfishly ignored by speeding drivers. You see them flout that sacrosanct Highway Code dictum on my page 127 with a ruthlessness that defies belief.)

Never exceed a speed limit, however, or the examiner must surely fail you for wilfully breaking the law. Where traffic calming measures are in place, demonstrate *calm* driving!

You will be unlikely to need to drive faster than about 55 mph during your Practical Test, unless perhaps on quite a long stretch of dual carriageway, it being one unmarked by any lower speed limit. To do so would probably be both unnecessary and unwise.

Always await a safe moment to check your speedometer (or any other instrument). You should soon learn the "feel" of your speed at each of the various speed limits, so that an untimely diversion of your attention – even of a split-second – need never occur.

After passing your Practical Test the temptation to go faster on the open road gets stronger! Unless there is more room still (than suggested under **Distance Out**, a few pages back) then, even on the straight, forget it. You need to be at an absolute minimum of one full metre off the kerb on the average, "open", single-carriageway trunk road, before even a speed of 60 mph may be safe.

More width than that isn't always available; which possibly makes some sense of why we have the boring (and, I would argue, largely unnecessary), "blanket", national, 60 mph maximum speed restriction on all such roads. By "open", incidentally, I mean a generally straight road, having good, all-round vision with wide, flat verges and/or empty fields both sides; not one, for example, winding through a forest, where such animals as deer or badger might without warning leap or scurry into your path. Twisting, bendy roads like that, with confined vision, are an entirely different matter. They merit such rigorously disciplined care that I have reserved for them an exclusive section under the heading **Country Lanes** in a few pages' time.

Many quite major country roads are little better, however, and faster cornering, even when, as sometimes, you are able to see that there are no traffic reasons around a bend to preclude it, also carries the obligation fully to understand skidding. That, and proper cornering techniques, I must also leave for now, until I return to SKIDS, in Chapter 7. Nevertheless, even slow cornering demands the right approach. So please study that chapter as early as you can.

At high speeds a car is many times more difficult to control – *and especially to steer or to stop* – so the extra room, which I have pleaded you do ensure is available, is essential. Just as vital is experience. Therefore, for your first several years – yes, even after you pass – keep higher speeds for visually well-landscaped dual carriageways or on motorways. My reason for urging such an extraordinary degree of patience is that even 100,000 miles' driving only gives you but a soupçon of the level of road-wisdom for which any serious emergency encountered at high speed can call. Though I recognise fully that you may well not believe me until you have driven that far, I also know that I would be in neglect of my duty, and my conscience, were I not to drive home to you the truth that speed, unchecked by that wisdom, does KILL.

KEEPING TO YOUR LANE
This section mainly applies to dual carriageways (and, in many respects, once you are fully licensed, to motorways), though what it says applies on every road with more than one lane for use in your direction. Whether your part of a dual carriageway is divided into two lanes or three (or more), the first, and principal, rule remains firmly based on the fact that we drive on the left. It decrees that you may only drive in the lefthand lane except when overtaking (or turning right).

Notice how this also matches the Highway Code rule that

you always allow others to overtake you if they wish.

The second rule – which follows from that first one – is that, after you yourself overtake (which I come to later), you must always endeavour to return to the most lefthand lane just as soon as you can. (If that involves getting across more than one lane, then you need to progress in careful stages, taking them one at a time.)

To block a middle or outer lane, unnecessarily, by just "sitting" in it (even going at the speed limit), whilst the lane to your left is free, is an offence. You become – unless someone ahead of you in your lane whom you are unable to pass is holding you up – a *moving obstruction*. (Note that the fact that you had been blocked was what had been happening could be impossible to prove in Court.) Notwithstanding any excuses, however, those behind will, not unreasonably if they wish to pass, hoot or flash their lights to tell you they are there. If a large lorry or coach, for example (or any vehicle with a trailer), is hot on your heels, remember that, although such vehicles are banished by Law from using the righthand-most lane of three (or more) on motorways, they are not so restricted on three and four lane dual carriageways. Its driver may have taken some time to build up speed; then, if you block him, wondering why he won't pass on your outside . . .

So don't become a blockhead! Tied in with the above overriding rules is another, fundamental principle applying to all dual and multiple-lane carriageways (and, incidentally, anywhere else where more than one lane forms, marked or not). This is that you overtake only on the right, except:

– when there are *slow-moving* queues and your (left) lane goes first
– to pass to the left of someone slowing down to turn right
– to *turn* left yourself whilst an outer lane is – at that particular time – having to wait for some reason
– if you are in a designated one-way street and wish to pass other traffic to its left.

Other than in one of the above specific circumstances, it is ILLEGAL to zoom past on the nearside of any moving vehicle. A *moving obstructor* does not give you any excuse.

Even with the sanction of one of the above prescribed

137

reasons, you are still barred from passing to the left, if that would mean encroaching upon a tram, bus or cycle lane; that is, during its period of operation, or whilst you are driving forwards rather than turning across it. Despite actions of an impatient few, never to be copied, I remind you here, too, of the Law that you must not drive on any footpath (e.g. pavement) or bridleway. So, never mount kerbs to blast past; wait, serenely.

As you have probably realised, the problem when you hope to overtake in normally flowing, multi-laned traffic will, more often than not, be that that driver in question ahead is, himself, being blocked behind others anyway – all waiting to take their turn to get ahead. In law, however, whether it is he or someone further up in front who may be wilfully obstructing, instead of moving in, makes no difference. *You still must not overtake along anyone's inside*.

In theory, this last rule should mean that, in free-flowing traffic, you will always be safe to move in to the next lane on your left unless you are at the time overtaking someone. It ought simply to go without saying that you should never have to worry that anyone will be belting past on that side. In an emergency (such as a roof rack shedding its load in front of you) freedom to move there at short notice might well save a serious accident.

In practice, however, with burgeoning traffic filling our roads to capacity, you have to worry very much that such a safe 'haven' will be denied to you at just such a moment when it is most needed. The stealthy, creeper-upper, inside-overtaker is just as deadly as the swooping, rocket-fuelled, practically airborne, undertaking ambusher. Either of these is at his worst on two wheels.

Whenever there is anyone worthy of suspicion in the vicinity behind you, you must therefore compensate. Do so by distancing yourself further back from whatever may be ahead of you. (That should defuse any immediate concern about potential trouble up front.) You can then indicate left, to signal your willingness to move in and let him through – that is, if he hasn't already perpetrated an undertake . . .

Such villains seem to breed with redoubled vigour amongst fast-hurtling, multi-laned traffic. Unless they are to be, correctly, so classified, we must presume instead that, somehow, they seriously believe queuing or waiting to be taking place –

in lanes to their right – at any speed up to 70 mph plus! Even that presupposes that they have read the Highway Code. How *the Law* might define genuine, slow-moving queuing conditions, as described there, you must judge for yourself but I am sure that in this matter it would not be the proverbial ass.

Your main protections from such illegality lie, firstly, in having my **Mirrors – Mirrors – Mirrors** drivestyle and, secondly, in adding a flash-look, backwards, across your inside shoulder – before ever committing yourself to moving in to a lane on your left. Believe me this precaution *often* saves lives, never mind paintwork.

Having branded those on two wheels as amongst the worst offenders in the above context, I must now leap partly to their defence. Motorcyclists, quite fairly, make good use of their ability to move up between lanes in stopped and/or slow-moving queues. (For some reason they almost invariably choose to populate between lanes, rather than to the far left or right of multi-line queues.) Few would grudge them that advantage. The pity is that so many of them are also prepared to take liberties, outside the law. You will see them daily, weaving in and out of, and squeezing through between, fast-moving lanes of traffic, in order to bypass whatever may be in front. At least, I hope you will . . . [see them].

Lastly, before I leave the subject of lane discipline for the moment, you will, I hope, recall how I earlier suggested that you would normally expect to stay roughly in the middle of any chosen lane; that is, except when changing lanes. Amongst *reasonably light traffic* on a dual carriageway trunk-road, you can sometimes add to your safety by means of a short-term refinement of this natural positioning. You can usefully shift a small fraction off that dead centre course, so as to gain the long view out ahead of whatever vehicle(s) may be in front of you for the time being. Your temporary shift can be to either side, whichever one most enhances your vision; however, only consider doing this when both your mirrors' running picture and the road width comfortably allow (you should not straddle *any* lane lines, for example), and *never* when there are motorcyclists loose around behind you. Always double-check your mirrors' information by means of a direct glance across the appropriate shoulder, before you begin. Don't let this technique become an excuse for driving too close, either!

COUNTRY LANES

Paradoxically, the narrowest lanes, where two cars cannot easily pass one another in opposite directions anyway, seem to be safer than those of middling width. On the former, even lunatics go slow. On the latter, quite sane drivers seem prone to chance it, cutting the corners and speeding far faster than, in reality, they could stop if someone came hurtling in the other direction at the sort of speed they are doing themselves. There seems to be an illusion of safety about these minor roads; yet, when accidents happen on them, they are rarely minor. Some *two thirds* of serious and fatal accidents happen on these very roads – proportionately, an alarming statistic indeed.

At "blind" corners and brows of hills particularly, you simply must be able to stop, come what may. That may be a countryman running late who rarely finds anyone on "his" lane; it may be a lone pedestrian, previously hidden on your side right at the apex of a corner, and met just as a maniac driver springs forth in the other direction; it may be an idiot charging the other way too fast and attempting to circumnavigate a pedestrian who had been similarly concealed from him; or it may be a herd of cows, or a tractor/trailer bulging with hay. Anything can happen, including the incredible.

You must discipline your speed on the basis that the incredible **WILL HAPPEN**.

If, say, through speeding along a winding, narrow, roller-coaster road, you killed a child on roller blades as quickly as you might swat a fly, WOULDN'T YOUR CONSCIENCE BLEED FOR LIFE?

You may feel I exaggerate with these examples. I hope you won't do so any longer after your first scare.

On country lanes keep in to your side closer than usual. Keep slow, always just a bit slower than instinct would dictate and, hopefully, you should always find you have some accident evasion margin when trouble strikes, as inevitably it will. Never be bullied by people behind or "back seat drivers" urging you on. Never cut corners. Evidence that you had so done would leave you "without a leg to stand on" in the event of an accident.

Blind, "single file", hump-back bridges, often incorporating a bend, can be death-traps. Slow right down as you approach, keeping well in to your own side and ready to stop

140

at once. Until you can see over the brow, you must be going slowly enough and watching for the instant the roof of an approaching vehicle may appear, so that you can stop – and possibly hoot, too – at that instant.

Various signs may dictate who has priority but they are hard ones to remember which means what. So, whilst making sure you know them from the Highway Code yourself (NOW!), assume other drivers may get it wrong. In any similar circumstance remember that your Highway Code says "Always give way if it can help to avoid an accident". It makes sense for whoever is nearest the top to go first. However, it is probably best to give way to the discourteous rather than have a silly hold-up.

At a hairpin bend (where the inside corner angle is less than a right angle) and other "tight" corners, a carefully timed hoot can be important to warn an oncoming racing cyclist, who is leaning in towards your side with his head down, that you are there. But I am afraid such a beep won't work if he has a Walkman on full blast. And it won't make any odds to a gaggle of geese around a corner. They keep coming regardless! So, never rely on your horn. Nevertheless, accident insurance claim forms usually have a question, "Did you sound your horn?", which shows the importance experts attach to the warning of your presence that a horn can usefully give in a great many different circumstances.

Hairpin bends are very often found in steep mountainous country. With such a tight corner, slow speed hardly needs emphasis. With steepness added, you need more than just slowness. Downhill, 2nd gear and footbrake control will be necessary. Uphill, the **Almost Stopping ... But Not Quite** technique of Chapter 2 may come in handy at the apex of the corner, if speed is down to a trickle but, if the hill is too steep, you will have to take 1st gear on the move.

Taking 1st gear On The Move
The change is easy when left to the last moment before the car stops. Carry it out smartly just like any downward change and "feather in" your re-acceleration afterwards. There is no need to jump on the accelerator and lurch forward. If the change fouls up for any reason, stop. Pull on your handbrake *firmly* and follow with a **Steep (up)Hill Start** routine. See page 71.

Ability to take 1st on the move successfully is essential, and not just for country, hairpin bends! You can suddenly need it at any uphill point where speed has had to drop to almost nothing, for example, when turning sharply into a steep uphill opening. Find some steep uphills to practise the change, aplenty, before you get caught unready.

Some hairpins are even worse. Never mind speed having to drop to a trickle, you actually have to stop half-way round – and then reverse back (**LOOKING BEHIND!**), before you can get round at all! And, if appropriate, wait for uphill traffic to get round first . . . See page 169.

On country lanes you need a sharp eye to watch for gates, stiles or anywhere from which people, animals, wild game, etc., may suddenly emerge on foot. You need to be prepared for pedestrians walking on the ''wrong'' side of the road not just the ''right'' side (see your Highway Code). You must also watch for tree roots, boulders etc., which may bulge from the edges on sunken roads. Obviously, you don't want to hit ones on your own side. But you must keep an eye on the other side too; because drivers coming the other way frequently swing out, apparently more worried about their cars landing in the ditch than them being smashed into you! On lanes flooded with large puddles they swing out to get around them too! Expect this and don't fall into the same error yourself. See page 163.

Having written of watching edges in country lanes, I must stress that one of the most dangerous faults you can acquire is over-concentration on where that edge is, to the exclusion of looking ahead where you are going! If you *ever* find yourself driving solely by reference to the edge – LOOK AHEAD AT ONCE. Equally dangerous is to steer on the basis of making sure you miss each oncoming vehicle. Watching them that closely lures you ever-closer to them! Close shaves frighten examiners. Train your brain, instead, to focus on whether the width that will be available to you ahead as you pass them by will be adequate. Never mind the edge or the oncomer; watch YOUR width . . . Aligning yourself correctly in the road will soon come naturally.

To return to animals on country lanes (or anywhere else!), be prepared to tarry behind a while, or stop whilst they walk round or pass by. Too few drivers, for example, seem to appreciate how inexperienced a horse rider might be, or how volatile a nervous, spooked or surprised horse can be. Moving on again is easy; a sudden stop could make a horse rear up and throw its rider. Besides, they can kick, too! Never rev your engine, hoot or flash your lights to hurry animals. Rather should you consider temporarily switching your engine off if having to wait.

FOLLOWING OTHERS

If the driver in front stops suddenly, can you? The space between you and the vehicle in front must allow for *thinking* and braking time. I will return to this **Gap To Leave** shortly.

TRAFFIC STOPS
Meanwhile, I should explain that in traffic hold-ups, if the queue moves only a little at a time, the gap which you leave can fall to as little as 6 metres between pull-ups, closing to under 2 metres when stopped. However, leave yourself enough room to be able to get round the vehicle ahead, in case it turns out to have broken down; some do! Also, leave extra space at uphill starts lest the car in front slips back. Finally, avoid like the plague ever becoming back marker in a queue immediately beyond a blind bend. Wait at the apex until sure the driver next behind you knows he must stop.

If there is a side turning as you queue on a major road, especially on your left, *do not move up and sit there blocking it off*! Think of the man from opposite you (who isn't neces- sarily in sight yet) who will want to turn right, into it, or of someone arriving to exit from that road. Why "put a cork in it" for them? See *Yellow Box Junctions* on page 244.

Normally, at each stop, use your handbrake, go out of gear and then release your foot pedals – the routine safety sequence which should, by now, have become "second-nature". Move on with a full **Smooth Start** (see pages 32, 71 and 78).

If it is obvious you are going to move on virtually *straighta- way*, it is permissible, instead of going out of gear, to keep your clutch pedal down and take 1st immediately, in readiness for **Key to Fig. 11, 5** of the **Smooth Start**. But don't make it a regular habit. If things change and you are going to have to wait, take the gear out and release your clutch. Sitting in gear with the clutch down is dangerous if your concentration slips. Especially avoid it at places such as at, or near, traffic lights, or anywhere where pedestrians are likely to walk across betwixt and between traffic queues, brushing past your bonnet. It also causes unnecessary (and expensive to repair) wear on the clutch thrust mechanism.

"Magic" Handbrake

For stops of *no more than a few seconds* on **level** road you can also omit the handbrake; simply, instead, holding the car on the footbrake all the time. For moving off you omit **Key to Fig. 11, 5** (because your right foot is on the brake). Then, when you come to the text to **Key to Fig. 12, 3**, (b) – having *substituted* switching your right foot to the accelerator for letting the handbrake off at (a) – you just do a quick juggle as/if necessary to get your feet right for (c) and then **Key to Fig. 12, 4**. *Short* duration downhill stops can be treated in a similar way. Again, however, although missing out the handbrake is allowed if carried out with ("magic") skill at the right time, the tip is not to be abused and allowed permanently to displace the proper, fundamental routine of two paragraphs back. When you are the front-marker having to stop at a junction or a zebra crossing, for examples, the examiner should certainly frown if you don't use your handbrake.

You may one day have to stop on a hill so steep you cannot trust the handbrake, alone, to hold the car. (Or you may have been parked on one.) You know (or your teacher will soon be telling you!) that your right foot is going to have to remain on the footbrake, holding the car, up to the point of moving, or you will be in trouble. (Note: If you left the car parked in gear for safety, your foot must go on to the footbrake *first*, before you return the gear lever to neutral and begin the normal safety routine for starting your engine.)

Facing uphill, simply combine the above foot-juggle with letting the handbrake *off afterwards*; that is, just as you reach your normal **Key to Fig. 12, 3** (c) and then **4**. Facing downhill, you just adapt your **Smooth Start Downhill** (see Chapter 2), by adding in having your footbrake on all the while, until you come to let off the handbrake. Then let both brakes off at once and follow by releasing the clutch as explained in that section.

THE GAP TO LEAVE

When you are in a traffic stream and the stream speeds up, you **MUST** increase your *THINKING* time, *braking* gap. (This especially if the long view ahead is hidden, for example, when you have a wide van immediately in front of you on a dead straight road. If curves in the road allowed you to see ahead of that van rather better, it might still be safe to remain moderately close behind despite a modest increase in speed. However, you would have to be *certain* that the extra vision gained by looking past the van was sufficient to enable you to predict accurately whenever its driver might have to stop, and you need to consider whether the van driver will know you are there. He has more chance of that when you are further back. If *you* cannot see his mirror(s), *he* cannot see you. Another time that you can, occasionally, remain closer than might otherwise seem prudent is when a car has exceptionally wide and low-slung windows, through which you can see clearly. Having noted these possibilities though, I should emphasise that any temptation to stay unusually close ought, unless you are looking for an opportunity to overtake, to be strongly resisted.)

Extend your *THINKING* time, *braking* gap for narrow or busy places, blind bends, when nearing obstructions, passing through junctions, where there are walkers, etc., and, indeed, *wherever potential* (and, perhaps, unseen) *danger exists*.

You are safer a little closer *only* where you can see ahead of the stream *well* **AND** where there are also no chances of other trouble coming in your way.

When room for manoeuvre is tight and lessened by parked cars, or traffic coming the other way, or both, *slow down*. Lengthen that gap. See READING THE ROAD later in this chapter. Nose-to-tail driving is a killer. Do not participate.

Adjust your gap as conditions dictate. N.B. That *includes* taking account of weather conditions.

Inability correctly to relate speed *and position* – see page 133 – to the all-round conditions is the number one failure of Learners. (Recently fully-licensed ones, unfortunately, being among the most prone to err . . .)

To the dismay of their teachers they speed on into situations fraught with danger. The idea of positioning so as to lessen that potential threat seems to escape them entirely as well.

In many town streets and similar places, I mean by "speed on", above, anything exceeding walking speed.

When people moan that speed kills they are being inaccurate. It is too much speed at the wrong time in the wrong part of the road that KILLS.

On any multi-lane (single or dual) carriageway all the same applies. Whenever traffic ahead of you starts to bunch up, hold back. Let your gap grow, until the bunching eases.

According to the Highway Code you need to leave an overall stopping distance or gap, in good conditions, of 6 car lengths at 30 mph; at 50 mph you need 13. Over 50 mph you need exponentially more.

Another way the Code suggests to judge, on good, dry roads, is to leave a 2-second time gap. If you can count slowly to 2 between the driver ahead passing a roadside mark and *you* reaching it, you're about right. My recommendation, to Learners especially, is to make that 3 seconds or, in bad conditions, as much as 4–6 seconds (or even, during your early days at the wheel, 8 seconds).

ON WET ROADS, because braking is so much more tricky, LEAVE TWO OR THREE TIMES THE STOPPING SPACE REQUIRED FOR DRY CONDITIONS; with other factors added, such as high winds, four times may be warranted. REDUCE SPEEDS IN GENERAL BY ONE THIRD OR MORE. For ice and snow such "maths" will hardly suffice; refer to SKIDS in such conditions, from page 287.

LEAVING ROOM FOR OTHERS TO OVERTAKE

To maintain your stopping room is only one of several, vital reasons you should allow those in front to become further away as the stream-speed increases. Unless it is your wish to overtake some of them, an increasingly long gap is needed so as to allow sufficient space for faster traffic to pass you.

When a stream of selfish drivers, who ignore this, forms, faster drivers can only pass at risk to themselves and you. A prime example of this problem occurring is when a long line of cars, caught behind a lorry, plods along for miles. Of course, all must be patient and wait for a safe time to pass. However, if the driver immediately behind the lorry has a slow car or is not prepared to plan to use overtaking opportunities, he really must help by dropping back, allowing others to "leap-frog" him one by one as they pass the lorry.

Such consideration for others is the essence of good driving.

On that score, being "menaced" by someone hard on your tail hardly endears him to you, does it? Never drive in such a way that someone ahead might feel threatened.

When you are being overtaken never act unpredictably; for example, never swing out or accelerate. Indeed, slow down, if necessary, if the overtaker has to cut in, no matter *what* your feelings may be. (This may be especially important if it is a lorry passing you. You may not be able to see *why* he's being forced to move in swiftly. You dare not risk being part-cause of a head-on accident. And besides, your own car could be smashed.)

However, use your judgement. If an overtaker has suddenly started to drop back instead of passing, you must keep going, so that he can quickly get in behind you instead.

EMERGENCY STOPPING FROM HIGH SPEED

Whilst I don't recommend you to drive much over 55 mph until long after your Practical Test, it is important for you to grasp at an early stage what can happen when you suddenly have to stop from a greater speed.

Get your teacher to demonstrate, on a dry day, on an empty, safe, dual carriageway (perhaps at first light), how the distances needed to stop rise out of all proportion once you are up to big speeds. (Any speed above about 40 mph I call BIG.) And how, downhill, the problems become even more acute.

Imprint what those extra distances look like into your own mind, ready for the day when you may need them. Be aware that when your car is heavily loaded down with passengers or goods or a (possibly) top heavy roof rack, such braking, particularly (along with steering control), is going to be severely affected. Conjure up in your mind's-eye too, how much worse it can all be in wet conditions with your tyres trying to slither instead of stopping. Study **Skids When Braking Hard** in Chapter 7.

SEEING BEYOND THE CAR IN FRONT

Notice how, the greater you make your *THINKING* time, *braking* gap, the better your vision out ahead of the vehicle immediately in front becomes, and the *less hidden you will be from oncomers*. A metre or two back makes a dramatic difference. It also gives you the chance to spot cyclists or pedestrians (or fallen rocks, etc.) that the man in front, and you, will have to move out to pass.

Also take your cue from the advanced driver and try to avoid following traffic directly in line. Drive, wherever *safely* possible, slightly to one side of the "footprint" of the vehicle in front of you, so as to improve the amount you can see round and ahead of it for danger. (This technique has similarities to that suggested on page 139 for dual carriageways; however, it must only be applied with even greater caution.) Tiny amounts off-line can count for a lot; your paramount concern, though, must remain to be certain no risk could be caused to anyone who might perhaps be closing up on your nearside or trying to overtake you or, even more so, to anyone coming the other way. So, never allow yourself to get carried away by your enthusiasm to maximise that forward vision, vital as it can be. Don't forget, either, those on two wheels, who just love to squeeze *between* lanes – even when those lanes are infested with traffic going in opposite directions.

WARNING PEOPLE BEHIND

Suppose you see, looming up, a reason for slowing down. For example, you might see, well ahead, a slow-moving vehicle correctly displaying an amber flashing light, or notice the brake-lights or an indicator signal on any vehicle up ahead going on. *Always* react early rather than late. Press your brake pedal lightly or as required. This puts on your own brakelights – at once warning anyone behind. If the prospective slowing up is slight (or even unnecessary) you lose nothing, but in an emergency:

(a) you are ready, "covering" the brake pedal with your speed in check, and

(b) the drivers behind have been warned, and

(c) if the road surface is unexpectedly skiddy or your brakes have failed, you will know straightaway, hopefully early enough to initiate an alternative strategy.

Sometimes – provided you are looking as far ahead as you should be doing – you will see the brakelights or an indicator on a car several places ahead come on, and be able to warn those behind you, even before a less alert driver immediately ahead of you has reacted! However, vital as the above levels of anticipation are, take care not to flash on your brakelights unnecessarily, especially in darkness; that can aggravate drivers behind, and constant, unthinking repetition can weaken their warning effect.

In non-emergency stopping make gradualness your byword. Aim to slacken speed gently, so that you avoid sudden stops. Frequent jamming on of your brakes is a sign that you are not anticipating problems ahead, early enough. Take the hint . . .

Once sure your brake-power is sound, aim to spread your braking across the full distance you have available, less a little safety margin. That way you never brake more than necessary. You always give those behind a fair chance to stop safely too – a policy that will serve you well.

If you are in a traffic stream which is stopping, say at a Zebra crossing, you will demonstrate better driving if you can also manage an arm slowing down signal. See page 225. This arm signal carries a bonus of alerting not only pedestrians but, also, *oncoming* traffic, as well as those behind you. It is especially useful if you are heading a traffic stream. You have to give the signal as soon as you start to slow down. This is because towards your stopping point, when you may need to be changing down the gears ready for moving on again, you will need that arm back so as to keep one hand on the steering wheel at all times. Only give such an arm signal if you have comfortable time. Remember that your priority, as you get near to any hazard, is to keep *both hands on the wheel*. You might have to swerve. This applies on your Practical Test just as in everyday driving. No examiner would expect otherwise.

GEARS IN TOWN

Always being in the right gear in the usually heavier traffic of town is quite an art! Re-study figs. 16–18 and the texts headed **Gear Speeds** and **How To Change Gear**.

If, on a level road in a built-up, 40 mph restricted area, you are travelling in a traffic stream in top gear and at about that speed, when everyone has to slow to 25 mph, the chances are, I regret to say, that no one will drop a gear for quick re-acceleration after the reason for slowing down has passed.

So, as you cannot then re-accelerate smartly anyway, it is reasonable to pick up speed more gradually, and without necessarily yourself changing down either. In circumstances like these, 3rd gear can also be used from lower speeds than usual, where it is yet unnecessary to drop to 2nd; and 2nd can be used from right down to a crawl.

However, if you are stream leader in a similar setting, you should avoid such dawdling off the mark when the position opens up. Definitely *change down* for quicker acceleration, and make sure you are never one to frustrate sharper-minded drivers behind. I'm not suggesting you develop habits of speeding in towns, or of ever going faster than safe or breaking speed limits but, whenever you are privileged to be at the front of such a stream, do get on with it as you pick up speed again.

If you are slowing down rather more – along with all the other traffic – but there is a good chance none of you will need actually to stop, make sure you get down into 2nd gear so that you can pick up the pace smartly as soon as the time comes. Be alert. Stay tuned! On your Practical Test you are expected to make normal progress, not dither around when you could be getting on.

It is usual to go up and down your gears in numerical order. However, with the speeds appropriate to most urban conditions, many drivers skip from 4th to 2nd gear or, maybe, go direct from 3rd to 5th. That's fine – provided you don't let lazy driving habits creep in. If, as a result, you become a sluggish driver, never in the right gear to add speed smartly when the traffic opens up, you become a menace and a root cause of unnecessary congestion and jams.

Should traffic drop to a snail's pace but *without stopping*, you can usually stay in 2nd gear and use your **Almost Stopping ... But Not Quite** routine as learnt on your open space. However, if the snail's pace continues for more than a few seconds, or, particularly, if you are on a steep uphill slope, it then becomes more appropriate to take 1st on the move. The technique is discussed in connection with hairpin bends on page 141. You are then ready to slow down even more, still without actually stopping! You can use the **Minimum Speed – Clutch Pedal Up** technique (again, from your open space practice) initially after the change, and you will still have clutch-slipping in 1st gear in hand, before you would have to give up and stop to avoid an engine stall. If all this seems a little esoteric and not worth knowing about, wait until you're in a long, hot, summer, uphill, traffic crawl and wish you had taken the trouble to practise! (Or rather, *don't* wait!) Because that's when you will save your clutch while others are "burning out" all around . . .

GEARS ON THE OPEN ROAD

Clear of the town you will spend much more of your time in top gear or, more likely, in your 5th gear to take advantage of fuel and noise saving. When you are going over about 40 mph, 5th is generally fine. However, if you need to boost acceleration from higher speeds, always return to top, or to 3rd if more appropriate.

Fig. 42 shows what gears you need when you go up and down dale, both for engine braking control downhill, and to keep your speed up, uphill.

Immediately you start losing speed uphill, take a lower gear and, unless there is a sound traffic reason not to, increase acceleration rapidly to maintain speed. The engine needs more acceleration – more fuel – to carry you up the hill. If the engine "labours", change down at once. (Labouring produces a metallic tinkling noise called "pinking", which your teacher can demonstrate.)

There is nothing worse, in conditions where overtaking is impossible, than to have a bunch of amateurs ahead of you, who allow the edge to come off their speed every time you all

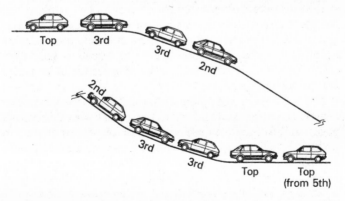

Fig 42   Using the gears uphill and downhill.

151

come to an uphill stretch. (As stopping is easier uphill, they can't even claim that keeping to a safe speed is the reason for their incompetence.) Don't join them! Go down as far as 3rd, then 2nd – or even 1st if the hill calls for it – each time dropping gear early rather than late. Return up the gears, of course, directly the hill levels out.

Approaching a steep hill down, take a lower gear to increase control and a lower gear still if the hill is very steep. At an *exceptionally steep hill* (take the hint if you see an escape lane sign!), always slow down and take the lowest gear you think you might need, at the top, before you begin the descent proper. You may also need to brake on the way down. Second would be the lowest gear normally required. Otherwise you can be faced, on the way down, with having to change down further, which may be tricky. If you have to do that, you must get speed down with your footbrake comfortably below the maximum of the lower gear, before making the change.

A refinement to your downward gear changing needs mention here. The same road speed in a lower gear needs a higher engine speed. Because of this, it is better driving and smoother for passengers if, when you go down the gearbox, you can always try to pre-match the engine speed needed in the new lower gear to whatever your road speed happens to be at the time. Refer again to fig. 18. The way to do so is this: during stage **2**, as you are shifting the gear lever, you give a quick blip on your accelerator to raise the engine revs. Continue into stage **3** as normal so that there is no delay. Doing this neatly, so that the revs are a perfect match for your speed as your clutch pedal returns up, soon comes with experience. You learn to adjust the size of blip to the circumstances; the higher your speed is in relation to the new lower gear, the stronger your blip must be.

The technique ought to be within the grasp of most Learners. However, an examiner would not mark it against you if you didn't use it. Nevertheless, you will see later, in SKIDS in Chapter 7, why a smooth transition down the gears is better driving.

Never, by the way, drive with your hand holding the gear lever. If you have second thoughts about a change, take your hand back to the steering wheel until you are ready.

READING THE ROAD

TOWN DRIVING – TRAINING YOUR EYES

In fig. 43, the lines fanning out from **A** represent your eyes scanning for trouble. **K**, immediately in front, is where most Learners, wrongly, over-concentrate. Some also allow their eyes to wander to the scenery **L**; they will not live long.

You must learn to switch your eyes rapidly about, near and far. In the near foreground, that means out to the sides, as well as right in front of you. Further out ahead, always keep an eye on your farthest horizon. Thus, approaching a bend or coming up to the brow of a hill, you watch the unfolding scene *as it opens up*; on the straight you keep searching afar, right to the point where the road fades from view.

Fig. 43, **K**, if there are no pedestrians, is possibly the safest area! You cover that instinctively, whilst you absorb the changing traffic situation further ahead. Your eyes anticipate the risk of a door opening from car **B** and someone jumping out. So, you steer a door's width clear or, instead, *slow right down* if you haven't room to do that because of oncoming traffic. In that event you may well even stop and wait, if necessary, rather than attempt to squeeze through on high risk. Remember, close shaves frighten examiners, too! If you saw someone preparing to leap out as you came along, you would probably toot your horn in advance but you would allow, nonetheless, that it might not be heard through loud, in-car music or by someone deaf.

Your eye-scanning takes in path **J**, to be sure no in-line roller-skater or child cyclist is about to zoom out into the road.

You watch the wagon **D**, which is, by all appearances, arriving a little too quickly to turn left and join your road, in order to be certain it does manage to stop.

E is a wet (and therefore slippery) patch you may not note until a split-second later.

You have in mind that the Learner driver **C**, indicating to go right, has not yet stopped, and that he may simply drive out in front of **F**! Is **F** watching **C**? If **F** swung your way in that circumstance, could you, even though he ought not to, manage to give him room?

Once you have seen the wet patch **E**, you slow down more

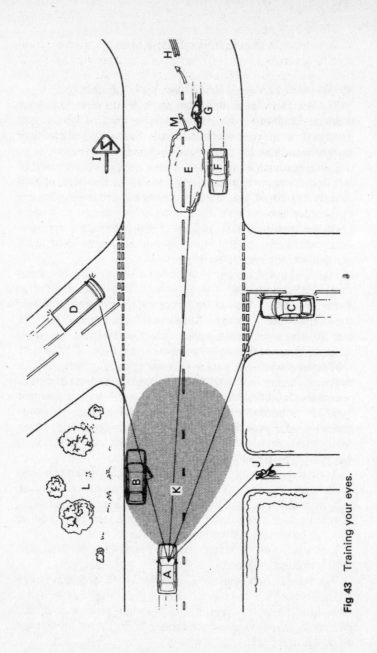

Fig 43 Training your eyes.

(than you ought to have done already), wary in case motorcyclist **G** attempts to pass **F**, skids, and slithers across "your road" towards **D**. Your glances include **H**, warned by arrow **M**, the start of a double white line and **I**, a double-bend sign.

You are lucky here that there has been no one behind but were you watching? A lot to be looking for? Yes, but a safe passage lies in your hands, for the *planned avoidance of danger is at the heart of safety*. Examiners expect you to maintain reasonable progress if a road is clear but, equally, to curb speed whenever you come upon a scene so pregnant with danger as in fig. 43; so don't be afraid to take responsibility:

* *YOU* can slow down;
* *YOU* can (within the confines of your side of the road and lane discipline) pick the line that offers you the maximum room for sudden manoeuvre;
* *YOU* can avoid always blaming only the other party in the event of an accident.

The experienced can always spot a lazy, thoughtless driver ahead, most easily, in town. He drives at a constant speed, too fast in danger, yet, often, too slow in the clear. Leaving adequate clearances hardly enters his head. Keep well away!

Whenever you share a road with more vulnerable users, **Slow Down**. A staggering 1 in 3 of our road deaths are of cyclists and pedestrians, children being the most at risk. It has been reported that **37%** of adults killed on foot would fail a driver's breathalyser – so skin your eyes for signs of any drunken haze.

TWO "EXPERT" TIPS

(a) In situations like that in fig. 43 keep a thumb or finger ready at the horn. See fig. 44. A toot can prevent danger – stop a jaywalker, for example, or save half-a-second and perhaps life.

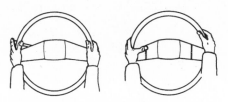

Fig 44   At the ready to toot, with one finger or a thumb as appropriate, but with both hands still in full control of the wheel.

(b) Also cover your footbrake, particularly, and the clutch pedal too, so that, in any emergency, no time is going to be lost in moving your feet for stopping. Let your feet "hover" over the pedals, as in fig. 45, *without necessarily pressing either one unless you need so to do*. Speed will reduce anyway – because your foot is off the accelerator. You can cut it further with a touch on the footbrake if you need to or, if it gets too low, your right foot can occasionally switch to give a dab of acceleration, returning to the "cover" position while the potential danger lasts.

Suppose, looking again at fig. 43, that, on your approach to the scene, some children had been tomfooling near the front of parked car **B**. Perhaps your only clue was tell-tale feet seen under the car at a very early stage before you reached it. You did look, didn't you? It is when such horrors, as could be those children, burst out into your path, forewarned or not, that you will be glad of my two "expert" tips. The UK still has one of the highest rates of accidents to children in Europe. Let's get it down.

MORE REFINED ROAD READING

In fig. 46, typical of a high street scene in front of you, you have a clear space ahead of *you* but traffic in the other direction is queuing. This is no time for wild acceleration or speed.

Here, the van, pulling out between the stopped traffic across

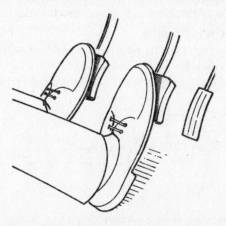

Fig 45 The "hover cover" position, at the ready for a quick stop.

Fig 46 A time NOT to accelerate wildly.

a "keep clear" section, nearly went right ahead. Luckily, he spotted the motorcycle which had suddenly weaved out to pound up on the outside, and he stopped in his tracks. (Whether he ever intended to wait for you – as he should have done – remains a moot point . . .) Potentially, a second later, that rider could have been thrown up in the air to land under *your* front wheels. The chances of a jaywalker wandering out through such stopped traffic, or of someone from your left dashing without looking, over to the bus, and of similar errors of judgement, are high. The situation demands single-file use of your side of the road and very modest speed. You will have drivers determined to barge past you, trying to make a second lane in their attempt to shoot ahead, much to the horror of the stopped traffic so close by. That you cannot prevent. Never join in.

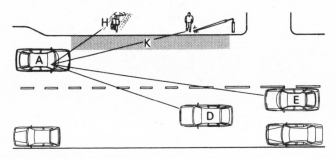

Fig 47 More refined eye-flashing.

157

Examine fig. 47, in which you are driver **A**. Apart from checking for jaywalkers like **H**, who may leave the pavement thoughtlessly, *especially in rain* – which always seems to cause those on foot to forget their personal safety – you need to glance at the oncoming vehicles. **E**, in particular, may decide to risk beginning to pass **D**, forcing you to use some of your *safety margin* **K**, between you and the pavement, or to brake. Watching his front wheels – *without dwelling on them* – is one way you can anticipate his pushy wrongdoing for, unless a car is skidding, it follows its front wheel direction.

Many roads occasionally become narrowed down without much warning. It is an amateur error to let yourself be forced out suddenly, as indicated by the dotted line in fig. 48. You can even find yourself having to pull up, as the dotted outline car has done, whilst better-positioned traffic passes by. That would be a matter of **Lane Discipline** to which we come shortly. Meanwhile the solid arrow shows how the more refined road-reader spots the problem way ahead and eases out smoothly to avoid being squeezed.

He also employs – cautiously – a very modest degree of vision-enhancing positioning, where there is sufficient road width to allow so doing. Travelling along a major road and coming up to a junction with a minor road at which vision is foreshortened by hedges or buildings, for example, he may lie out in the road or move in to his left a small fraction more than would be normal. This would be so as to see better or earlier in a particular direction from which traffic might suddenly appear; however, he would never place himself so far out as to endanger other traffic. Similarly, as he rounds the apex of a wide but mostly blind, righthand bend, he may choose a line

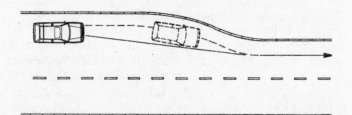

Fig 48   Road narrows. Ease out early as continuous arrow shows.

closer to his nearside edge than strictly appropriate for his speed, if that is likely to enhance his view ahead, out of it, and/or to keep him better out of the way of anyone, yet unseen, coming the other way.

PEDESTRIANS CROSSING

Wherever a pedestrian chooses to cross the road he has *priority*. He may step out without looking; you may consider him to be utterly foolish; but you cannot wilfully just carry on and run him over. You are morally and legally bound to take the best evasive action you can. In that sense he *must have* universal priority.

So, it is not only at a Zebra, Pelican or Puffin crossing that you must assume the pedestrian is king; you must be watching everywhere, and remember that it may not be immediately obvious to you when someone is slow, mentally disturbed, deaf or blind. Especially consider the elderly, teenage exuberance, and that tiny tots may do *anything*, even when parents are there. And beware the inebriated, too.

Zebra, Pelican and Puffin crossings give pedestrians particular priority. A Toucan is another variation, designed also to allow cyclists priority to *ride* across. (Drivers should see a full size bicycle frame, painted in white, across the carriageway where cyclists ride over. Be alerted; mounted bikers come fast!)

Zigzag lines either side of pedestrian crossings define the area around them in which you may NEVER park and where, on the approach side, overtaking the nearest vehicle towards the crossing is banned under ANY circumstances. Assume the bans even where the zigzag lines may be faded or temporarily absent. Whether, when there are two lanes, you should define moving up alongside as "overtaking" in the above context is unclear in the Highway Code. However, I wouldn't push your luck, whether there are pedestrians you are both stopping for or not.

At a Zebra crossing, if people are still standing on the pavement, you don't have to stop. *But you must show awareness and be ready so to do.*

Once anyone has stepped onto the crossing, then, even if they are still waiting, you must STOP, unless too sudden a stop risks a pile-up from behind. Otherwise, if you drive where they are about to walk, *you are at fault*.

Should someone rush across quite without warning – so that you have no chance to go through safely – then you *must*, of course, EMERGENCY STOP TO SAFEGUARD LIFE even at risk of a hit from behind.

For normal stopping at a Zebra (or, indeed, at any type of pedestrian crossing) it is *better* to stop a little short of the official stop line. Pedestrians will appreciate your care, and it helps them to see round and behind you, in case someone else isn't paying attention and stopping.

Train your eyes to look at both pavements on approach to a Zebra Crossing. (Flashing, orange "Belisha" beacons should highlight the crossing for you, from a long way ahead.) If anyone is crossing you must stop, or slow sufficiently, using speed judgement and common sense, so that he has passed *well before* you get there.

When you have been the first to have to stop, and the last walker has crossed the Zebra crossing far enough for you to continue, you go, but not so soon as to frighten him. Never rev your engine to try to hurry him up; never move your gear lever into 1st until he has just passed.

Where there is a centre island in a Zebra crossing, each side is, technically, meant to be treated as a separate crossing. However, as a centre island is not a very safe place to stand and wait, it is best for anyone waiting to cross your half of the Zebra from that middle point, for you to give way anyway, regardless of whether they may have actually stepped off the island. This distinction does *not* apply, however, to Pelican or to other traffic light controlled crossings, unless they are *staggered*; that is, with an extra set of pedestrian push buttons and a waiting area, kept safe by railings, in the middle of the road. Any *straight* such crossing – even one *having a centre island* – is, instead, legally deemed to be a *single crossing*; give way according to the rules below, even if the pedestrian(s) to whom you so do are crossing from the other half of the crossing from yourself (i.e. beyond that island).

Pelican, Puffin and also Toucan crossings differ from Zebras in other ways, too, mainly because traffic light signals are added to control the actions, both of drivers and of those using the crossings, respectively. But remember, the pedestrian (or cyclist on a Toucan) is *always* king, at fault though he may be! The rules for drivers are set out below, in the same sequence that pedestrian traffic lights always operate:

(a) Green.

GO. However, YOU *STILL* HAVE, **FIRST**, TO GIVE WAY TO ANY STRAGGLERS. (Use normal care. Pedestrians and cyclists should wait; *don't trust them*; watch them too!)

(b) Continuous amber.

STOP (unless already so close it would be unsafe so to do).

(c) Red (a high-pitched pulsating tone may sound to inform the blind they can safely cross).

STOP! (Walkers have right of way, even if they have yet to set foot on the crossing itself.) **N.B.** *You still have to* **STOP**, and wait for (d)$_1$ – or (d)$_2$ – *even if there are none, or if those there have finished crossing already.*

(d)$_1$ *Pelicans*: Flashing on-off amber.

GIVE WAY to pedestrians still crossing (however, if the crossing is empty, or the last pedestrians are comfortably clear before green comes on again, you should go).

(d)$_2$ *Puffins* and *Toucans*: *Always* WAIT FOR GREEN.

Neither of these crossings have, in their sequence, a flashing amber mode. For drivers, they are more akin to an ordinary traffic light. Their "secret weapon" is the inclusion of electronic sensors to hold the lights at red whilst anyone crossing still needs more time. The sensors should shorten or avoid traffic hold ups, because they detect the presence or absence of people crossing, accurately, whereas, for example, a Pelican stops traffic for a set time, even when a pedestrian changes his mind and decides not to cross after all. At a Puffin or Toucan crossing, therefore, *you cannot go until green appears*; and then only *after observing* the caveats in (a) above.

At all these crossings, if there is *any* doubt that a pedestrian or cyclist will stick to the rules, always stop. Never wave at or toot at someone to encourage him to cross, even if he has every right. That is unlawful and can be dangerous. It is for him to look out. A slowing down arm signal, however, is correct. Given early it is helpful, and it informs him that you are stopping.

Any type of pedestrian crossing, come upon whilst you are in queuing traffic, presents traps to Learners and amateurs. Unless you are *thinking* and looking ahead, you may not notice the cocky pedestrian who strides out dangerously between stopped or slow-moving vehicles rather than using the crossing. Likewise it is easy to move up with the queue, only to block the crossing because traffic beyond it is stuck! Your examiner would not be amused . . . notwithstanding ugly looks you may receive from pedestrians. You may not stop on the crossing itself except, in emergency, to avert an accident.

STOP! SCHOOL CROSSING PATROLS, ETC.
When the patrolman steps out displaying his hand-held sign, you **MUST** stop. Apply the same care as for a Zebra. Policemen or traffic wardens often do the job too. Be sure you already fully understand from the Highway Code the authorised signals that they use. Near schools, look out for the twin, orange lights, mounted one above the other on the fixed school

162

warning sign-pole, to be flashing alternately. It's the patrol-man who switches them on . . .

Uniformed, legal authorities are not the only people for whom you may have/need to stop. You would stop, for examples, if a shepherd made the request because of his flock, or for a schoolmaster with children in his charge. Not stopping, whoever requests it, can put you in considerable legal difficulty; however, if you felt highly suspicious of some apparently strange request, you could be well-advised to keep your doors and windows locked for the time being. Remember: you cannot risk any accident or running anyone down.

GIVING WAY

EMEGENCY VEHICLES
Make way, where safe, for ambulances, fire and police vehicles sporting flashing blue lights and sirens. Expect other vehicles to scatter for them; e.g., on a two-lane dual carriageway, by shifting in or out to leave them a clear run up the middle. Do the same for a doctor with his green flashing light. Allow a disabled person who ventures on the highway on a powered buggy extra room. Did you know that – provided he displays a yellow flashing light – he can go on dual carriageways, despite having a top speed of only 8 – 10 mph ?

PASSING STATIONARY OBSTACLES
When passing any obstacle on your side of the road, the *rule of the road* is that, if there is no room because of approaching traffic, YOU *must give way*. You slow right down and, if necessary, wait until you can pass safely *without any approaching vehicle having to decelerate, brake, or – worse – take avoiding action*. The test is, will the oncomer have to slow or move over? If so, GIVE WAY. Nevertheless, if someone is approaching you *uphill* and with a blockage on his side, it is courteous if you are able, instead, to wait for him.

In fig. 49, **U** wait for approaching cars **A** and **B** to pass. Should a fool or a cad, on finding himself in the opposite situation (i.e. when you are driver **A**), misjudge getting round the tree and force you to brake, don't accelerate or swing out

Fig 49 Giving way at a fallen tree.

in hostility – as too many drivers do. *Slow up*. Two dead cads do not make a gentleman.

Treat roadworks similarly. Signs usually alert you before you arrive. Always wait well back and well tucked in to your left, if you have to, so that the largest of lorries could get through the other way should one turn up before you can go. Likewise, wait well back if temporary traffic lights stop you (learn the lights' sequence from your Highway Code) or if a workman using a temporary, hand-held sign instructs you to wait.

In fig. 50, you are **A**, and need to move out to pass parked car **D**. Mirrors' watching shows car **B** close behind. You think

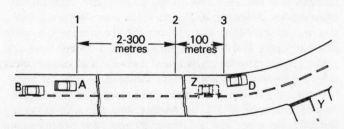

Fig 50 Passing a parked vehicle.

B wants to pass. He may not have yet seen **D**, particularly if your car hides his view.

Imagine your speed is 35 mph. Because of **B**, you give a brief right indicator signal from **1**, until your mirrors show that **B** realises and accepts that you are both going to need to move out. If no one is coming the other way, and you can see that you will be able to pass **D** without any complications, cancel it by **2**. (Otherwise – you may find yourself, by the time you reach **Y**, behaving like the car in fig. 52!) You make it brief to prevent **B** – or anyone else – from thinking you are going to turn at **Y**.

If no vehicles are close behind *and* none is coming, there is no need to signal.

However, if someone *is* coming, or you cannot be sure that there isn't going to be anyone, *do* signal, and maintain that signal as you slow down and assess the situation.

From **1**, in fig. 50, having signalled extra early if there is a **B** on your tail, begin easing out gradually so that, by **2**, your righthand wheels are running parallel with, and just inside, the centre line on your own side. You are thus already in position, by **2**, to see past **D**, and to decide whether you will have time to go or will have to pull up and wait at **Z**. Learners often leave moving out *too late* and eventually have to stop, hard up behind **D**, unable to see round, and being passed and hooted. Ease out early, gradually – never suddenly.

At 35 mph, point **1** would be 300–400 metres from the parked car. Always drop speed by **2**, ready for stopping at **Z** if necessary. Between **1** and **2** you take 3rd gear and remain ready to drop to 2nd should it become needed. The decision to be made by **2**, whether or not you will have to wait at **Z**, depends on conditions; however, if you decide stopping will be necessary, then you must plan to ensure that your **Z** position will be both fully on your own side, and *far back* enough from **D**, for you to be able to see ahead properly whilst you are waiting. Make sure any necessary waiting will be done neatly placed and within your own side of the road.

Directly it becomes obvious – if it does – that you are clear to go on without needing to stop, cancel your signal if given. However, if you are going to have to wait, keep the indicator on whilst you pull up at **Z**. Then it continues to warn everyone that something unusual is happening – i.e. you are stopping. Only cancel it later, just before you are able to move on again.

Either way make sure your signal is *off* by the time you pass the car **D** – or, if there are several vehicles, once you reach the first one. Even if there is no road such as **Y**, as in this example, signalling beyond that point is unnecessary and confusing. (Incidentally, were you *intending* to turn into **Y**, an arm signal, given just before turning, should ensure no misunderstanding.)

To return to fig. 50, early *positioning* is vital on several more counts. Followers are forewarned well ahead. Oncomers see you sooner. You will be able to pass parallel to car **D** and, therefore, with less of a "detour". (A great swing round any such car could well mean that your own car would then be off-balance if you suddenly had to brake. That could become the cause of an unnecessary skid. See SKIDS in Chapter 7.)

Quite often, being nicely "lined up" also allows you to go on safely at times where, because of someone coming the other way, you otherwise could not consider it. This is because road widths frequently turn out to be such that, when the oncomer has been able to see you early and it has been safe for him courteously to move in to his left a little to help, and he *has* so done voluntarily, there is *then* room for everyone; correctly positioned, you are ready to use it.

However, you should beware any risk of becoming the meat in the sandwich! In fig. 51, you are **A**. There seems to be plenty of room to pass the parked goods vehicles without crossing the centre line, but **E** is coming fast, overtaking the other traffic. Should you go through? The answer, in all similar situations, is never go on where there is the slightest

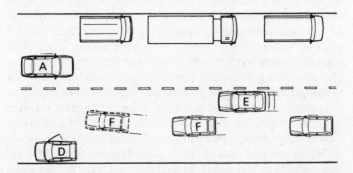

Fig 51 Meat in the sandwich.

chance you might be squashed. Car **E** could be forced out by car **F**. (**F** may not have seen **E** in his mirrors, and may suddenly swing out – shown in broken outline – if **D** opens his door.) A pedestrian might step out from between the parked commercial vehicles on your side, or one of the drivers thereof might suddenly jump down from his cab. Equally, one of the latter folk, further deliveries being foremost on his mind, could, in a moment of carelessness, pull out without warning. Examiners watch whether you leave adequate clearance for such shocks. Larger obstructions that may hide people, like the three lorries here all close together, demand more safety margin.

Slow down ahead of the sandwich risk. Time it so that you need not necessarily commit to going through until **E** has gone. Stop if needs be; although, once your anticipation and judgment of speed improve, stops are often avoidable. Despite mistakes by **D** and/or **F**, **E** shouldn't anyway be trying to pass when you are coming, should **E**? More fundamental, should **F** stray out, is that **E,** already in the wrong, should *always pull back* rather than attempting to swerve past.

If you were too close to the centre line or had not already slackened speed and covered your brake, you would be at fault too. Guilty, though not necessarily in legal terms, because you had left yourself no room for errors, albeit other people's; but ones which are so common they *must be expected.*

Many urban roads are really wide enough for two lanes in each direction – were it not for the fact that they are littered with parked vehicles punctuating that freedom. The road in fig. 51 is an example. Dual carriageways are frequently choked down to a single lane each way for the same reason. In these circumstances it makes little sense to flip in and out again in order to use every short gap between the parked vehicles. Indeed, so doing would considerably disrupt the general flow of traffic. You are expected to use your judgement. In queuing conditions, you would move back in after passing a solitary, parked car, even if the next one were only to be 75 metres up the road. Whereas, in free-flowing traffic, you would ignore smaller gaps and keep to a line that gives you ample clearance from any rows of parked vehicles. Nevertheless, if someone were clearly wanting to pass you, you *would* make use of any longer gap of, say, 250 metres or so, thus letting him through and upholding the spirit of courtesy in your Highway Code.

Remember my pleas that you switch your eyes rapidly everywhere, look far enough ahead, and *plan* to avoid danger. If you follow them without fail, you will always drop speed whenever risks escalate, and you will always position accordingly; as a result, untimely actions by others ought never to catch you off guard.

You will have already taken the optimum line for a safe passage, invariably have speed sensibly in check and, rarely, if ever, find yourself without a safe margin of room for sudden manoeuvre.

See fig. 52. If, like this driver, who has no thought of turning, your indicator still flashes away merrily long after some previous use, cancel it. Others may try to remind you by gesticulating or by a toot or headlight flash; but the warning light and ticking noise inside your car should be enough!

PASSING MOVING OBSTACLES – e.g. CYCLISTS AND ANIMALS

Leave cyclists extra room (1½ metres plus) even if that means slowing and tagging *a respectable distance behind* – for *as long as it may take* before you can pass with the clearance you need. Stay alert! Cyclists often suddenly dismount when the going gets steep. They also wobble in gusty wind or its eddies, or perhaps to get around uneven sections of road, tram lines or "larger-than-life" (to them) pot holes

Fig 52 If your indicator has failed to return to normal by itself, cancel it! Here, someone might conclude you were going to turn into the driveway or the lane.

or drain covers (motorcyclists sometimes swerve for these, too); or, maybe, it will be a bicycle pump, poking through the spokes, that pitches them off altogether. Make due allowance for age, too, whenever you come across children (under or over 100 years old) on bikes.

If you reach an obstruction, a junction where you are about to turn left or any other place a cyclist is at his most vulnerable, at the same time as he does, always let him go first. You dare not risk squashing him. He may well swing unexpectedly widely around the roadworks or whatever; he may not, himself, be turning at the junction . . .

Leave even more room and take more care when you need to pass animals. Their unpredictability demands it. See also page 142.

Always signal these passes in advance even if, on a wide road, you won't be moving out much. This alerts people, ahead or behind, that there is a problem they may not yet have noticed or be able to see. At night, when vision is hard anyway, particularly out in the country, your signal may be crucial to safety. On the subject of cyclists, these quintessentially vulnerable, venerable creatures (yes, even the lawless types . . .) can also benefit from your common-sense help when/if they move to a crown-of-the-road position for turning right. If you can just hold *extra* well back or keep *extra* well to their left, other road users, from every angle of view, will have a greater chance of seeing them in good time and of keeping clear themselves.

SINGLE TRACK ROADS WITH PASSING PLACES

Glaringly obvious examples of these are invariably signposted. Where you must take extra care and follow the same basic rules is at *unmarked* narrow places!

The general rule is that traffic going uphill has priority; if you are going downhill you should wait in a passing place on your side – or just opposite one if the inlet is on the other side – so as to let the uphill driver(s) pass by. However, there is little point in someone who is coming down (or several people who are so doing) having to reverse a huge distance uphill when you are coming up, if the nearest passing place is much nearer for you to drop back in to. Apply sense! Unfortunately, you cannot force others so to do, but they usually do. Naturally, you should never park in a passing place, whether so marked or not.

At the point of squeezing past you may, if it is a very narrow "squeak", be better, as a Learner, to do the waiting, so that the oncoming driver runs the risk of touching your paintwork, rather than the other way round – even when the theoretical priority may be yours.

These rules should be applied much in the same way in narrow residential or commercial streets where cars, skips, etc., are parked all the way down both sides, leaving only one vehicle width down the middle. Treat the occasional parking spaces (of which there are bound to be some) as passing places, and act accordingly. Kill your speed, too. Such streets are death traps waiting for drivers who go criminally fast. A car door only needs to open; an infant to crawl between parked vehicles . . . 20 mph may well be too quick to go.

Narrow bridges, over or under, and humpback bridges – at any of which opposing traffic may be unable to pass – are often found on roads or streets of otherwise reasonable width. They need similar, commonsense treatment. Even if signs or traffic lights allow you priority, always be alert and prepared to wait for oncoming traffic which may come on through regardless. Where you cannot see the other side, you may need to wait, listen and hoot before moving on slowly and with considerable care. Think in terms of a bus or demolition lorry suddenly appearing in the middle consuming the whole available width – as much as of a lone cyclist chancing his luck at full tilt.

LANE DISCIPLINE

With two or more busy lanes for traffic in your direction you may need to move to another one prior to making a turn, or perhaps in order to overtake. Another reason for wanting to move can be that your own lane "fizzles out". Perhaps you are in an outside lane when someone ahead is having to slow and then wait before turning right. Perhaps, as can happen to any lane, roadworks intervene. A parked car may mean you have to leave a lefthand lane temporarily. It all requires constant anticipation, and that means looking a surprisingly (to most Learners) *long way ahead.*

You cannot just barge across into a lane next door to yours whilst that one is full of flowing traffic, whatever the reason for so doing may be. None of those drivers or riders should ever be placed at risk or forced to slow down, because of you. *The rule is* GIVE WAY *and let that traffic flow on.*

You wait your turn before you join it. That will probably at least mean having to slow down. Ultimately, it can mean having to stop. How it turns out will depend upon when a safe gap to merge into that flow becomes available. Your anticipation has to be good enough to allow time to signal your lane change and, depending on the circumstances, perhaps for others to "accept" that signal, too, before you can move across.

Whenever you change lane, for whatever the need may be, give a brief indicator signal beforehand. Check your mirrors *first*; don't begin to signal unless/until there is, potentially, a gap for you in the new lane. Double-check your mirrors after beginning your signal. Your final check has to be with a flash-look over the appropriate shoulder. No more than a glimpse, just from the corner of your eye focused through the lower half of your rear-passenger-door window, can be enough to save you from a mirror-hopper on either side.

Cancel the signal directly you start moving over, unless it needs to continue prior to a turn you are making. (As you rarely need more than half-a-dozen flashes for a simple lane change, it is worthwhile developing a habit to prevent you forgetting to cancel it! Keep a finger holding the control stalk on or, if you cannot reach it without taking your hand off the wheel, keep a finger outstretched towards it. "Flick" it back off again, against its spring loading, directly you have moved over.)

So often, in my observation, it is only the very advanced drivers, who genuinely look far enough ahead, who manage to re-align themselves in time, easing across into the necessary lane without affecting anyone else, long before a turn or a blockage is reached. For the rest, the turn is upon them, or double (or more) queues are already forming because of whatever the problem is, before they even realise that they may need to change lane.

If there is suddenly *a whole queue* having to give way to an adjacent flowing lane, as is all too common when a lane becomes temporarily blocked, each member of that queue must then wait, in turn, as necessary. (That is, unless the obstacle clears, in which event they can, probably, promptly revert to continuing in their original lane.)

Double queues and even treble ones, or more, of course, form all the time near traffic lights, roundabouts and other junctions. Always choose and move to an appropriate queue for your direction *early*. Otherwise, you can find yourself "pinned" in the wrong lane, unable to get across to the right one. (**Note:** You must obey traffic lane arrows, on the road or on signs; not so to do can be construed as careless or inconsiderate driving.) You may then have to pass by a turn or go in a wrong direction. This is because (even if it were safe and not in conflict with directional lane arrows) you should *not* – in an attempt to swap lanes – selfishly cause an unnecessary blockage to those behind who are correctly laned for where they want to go. In the absence of any reasonable opportunity to move to the lane you need, you must stay with the direction of the lane in which you are "trapped". You must be patient; even if it will mean having to rejoin your route later, after a detour.

I remind you that the Highway Code specifically bans cutting from one queue to another in order to jump traffic. However, cyclists and motorcyclists *do* – not always unreasonably – weave in and out of crawling traffic queues. They may push their luck but you are always best to yield. This involves good mirrors' watching and, at first, advice from an alert teacher.

Although, in multiple-laned traffic streams or queues, you should always signal before moving to an outer lane and, equally so, before crossing to an inner one, you need not apply this rule robotically when all you are doing is simply moving back to the left after overtaking in lighter traffic, or after passing a parked vehicle. This is despite the fact that, "technically", you may, nonetheless, be changing lanes.

That said, however, it can be vital so to do after overtaking fast on a three-lane two-way road, or on a *treble*-laned dual carriageway (see pages 183 and 185), or on any motorway having more than two lanes for traffic in your direction.

Where a dual carriageway reverts to a single one there is often a bottle-neck, with queues forming. At the very least, drivers from each of the two lanes must manage to merge together amicably! Generally, the above principles are applied without any hiccoughs, depending on which lane comes to an end. However, because of possible, fast-moving, oncoming traffic shortly to be faced directly on the single carriageway, it is customary – and sane – always to let outer lane drivers in – regardless of whose lane it is that peters out. Expect this. Conform. Never risk placing anyone in dire jeopardy.

OVERTAKING

I will deal first with single carriageway roads, those having a *single-lane* each way.

SINGLE CARRIAGEWAY OVERTAKING

The secret of safe overtaking, of passing anyone driving along ahead of you, lies in staying sufficiently *well back* from that driver's vehicle, while you plan the pass. You have to learn from experience how close you can get while still maintaining optimum vision but you can be certain that to get cramped up in behind will be folly. From there, easing out for a peep ahead becomes like "Russian Roulette". From further back, it is comparatively safe to move out a fraction for the best view, always at-the-ready, of course, to pull back in promptly if/when traffic is going by the other way. The extra separation also makes it easier to take advantage of curves in the road in order to see ahead.

Once clear, assuming no one following is about to pass you, you signal with your right indicator, take a final check-behind-flash-look over your right shoulder, and then move on out for your overtake, gradually, never in a swerve – and accelerating powerfully as you do so.

Remember that, if someone is already passing you, the *rule of the road* is to *GIVE WAY. Let them go first.* No one should ever need to slow – or even hesitate – because of your plans. So, don't even take a peek, *still less signal*, until sure that you are clear of overtakers from behind.

Starting further back for best vision delivers another vital bonus. It enables you to begin building up the maximum appropriate acceleration *early*, so that, when you go, you will be exposed to danger on the wrong side of the road for the least possible time. You have no "rights" out there. You may only use that wrong side if it is free.

Very often, you will be able to time things so that you will be both in the right gear to accelerate further and have all systems on "go", all from the precise moment a gap opens up for you, just as the last vehicle passes by the other way. But don't overdo your pre-build-up of speed. You still need to be able to drop back in, if a problem appears at the last moment. The above being stated, however, the facts are that if you never plan your passes on our crowded roads, it is likely you will find yourself forever adding to those awful, trailing-along traffic jams we see most painfully behind caravans in the Summer.

It is suicidal to take a moment longer than necessary to overhaul whatever you are passing. If you dawdle, you can be sure some unexpected disaster will turn up. Whatever it is you are overtaking, you need to be going a good 15–20 mph faster as you pull past, and to have plenty more acceleration in reserve. Never try to pass if you can only do so by going "flat out"; having no spare margin is a sure road into disaster. Passing long lorries needs superior judgement of pace and even more speed in reserve.

To be sure maximum acceleration *will be available, you must use low gear* in order to overtake any vehicle doing less than around 45–55 mph. It is then usually unwise to change gear up again until after the pass; this being in case you misjudge the upward change and lose speed sorting that out. Choosing the right initial gear is therefore important:

(a) Starting to overtake from below 20 mph, use 2nd.
(b) Otherwise, from anywhere below about 50 mph, use 3rd.
(c) If speed is still higher and you are in 5th, always come back at least to top (or 3rd if more appropriate).

VISION and "timing" are further keys. In fig. 53, you are doing a little over 45 mph, ready to overtake the van, and he about 35 mph. Your checks have shown nothing is trying to overtake you. You are signalling. You have begun your gradual moving out. Your acceleration is well under way, correctly in 3rd gear. Space Y, to your left, remains available as a safety margin, into which to drop back should any oncoming vehicle, coming fast, suddenly appear. You can now see well beyond the van. You are still at the stage of judging whether you will have sufficient time and room both to pass and to return fully to your side safely.

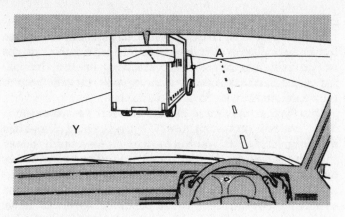

Fig 53 Overtaking.

Not only do you have several mph ready, "in hand", for achieving your objective of dispatching the pass in the minimum time, you have the maximum, reserve acceleration at your toe. But you are not yet committed. You can still switch to a left signal, drop off speed and pull back into **Y**, in a trice, probably without even needing to touch your brakes.

For thousands of miles and a great many overtakes, you should be guided at this point by your teacher, to confirm (if necessary) whether you are now safe to go on, or need to pull back. (Occasionally, you may just stay ready for a short distance before deciding one way or the other but it's not a safe place in which to hang around long!) He must help you judge whether you have sufficient speed and acceleration available. It may still be safe, for example, despite oncoming traffic already appearing in the far distance. That could depend on how far away it is in relation to its speed. Or it could already have become unsafe, perhaps because you are now too close to the blind brow of a hill or you believe a concealed dip may lie ahead.

Assess approaching traffic. Will they have to slow down, even slightly? If the answer could be "yes", don't go. To cause evasive action is dangerous. Allow that, *downhill*, pulling back would be enormously harder (though this should be correspondingly easier uphill). Equally, *uphill*, whilst *you* might be able to pull back quicker, oncoming downhill traffic may well be gathering speed rapidly and will certainly find it harder to take evasive action if you get it wrong.

Correct judgment is much harder at night, and it is then further bedevilled by the assortment of illegal lights one can meet coming, e.g. cars with one headlamp missing! Overtaking during darkness is better avoided until you have become fully comfortable with daytime overtaking.

Once you decide, rattle on and GO – if your decision is "yes"; or pull back straightaway – if it is "no". Avoid half measures. Hesitation, you will have heard, can cause you loss.

From your fig. 53 position, things can still go wrong. It may turn out safer to cancel the operation *after* committing yourself, than to try to pull it off at risk to lives all round. Your teacher must be alert to advise or confirm at once what to do; he dare not abandon you to hesitation. For example, the van driver may drift or even swing out because of a cyclist – hitherto unseen by you – on his inside, or perhaps because of a child running out from his left. So, as your eyes continue to scan ahead for danger, also flash them to his front road-wheel. If that doesn't turn outwards, he can't hit you. An empty heavy lorry may regain speed alarmingly quickly once it begins a descent – changing the whole dynamics of what began by looking like a safe overtake!

Such possibilities make an *advisory* warning hoot, *before passing*, very wise, especially where the road width means you need to be closer alongside than, ideally, you would like. Normally, allow a good bit more than a door's opening width, between you and whatever you are passing; this must be done without, to your offside, sacrificing the same safety margin that you would expect to keep from your nearside edge at a similar speed. Otherwise, as the Highway Code commands, you must not overtake where the road narrows.

GET BACK TO SAFETY

Though you must avoid "cutting in" after passing, you MUST return to your side promptly. *Do not stay on the wrong side of the road just because it is clear. Get back!* A quick glance over your left shoulder confirms beyond doubt how soon you are clear to come in. At first ask your teacher to guide you as well. It is nearly always safe far earlier than you expect. So, a direct look is vital. Provided the man you pass

176

doesn't have to slow down, you can get in as early as you like!

Do.

But don't then slow down on him (unless unavoidably and owing to something unforeseen).

Finally, check that your right indicator did cancel. It ought to have done so automatically, as you moved back in.

Let's suppose that, despite all this instruction, you still make a misjudgement one day. We all do sometimes. You are almost past someone, getting rather too close to the next corner but already *too late to drop back*, when an oncoming car appears around that corner at breakneck speed. Indicate left at once. (You could have had a finger at the ready so to do, having already realised that you had mistakenly run things a little tight . . .) This should immediately alert the driver you are passing that you are going to be forced, unavoidably, to cut in. And it tells the oncomer exactly where you are heading to get out of his way. Simultaneously, GET IN, as fast as you then can.

In potential danger like this, don't be afraid of cutting in quite fiercely. In the split-second that this sort of emergency can arise, if the man you are passing is awake (which he should be if you hooted), he will drop back out of your way anyway. Believe me, your greatest crash risk is unlikely to be touching his front wing with your back one. Even if that does happen, it will be better than risking obliteration through hitting that breakneck-speeding, oncoming idiot who, incidentally, cannot possibly have been following that Highway Code dictum given on my page 127. Can he?

THAT WARNING HOOT

Whenever you decide that an advisory hoot is going to be appropriate, announcing your presence, make it when you are close enough to be heard but still have time to drop back. Some "thou shall not pass" types may actually swing out when they hear you! Perhaps – to be kinder to them – they hope to warn you of danger ahead, though it is a dangerous way to try so to do.

Always hoot weavers or drivers whose mirrors are plainly askew. Always atune your thinking to that of drivers of vans, lorries, articulated vehicles, and any unusually shaped, widely loaded or specialised commercial vehicle, for whom very substantial mirror blind spots may, at times, reduce their coverage to NIL.

If passing two or more vehicles, one after the other, hoot each one in turn. There are still plenty of drivers around who, before pulling out to overtake, clean forget either to check that no one is passing them or to signal. There are also drivers who, if they are not deaf, are deafened by their radio . . .

When someone ahead has been signalling right for some time, perhaps even passing by several possible turnings, you must never assume that they have forgotten to cancel the signal and that it is, therefore, safe to pass. Hold back until that driver has cancelled it, so confirming that he is not about to turn, change lane, or, himself, to overtake someone further ahead.

ONE PLUS ONE DOES NOT ALWAYS = TWO!

Suppose the driver first in line ahead of you pulls out to overtake. Can you "convoy-pass", too, just by following him? Most usually not, I would suggest. However, a guarded "yes" may be possible, even on a single carriageway road, *provided* you can, *continuously*:

(a)   see that the road out ahead of him manifests no potential problems for you, whether or not he accelerates sufficiently fast for your liking

(b)   maintain a respectable gap between you and him

(c)   remain unthreatened by any idiot "stuck to your back bumper" trying to "convoy-pass" as well, and

(d)   be certain of *Room For Me Too*.

What, precisely, I mean by (d) will be made very clear in the remaining pages of this chapter. Meanwhile, be advised that, when it comes to overtaking, one plus one does not – if (d) is absent – always = two . . . [successful, safe, overtakes].

THREE "OVERTAKING" QUESTIONS

Ask yourself:

1. "Is there a *gap ahead* for me to return to?" In fig. 53, the van is not close behind and therefore concealing some other vehicle just ahead of itself (absurd, close-up driving which daily goes on). Neither is the van catching up any traffic further ahead. It is therefore safe. If there is such traffic, then, *provided it is moving on well*, you should continue to be safe. Watch it like a hawk because, if it were to slow down before you have moved safely back in, you could be in serious trouble – whether or not you know its reason for slowing up. Never overtake a nose-to-tail stream of traffic, without the safe-refuge of a specific gap, clearly at your disposal ahead. *That* – is madness.

2. "Even beyond the point of commitment, could I still hope to brake and pull in behind the van – if something went wrong and I had no choice?" If a driver following you is already moving up to block what you earlier considered to be your safety margin – **Y**, fig. 53 – that option may no longer exist. Many evil, or plain stupid, drivers do exactly this. If you see this happening then, unless there is absolutely no doubt all is clear ahead, it is better to slow and drop back to safety. Let the fool pass you, before you even consider trying again.

3. "Are *none* of the "**MUST** or DO NOT OVERTAKE"" rules listed in the Highway Code going to be broken?" Check now – that you know them *all*. If any of those commands would be breached, *wait* for a safer opportunity.

The Code urges you, for example, *not to overtake* at, or approaching, *any* type of junction. Discipline yourself. Be it a road or just a lane, on *either* side, that carries a threat to your safety, hold back. It could, otherwise, if someone suddenly noses out without looking, just be your (un)lucky day. That a driver in front of you may be slowing down, apparently to turn left, is not an excuse for spurting past early without due caution. His vehicle may mask something you cannot (yet) see. Just as may such a vehicle turning right, equally, be masking unseen danger: never be in too much haste to pass by on its left. Indeed, never try to pass in this world by risking passing into the next.

I now come to the question of what to do *whenever* someone is overtaking *towards you*, on a single-lane carriageway. If he has plenty of time, that is fine. But you MUST REACT INSTANTLY to any chance, *however remote*, that he may not regain the safety of his own side in good time:

EASE OFF YOUR ACCELERATOR: COVER YOUR BRAKE: REASSESS.

179

This way, you are already curbing your speed; you are poised to add braking with lightning quickness. If he has made a horrendous misjudgement, you should still stand a chance of stopping or steering out of his way.

The key to staying alive is that instant reaction. That is what allows you to get *your* speed under control. Without it, you may be a no-hoper before you know it. If there is a smash, you may blame him if you will; but – if you failed to react instantly – blame yourself more – for not protecting him.

For a moment I turn to single carriageways which have *more than one lane* each way and may have occasional, KEEP LEFT bollards in the middle but no continuous, central barrier separating opposing traffic as there is on a full dual carriageway.

Conjure up in your mind a common situation on such roads; where you are in the righthand lane of two, flowing past slower traffic in the inner lane. It is easy to forget, momentarily, that, in reality, you are overtaking those slower vehicles rather than merely keeping up with faster, outer-lane traffic. It follows, from such lapses of concentration, that you will, inevitably, find yourself overtaking at some of the places at which overtaking is *forbidden* by the Highway Code; unless, that is, you are very fastidious about holding back when you should and/or getting ahead in good time if that is more appropriate. The most obvious examples are junctions and pedestrian crossings of all sorts. Remind yourself, from the Code, of all the less obvious, ''no-go'' (overtaking) areas. If you carry on, regardless, forcing the squeezing of two lanes through such places, *you are in the wrong*. You may feel you are in good company with the majority (who do such things) but that is no excuse for dangerous driving.

DOUBLE WHITE LINES

These ban overtaking at hazardous places. Parking, wherever there are double white lines of any sort, is forbidden *on both sides of the road*. Stopping while passengers get in or out is OK (but foolish!). If the line nearest you is *continuous*, do not ride on or cross it. If you do, you will be breaking the law, unless this is to pass an obstruction (e.g. a broken-down vehicle) or, in emergency, to avoid an accident. However, there is one exception to this blanket prohibition on overtaking: you are allowed – with suitable care – to pass a pedal cycle, a horse, or a vehicle equipped for road maintenance – provided that its speed of progress is not above 10 mph.

Where the line nearest you is broken, you may cross it in order to overtake but with two provisos: (1) the manoeuvre must be safe; (2) it must be complete *before* you next come to a continuous line that prohibits your remaining over that side of the carriageway.

Fig. 54 shows an arrangement of double lines you will often find. Two lanes are allocated to traffic in one direction, only one lane to that from the other. This would typically be on a long hill, to enable cars to pass slow lorries, etc., in the uphill direction. Don't be lulled into thinking no one will come out of the single lane when you are in the outer, overtaking, lane of the two-lane side. Sometimes the *single lane* has a broken line on *its* side entitling drivers to come out if safe ... *Sometimes* drivers break the law.

In fig. 54, **U** would be safe in the outer lane, only if **U** could see all was clear through behind **A** and well beyond the next bend(s).

Where you need to cross double white lines in order to make a turn to the right, you may so do even if the continuous line is the nearest one to you; however, it is normally only for access to or from a tiny lane, or a private entrance, that such a need arises.

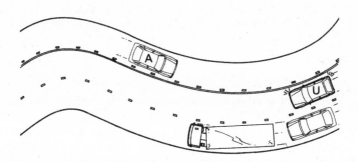

Fig 54   A double white line with a false impression of safety.

OVERTAKING ON THREE-LANE TWO-WAY ROADS

Traffic on these roads frequently drives very fast. Quite often, three lanes are not actually marked; there is a single, dividing, centre line in the middle but the width of the road, and the weight of the traffic commonly using the road, make three-lane usage the accepted norm for that particular road.

Custom, and common sense, largely dictate the practical rules for overtaking in the middle of these perilous highways. The Highway Code contents itself merely with saying that you have no more right to use the middle lane than does a driver coming from the opposite direction.

My approach to them is as follows: **ALWAYS** *give way* to an oncoming vehicle *already in the middle* (as well as to any

Fig 55 3-lane(s) 2-way.

driver already there coming from behind you!). For example, in fig. 55, **K** is contemplating passing **J** but **A**, oncoming, is already *in the middle lane*, here half a mile distant. It is difficult to show the full distance within the perspective of a small line drawing, so I must ask you to imagine that **A** is further away than I can draw his car. If you were **K**, you might imagine, "I will be safe to move to the middle lane and begin my pass, because **A** can drop into the gap, between **C** and **D**, well before we could come within striking distance of each other." *Don't do it.* Let **A** come on. He may wish to keep in the overtaking lane to pass **D**, **E**, and **F**, especially if the road behind you is clear.

There are more reasons. Courtesy is one. Others include the fact that your stream has no safe-refuge gap, ahead, for you to drop into; the only way to get in might be to "force the issue", which could leave you in danger if one of the drivers was nasty. **C** might close up on **D**, and leave **A** similarly caught. Or, **A**'s gap could shrink anyway; for example, because of **F** having to slow down rapidly due to some cause, now already behind you, and therefore possibly unknown to you.

The result, if both you and **A** were left high-and-dry in the middle lane, would be a potential disaster. You would both need to brake hard but there might not be enough time to avoid a crash. The fierce braking might throw either of you into your respective opposing line of traffic. There might be a car **Z**, following close on **A**, *but unseen by you* until **A** had filled the gap **C–D**. By the time you had realised that he was coming too or, indeed, he had even seen you, it could be too late for either of you to take avoiding action. **A** may *not* be overtaking. He may be stopping – ready to turn right into the gateway . . .

When you are in the middle, yourself overtaking, you must be prepared for someone coming the other way to pull out into your path, regardless of custom or sense. Therefore, whilst in the middle, you must *always* have – specifically targeted as already emphasised elsewhere – the "bolt-hole", safe-refuge gap which you intend to use; never enter the middle lane in any other circumstance; if your gap shows signs of "melting away", abort your overtake at once.

If you are going to overtake more than one vehicle, keep your right indicator flashing all the time. Always switch to the left indicator, briefly, when you are about to move in. During daylight overtaking of this sort many drivers add dipped headlamps, keeping them on all the while that they are in the middle lane. It is wise because it helps to draw oncoming drivers' attention to what is happening.

By using speed judgement you can often avoid the situation in fig. 56. **W** is passing **X** at the same instant **Y** goes the other way. For a moment he becomes the "meat in the sandwich". The slightest miscalculation by any party could bode trouble, as might a mechanical fault, burst tyre, etc.

Faced with possible, though not actual, danger like this, choose the lesser risk. Thus **W** should stay nearer **X** than **Y** because touching **X** would be safer than even a glancing blow, never mind a head-on crash, with **Y**. **Y** should keep closer to his edge than to **W**.

This is defensive driving, the importance of which is, even today, scarcely realised. If more cars are close behind **Y**, **W**'s risk is greatly increased, as any one of them may pull out.

All this is taking refinement too far, you may feel, but it is precisely these finer points of driving that distinguish the master, whom I expect you to become, from the amateurs who are everywhere.

Room For Me Too?
Never blindly follow another driver who is also overtaking in the middle, in the hope that, "somehow", there will always be room for both of you to return to your own side. If he is suddenly forced to brake to get back in, where do you go?

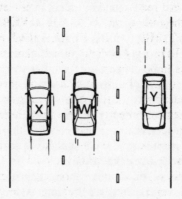

Fig 56 3-lanes, 2-way, clearance considerations.

Once more, you must be certain of your own safe-refuge, bolt-hole gap, and that it is not suddenly going to turn into his!

You've got to be looking far enough ahead, too, to *know* that the whole (double) stream in your direction is not about to come to a forced halt. Nothing shrinks your safe-refuge gap faster, nor deposits you at the "pearly gates" more quickly.

DUAL CARRIAGEWAY OVERTAKING

This "disappearing gap" risk applies with a vengeance on dual carriageways as well as wide, single carriageways, with more than one lane both ways. At the higher speeds typically driven on such roads, if you are too busy eyeing whatever you are passing to notice that traffic ahead is crunching to a stop, you may find yourself joining that crunch.

There is no substitute for watching, right the way to the horizon, that *all* the traffic ahead *is* moving. If the distance to that horizon telescopes down because of a blind bend, going up over a brow or, more dangerous still, because of a concealed dip, HOLD BACK.

Whatever anyone else may be doing, **YOU** *have got to be able to stop if, when you get round that corner, over that brow or into that dip, you are suddenly faced with stopped traffic or a crash.* Suppose someone is sitting, stopped in the outside lane there, waiting to make a little-used right turn . . .

On duals you *must* remember your **Lane Discipline**, and use your mirrors carefully. No speeding up or pulling out whilst others are ready to flow past! Don't even begin your signal until they've gone. **WATCH OVER AN AMPLE PERIOD OF TIME, TO BE SURE THAT NO ONE CAN BE THERE**. Take a last-second, direct, glance over your right shoulder, so as to be *certain*.

If you plan to move out to a middle lane of three, beware of someone thundering up past you in the *outside* lane, who then chooses that same moment to return to the middle lane. It's a common crash scenario.

If you are overtaking several vehicles, all of them before returning to the left lane (or to the middle and then to the left lane), of a dual or multi-lane carriageway, then cancel your right indicator once you are beginning to overhaul them (unless you are intending to move further to your right). Don't forget, when you finally come to move back in, that you should give notice of your intention, doing so by giving a brief, left indicator signal in advance.

If it is only to a middle lane that you are returning initially, look out for an inside-lane man who picks that same time to pull out! Although, in theory, he ought to GIVE WAY to let you come in, you don't want to slap your sides in the middle. It wouldn't be funny enough for that!

Remember that outer lanes are for overtaking, only. When using them, get on with the task in hand. Nothing perpetuates dangerous bunching, nor irritates more, than someone who, with a clear road ahead, nevertheless creeps past whatever he is passing, snarling up faster traffic behind when he could perfectly well have finished the job long ago.

Mile after mile splendid three lane dual carriageways in the UK are blocked as "middle-lane-man" slowly edges past "inner-lane-man" – as Mr. 46 mph dices with Mr. 43 mph. When "50 mph-man" hits the outside lane to overhaul these brethren the all too familiar "sheer-weight-of-traffic" syndrome sets itself up behind them. Within moments drivers in all three lanes vie with each other to crawl, stop or speed up in random order until "Mr. 46 mph" or "Mr. 50 mph" finally deigns to move over. Meanwhile – within this "Mr. man"-made jam – drivers inevitably find themselves travelling lengthy distances trapped in each other's mirrors' blind spots, the very thing common sense tells them they should avoid whenever possible!

When you are overtaking a row of slower traffic, take very great care that no one from that stream will pull out on you. (**Note:** A toot in time is sometimes divine!) Never fall into the trap of assuming that you need not worry so much about this if you are in a middle lane, perhaps relying on some vague idea that you could always move out a bit. To swing out unexpectedly, like that, could put both you yourself and an outside-lane driver, who was already committed to passing you, in instant peril.

I must add that, were any such driver to be passing you at some ferocious speed hugely above yours, as well as just at the very moment all three parties are destined to come into line abreast, then he would be certifiable as insane; but it would in no way excuse your share of the blame for a severe accident.

A sudden lurch sideways at high speed could cause you to lose control anyway. Make sure all your lane changes are smooth and gentle. IN EMERGENCY, ABOVE ALL, YOU MUST STAY IN LANE. Not to, risks your all.

Having exposed several reasons for the sudden crunch-ups all too common on dual carriageways, prompts mention of what to do if you see with horror such a tangle erupting ahead. On duals restricted only by the National speed limit, you can switch on your hazard warning lights at once – in tandem with your rapid braking to bring your speed well under control. Keep them on until other drivers around and behind you have clearly seen the problem too. Regrettably the law implies that you may not do so on any other roads apart from motorways.

Raised "rumble" strips, equally spaced and usually in yellow or red, are often "painted" at right angles across all lanes for a considerable distance before your half of a dual terminates at a roundabout, or perhaps before a long slip road exit reaches its junction with an ordinary road. I trust you will never accelerate to overtake where these warn you visibly, by ear and via your car's suspension, to *reduce* speed in good time. They are now found on ordinary roads at the entry to villages, too, alerting you to slow down appropriately.

Overtaking – Headlamp – Customs
On dual, and other multi-lane, carriageways, a headlamp flash – seen in your mirrors – has become customary for two different purposes:

1) As a request from a faster driver, who is behind you and waiting to overtake, that you move in from an outer lane as soon as you can.

2) As an "all clear" signal from someone you have just overtaken, telling you it is now safe to pull back in, in front.

These flashes are not countenanced by the Highway Code; indeed the Code attempts to deny their use. Nevertheless, they exist. Let them be advisory only. Make certain, whichever type of flash you may receive, that you are sure it is safe to move in, before you so do. Beware the rat who flashes, immediately prior to whizzing past on your inside! Look out for the motorcyclist who weaves through from further behind, unaware of an "all clear" flash having been given to you.

187

6

Junctions

WHO GOES FIRST?

Martians looking down from Space might conclude that on Earth a driver has a general priority whenever driving forwards on his side of the road. This, in theory, in the UK, he does. Pedestrians ought not to step out in front of him; oncomers intending to turn right should wait for him to pass; side road traffic should await his passing [by]; and so on but reality is punctured by exceptions *disproving* this "rule", as I shall show.

Almost all UK roads are classified as being major or minor.

You always cede priority to anyone on a major road.

The essence of our road Law, however, is *not* that being on the major road confers any "right of way"; rather it is that those on minor roads must expect always to yield precedence. To conclude, therefore, that your occupation of a major road provides you with any "right" to proceed is wildly mistaken.

At the vast majority of junctions it is made obvious which is the major road; the minor one having a characteristic layout of broken white lines painted at right angles across it where it meets the major one. This layout, in effect, "rules off" the neck of the minor road, and comprises a double broken line across the left half of it, with the line nearest to the major road extended right across both halves (see fig. 43). These lines are the *basic instruction* that informs minor road drivers that they MUST GIVE WAY.

At little-used junctions (unless wholly unmarked – for which see page 263) they may be your only clue as to status.

However, most often you will find in addition a GIVE WAY sign posted near to the end of the minor road, facing traffic coming along it. There may also be a large, white warning triangle painted on the road surface close to the end of the minor road itself, inverted so that its narrowest angle points back towards drivers thereon; or, you might find that (either) one of these two has been used to reinforce the broken lines across, but not the other. (**Note:** Where a minor road driver cannot see a junction very clearly until he has almost reached it, perhaps because of tall hedges lining a bend, he should find a blank, inverted, red-triangle warning sign – with the distance to the junction posted underneath it – conspicuously displayed well before that final bend.)

Alternatively (invariably at more dangerous junctions with extremely limited vision altogether), there will be, as in fig. 57, a single, extra thick, solid line substituted for the double broken ones across the lefthand half of the end of a minor road, and a STOP sign facing drivers therefrom. In addition, the word STOP may be spelt out on the road just before you reach the line. (Again, there may be an advance warning sign – exactly the same sort as just described – if the major road is at all concealed from those drivers.)

The STOP sign *means*: **STOP**. (Should you be clear to move on at once, you can, but only *after* having stopped *at the line* first, regardless of all other considerations.)

Where roads of equal status meet, traffic lights switch the priorities alternately or there is a roundabout. I shall come to these last because special rules about priority apply to them.

Police or traffic wardens may intervene at any type of junction, taking over the orchestration of priorities for all the traffic (and temporarily revising those priorities, if needs be), in order to clear congested traffic. Learn the meaning of *their* signals and the correct ones to give *them*, from the Highway Code. Remember that any officer can make a mistake, though it happens rarely. However, an accident could be deemed your look-out; you must obey but with your own care added.

Throughout this book I have urged you to accept that the pedestrian is (like a customer) always right (even when wrong!). He could be you . . . It is vital that you understand his – probably subconscious – feeling, that he has a superior status when walking along the pavement of a major road and reaching a junction. He feels entitled to walk across the neck of the minor road just as if the pavement extended across it. Though expecting him to act cautiously and responsibly, the Law – in extremis – agrees: because it can hardly sanction your knocking him down. From whichever direction you may be coming, you MUST therefore, if he wants to walk over now, reasonably or unreasonably, wait for him.

189

CORRECT POSITIONING AND RIGHT SPEED

Wherever you meet other traffic or you turn, being in the correct position and having the right speed are the critical factors which save accidents. It is not just the doing it right that counts; it is the fact that your intentions are also thereby made beyond doubt to everyone in the vicinity.

Proper POSITIONING and the correct CONTROL of speed are of greater importance for SAFETY even than signals (not that I'm suggesting you fail to give any!). However, *I would rather be driven a million miles by a driver who grasped this fact, than a single mile in an indestructible army tank with one who had no grip on these cornerstones of safe driving*.

At many junctions you may not have priority but are entitled to go on without a stop if the roads are clear. Whilst it is paramount that you check adequately for other traffic (as my following pages make brutally clear) and *do stop* when necessary, an examiner may frown if – when the way is clear – you are often hesitant and thus miss safe opportunities to go. Equally, where you do stop at such a junction, he will expect to see skilful preparation *just before* the main road clears, so that you normally make use of the first available safe gap in the traffic. Good judgment at such moments only comes with gaining enough experience but always err on the side of caution; no examiner should fail you for that.

TURNING LEFT

LEFT TURN *OFF* A MAJOR ROAD

In fig. 57 you are going to turn left *off* your (major) road. At **A** you are doing 35 mph, some 250 metres from the turn. For clarity, I have omitted other traffic for the moment.

From **A**, you double-check your mirrors, put on your left indicator, and then start to reduce speed. At **B**, about 175 metres from the turn, you take 3rd gear. By **C₁**, with about 30 metres to go, braking gently if need be, you should be down to a running pace. Then you take 2nd. Aim to arrive at the turn at *walking pace or less*. With good judgement any braking you need to do will be hardly noticeable. Last-second, fierce braking is bad.

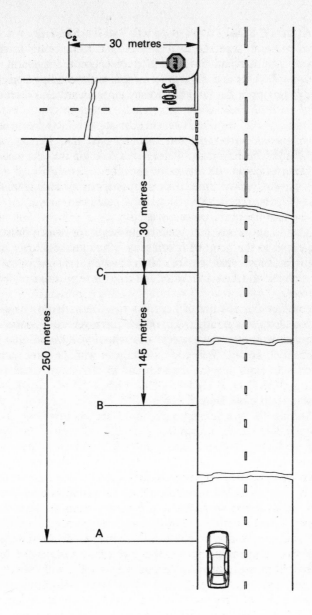

Fig 57 Making a left turn into a minor road.

At many, tighter, turns there will – at least to begin with – have to be a stage shortly before you begin to steer round, where you **Almost Stop . . . But Not Quite** (as learnt in Chapter 2). This enables you to recapture clutch-slip, momentarily, just prior to moving forward again gently, *and under total control*, into the minor road. If the road is steeply downhill as the turning is reached, it may be a case of using the *Downhill* **Mile-An-Hour** technique of page 67, instead, just for the final moments before you drive on into the turn.

Otherwise you will arrive too quickly.

You won't have time to steer in properly or straighten up smoothly, and there will be a general panic and danger as you sweep into the turn "on two wheels".

This is not to say that you should begin the whole process too early, to the point of holding up others unnecessarily but, until you know what you are doing, the greater danger by far is of arriving too fast and without being in a position of total control.

Another classic fault of Learners to avoid is failing to look ahead along that minor road you are turning into. Is someone about to walk across the neck – to whom you *would have to give way* if he did? Will you have to wait whilst a lorry with a wide load exits into the major road? In other words, are you still **LOOKING WHERE YOU ARE GOING** despite all you have to think about?

During the whole approach, from the moment you first change down, have a continuing eye on your mirrors, as ever, and hold a steady course well to the left. Pavements are always rounded at turnings, so there should be no need to make any outward "detour" before you go round. Just steer round (using rapid steering movements) *at the exact right moment*. This will present no problem, provided you are going *slowly enough*. You should be no more than 2–3 tyre widths out from the edge as you drive round. But don't get too close either; you will risk sweeping people off the pavement or hitting the kerb itself. Straighten up equally rapidly so that you will have neither under- nor over-steered for the turn, and resume your normal distance out as you re-accelerate, still in 2nd gear, towards C_2, before taking 3rd and so on. Once into your new road, don't linger. Get up through the gears to a normal speed promptly, unless traffic reasons prevent you. Resume mirrors' watching straightaway. Cancel your indicator if it has not self-cancelled as it should.

The Highway Code warns you never to overtake a cyclist just before turning left. You have to watch your mirrors as well, in case one tries to slink up on your nearside as you slow down; especially keep an eye if you are having to wait before making your entry into the minor road. Always make a final check over your left shoulder. Be warned! Two-wheelers, especially the motorised variety, are always doing this despite the danger they run. Wait. Let them go.

On bigger roads, a deceleration "slip road" lets you pull off the major road earlier, as you reach the turn; drivers following can pass you safely, sooner. Use it!

(Let me here sound a warning gong for times when you are following someone who seems exasperatingly slow when he turns off left (or right for that matter). Don't get up too close to him. Never, whether you are going straight on or turning also, presume that he will pull off your road completely in one go. Frequently, this sort **STOPS**, with the back of his vehicle *still blocking the major road*. Perhaps he has misjudged getting into a gateway. Perhaps a chicken has decided to cross the road he is trying to enter. It may be no fault of his own this time. "Why?" doesn't matter! Unless you assume that he WON'T GET CLEAR until you see that HE HAS DONE, and hold back accordingly, you are likely to finish up hitting him. Hold onto a gap in which you can stop, until it's 100% positive you won't need so to do. Such a driver may well be either elderly, a Learner or one still inexperienced; regard him not in anger but as presenting an opportunity to practise your good driving and tolerance.)

LEFT TURN *ONTO* A MAJOR ROAD

This time you are on the side road, in fig. 57, about to turn left into the major road. Again, I assume there is no one in front of you to worry about.

If the sign says STOP, as in this figure, you *must* **STOP** *completely* at the line, no matter whether all is clear or what a driver in front did, were there to be one.

Failure to **STOP** = breaking the Law = Practical Test failure. I will deal with what to do if the sign says GIVE WAY a few pages on; for now, please assume it's a STOP sign.

Imagine the same distances **A**, **B** and **C**, each from the turn, along the major road in fig. 57, now applied to the minor road. Double-check your mirrors; then start signalling with your left indicator, before beginning to slow down. Reckon to take 3rd as before, approximately at **B** but, here, because you will have to stop anyway, you need not go down to 2nd gear. Brake gently in 3rd and stop when the front of your car reaches the line. Keep well in to the left as before. The same 2–3 tyre widths out when you come to the turn itself will be correct.

As you arrive at the end of your road, prior to reaching any major road, particularly watch out for pedestrians from either side stepping across its neck as you reach it. They see you slowing up, and take this as their permission to walk across! Let them if they do. In addition, remember to take all the same care previously mentioned about cyclists.

Whenever a stop is going to be REQUIRED, as here (by Law), or is otherwise necessary, remember to put your clutch down during the final moments, so as to prevent stalling. Once stopped, apply your handbrake and slip into neutral, before releasing your foot pedals. The handbrake must be on to prevent rolling forward or back. Forward could be deadly; and it is easy to slip back and hit a car behind unwittingly!

You stop with your front bumper *at the line*, not "miles" before; otherwise you won't be able to see properly both ways along the major road. If, after stopping, you still can't see – perhaps because your zones of vision right and/or left are cut off by parked vehicles lining your side of the main road – edge forward extremely cautiously until you can, and stop again.

As you do so, be looking to your right, from where any most immediate danger is likely to come; however, you *must* allow time to take a quick glance or two to the *left* as well, in order to make sure that your car's nose is not going to be chopped off by someone cutting the corner as he turns right, off the major road! Once more, I cannot over-emphasise the necessity to be **LOOK-ING** – at any given instant – **WHERE YOU ARE GOING**.

For all the above reasons, always make your final glide to a stop reasonably gentle. That is what will make sure you have time to see whether, for example, you will have to make an extra stop, *before* the line, initially, for a walker (as you *would* have to if he stepped out) or whatever. It also gives confidence

– to anyone coming along the major road – that you are in full control for stopping.

Once the major road is clear for you, make a **Smooth Start** in 1st gear, and go. Remember, just before that, to double-check with a flash-look over your left shoulder for any cycle or motorcycle trying to squeeze out between you and the kerb.

It is sometimes appropriate, if traffic and any pedestrians have already dispersed, to select 1st gear straightaway – as you complete your safety stopping sequence on the controls – in readiness to go on. Your teacher can advise. Otherwise, it is, without doubt, safer, if you have to wait because of traffic, *not* to prepare for your **Smooth Start** by moving the lever into 1st gear until just before the last vehicle for which you need to wait passes by. However, unless you do so by then, you will lose countless opportunities – with someone else always seeming to come up before you are ready.

When the right moment comes, keep *well* tucked in as you steer out. Make sure you straighten up, so as to reach a normal distance out, in one neat operation – all done as you accelerate – without dithering, up the gears to an appropriate speed. Look to your mirrors. Check that your signal self-cancels.

"Clear for you", above, means not only that both your immediate path into the major road is free (of pedestrians or stopped traffic, for examples) and that no one coming from your right will find they have to slow down – even a fraction – because of your coming out, but also that you *will have*, in particular, *checked* in case there are *two* vehicles, one overtaking the other, coming from your *left*. WAIT OR DIE... (**Note:** Pedestrians frequently wander across *major roads* at corners of junctions; indeed, they often do so regardless of the availability of a perfectly good pedestrian crossing nearby . . .)

Looking Right and Left
A common, eyeball instruction for emerging at junctions is "*look right, left, and right again*"; the theory being that *if it's safe, you go*; and, if it is not, you continue to repeat *the whole sequence*, until you can go.

Such systematic care is, I fear, enormously more efficient than are all too many drivers; but even more is needed.

For example, one-ways deceive followers of the above rule.

195

The traffic nearest your bonnet may then whizz past from your *left . . .*

Not only must you *move your head and neck* (forward or back as needed), as well as your eyes, you must begin looking both ways *well before you reach the line*. Otherwise, you will be liable not to notice pedestrians stepping off the pavements either to your left or to your right. They are usually the *first* potential snag for which to be prepared to give way. Nor will you spot those right-turning, corner-cutting, nose-choppers from your left, in time. What happens (if you don't swing your eyes out on stalks) is that your roof pillars, lamp posts, or whatever, create blind spots, which conceal danger. Fig. 2 showed the areas such things can so easily mask.

Again, if you merely glance too quickly, your eyes will miss joggers, or two-wheel riders trailing along the pavement edge from your right, and so on. Believe me, never minding all of them, whole *lorries* can be concealed, not only by your roof pillars, but also by apparently trivial dirt on your window(s) or on your glasses, or even by your passenger's nose! The human eye, remember, has its own blind-spot too.

Take life-loving-length looks both ways.

A second look – a sweeping, long enough, look – picks out any previously hidden moving vehicle. And keep your eyes skinned all around as you set off.

At night, when sideways looks are away from the pool of light from your headlights and, instead, into darkness, allow even longer for each look. Your eyes need extra time to adjust, before they can pierce the darkness properly and see the unlit, black clothed biker, or the dark horse.

Make No Assumptions about anyone who is signalling left to enter the road you are leaving. See page 229.

In fig. 58 the car driver followed the common eyeball rule, as first given above, but still crashed. The major road rose more steeply towards the middle than he had anticipated. He had also, admittedly by mistake, started off in 3rd gear when he had intended to be in 1st. As a result, the engine had started to labour on the way across – almost stalling – and he had then taken longer to recover, whilst he fumbled trying to get the lever back into the right gear, than he had expected.

Had he continued eye-switching right, left and ahead *while this was all going on*, he would have seen the lorry which had

Fig 58 "Feeding the engine" when crossing danger areas.

by then appeared, and could have stopped in his own (first) half of the major road. Had he moved more smartly in the first instance, he might have made it anyway.

The lessons of this story, should anything like it ever happen to you, are:

1. To linger on, in hope, in the wrong gear is almost always asking for trouble: you need 1st to cross a major road; therefore STOP and put that right first, without more ado.

2. Keep eyes "in the back of your head" looking all around, as you go.

3. Stalling can be a killer. Even in 1st gear it can still happen if you are too casual with your footwork. Make certain that you get your accelerator going *resolutely, before, as, and after* you let the clutch up, to be sure to get you over the danger area, safely, quickly. Feed that engine!

4. The lorry driver, in fig. 58, ought to have anticipated that the car might falter. He had a duty to slow down earlier – making himself *ready to stop*. Then, as the scene unfolded so potentially disastrously, he could have pulled up in safety. There were plenty of clues for the observant: the rate the car was moving off; its driver failing to look his way; even the realisation, perhaps, that too quick a look by that car driver

might not have focused and *seen* . . .

That lorry driver was Part II of the accident.

Being on the major road does not, as explained at the start of this chapter, give him any "right" to plunder on regardless; nor would it you – the possession of a full driving licence is *not* a licence to kill, any more than is the holding of a provisional one.

Tolerance must be your watchword, again, should someone pull out too close for comfort, to get in ahead of you. Drop back. Don't close up, blast your horn or blaze your headlights in anger. His error is more likely to be caused by your being in his blind spot – especially where a junction is swamped by illegal parking – than to be deliberate. Menacing someone in anger is only one step from "road rage"; see page 7.

Correct "Line" When Turning Left
Fig. 59 shows bungled "lines" through left turns. You see them happen every day.

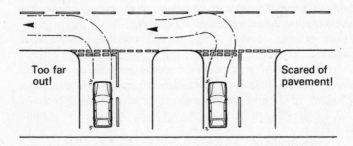

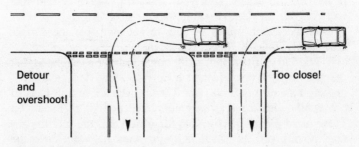

Fig 59 Bungled "lines" turning left.

Fig. 60 shows the right "lines", tucked well in, both in order to make the direction you are taking abundantly clear, and to keep you well away from other traffic. (If there were to be an oil spill or black ice at the junction, you might skid; you would be grateful indeed, then, if the space you had gained by taking the proper line saved you from an accident.) Proper positioning at the end of a minor road is also essential so as to enable a cycle or motorcycle, catching up from behind you, who is turning right (or, perhaps, if it is a crossroads, going straight across), to come up alongside unhindered.

See fig. 57 again. I now return, as promised, to what you should do when turning left onto a major road at a GIVE WAY designated junction, rather than at a STOP signed one.

Here, you *do* take 2nd for the last 20 or 30 metres before your turn. This is because there is no need to stop if the junction turns out to be clear. Being in 2nd *and* at slow speed, you are, accordingly, *prepared*, when you arrive at the line, *to stop or go*.

If vision either way along the major road at the junction is poor, or even if it is partially obscured at just one point, you will probably be wise to stop at the GIVE WAY line anyway. However, if the road-end and the major road are open-to-view, your careful control of your speed and positioning on approach should enable you to gain the necessary time to look *both* ways just as efficiently as has already been described – but to

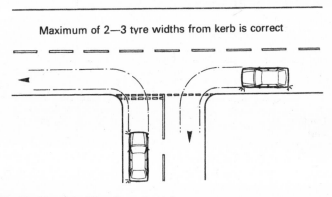

Maximum of 2—3 tyre widths from kerb is correct

Fig 60 The right "lines" turning left.

have *completed* so doing from comfortably before you reach the line.

You get to the line, poised – ready safely to make your final decision as to whether or not you need to stop:

1. If there is any traffic coming from your right along the major road then, as instructed by the sign, you GIVE WAY. You MUST let them take priority. That's the Law. STOP, unless that traffic is far enough away not to be affected anyway. Once stopped, treat the situation exactly as you would have after having stopped at a STOP line, remembering first to put your handbrake on and your gear into neutral, before relaxing your legs/feet by bringing the latter back up off the footpedals.

2. If vehicles from your *left* are overtaking each other, or there is the remotest chance they might do, again, STOP!

Note: Were the junction in fig. 57 to be, instead, a cross-roads, you may well be faced opposite with someone arriving there who is turning, or may be about to turn, right. You are probably best advised in these circumstances to STOP anyway. In theory, in the absence of any other traffic, you have priority over him to make your turn out to the left, first. You are directly "entering" a traffic stream, even if there is none there; whereas he would have to "cross" one – the one from his right (your left) – again, even were no such stream to exist, before he could so do. In practice, many drivers fail to understand these priorities correctly, which is why I advise the additional care of making a stop. Remember, your prime concern is to *avoid* accidents; not to finish up defending how "right" you were after another driver makes a mistake. Your STOP gives you time to be sure he won't attempt to pull ahead of you in error. Equally, the presence of a right-turner, already waiting opposite you, should always trigger similar, added caution.

3. If, on the other hand, there is no traffic from any direction that will affect your turn and no chance of danger to pedestrians, then you can – and should – carry on without any stop. It is your early signalling, sensible speed, and taking the correct "line" – so that everyone else knows exactly your direction and your intentions – that is so ever-important here and, perhaps I should emphasise, even more so when you don't need to stop.

Take care – not forgetting your mirrors and a glance added over your left shoulder – and with those eyes ranging, as you move on. Keep reasonably slow, so that, if a vehicle suddenly appears, you can easily GIVE WAY at the last moment. (Were you not to, and that driver had to brake or slow down, you would be at fault. Your Practical Test pass could be in doubt. That result might depend on whether it was safer, in the particular circumstances, still to go, than to try to stop in your tracks.)

Having decided to go without a stop, if you do, remember to pick up speed again smartly once you are on the major road. As always, confirm what is in your mirrors at once, and make sure your signal has stopped flashing.

You must learn to avoid stopping studiously at the line where there is no need. Doing that not only creates an unnecessary hold-up; you can also be bumped by someone following you, who is likely to be seriously miffed that you stopped – someone who was looking both ways (and seeing them clear) but forgetting to watch *you* as well. Silly of him you may think – until you've nearly done it yourself . . . People are entitled to stop at junctions for no better reason than that they haven't yet looked properly. You will do it yourself at times – so why shouldn't others?

If you bump someone from behind, the matter will, almost certainly, be judged to be your fault. However, that person will have due cause to be seriously miffed too. Losing your "no-claims" bonus (it is not a "no *blame*" bonus) can be costly!

LEFT TURNS AT CROSSROADS

I exposed in no. 2, above, and earlier, a potential snag as you *join* a major road at crossroads. In fig. 61, you are **C**, positioned ready to turn left and *leave* one, travelling slowly, and within 10–15 metres of your turn, as I expose another, common snag.

Assume for the moment that there is no car at **A**. Because you are turning left, **B** thinks he can nip across in front of you at the last second, and does so. Or, perhaps, *there is* a right-turner waiting, like **A**. He, equally, sees you are slowing down to go left, and thinks "If I am quick, I can swing across

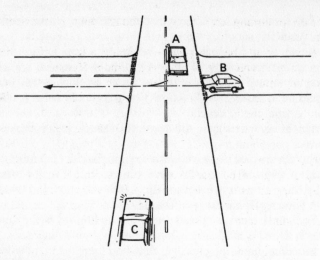

Fig 61 Crossroads snags.

and complete my right turn first''.

Either of them would be in the wrong to put your precedence along the major road in jeopardy. (If it were to be both, they would probably smash together!) Neither their cheek nor their incorrectness can be condoned but, I would be at the ready to let *one – or both* – of them go, if he – or they – were to start. Your forgiveness is likely to prove by far the safest plot. The last thing any of you want is to become involved in some shemozzle, with any of you stuck, marooned across the major road and at the mercy of excessively fast drivers appearing thereon. (On that score, see also ''lesson'' 4, page 197.)

TURNING RIGHT

RIGHT TURN *ONTO* A MAJOR ROAD

In fig. 62, U have almost reached a GIVE WAY line, where you are going to turn right. For simplicity, in this drawing, there is, again, no one else in front of you. The general routine, prior to arriving at the position depicted in fig. 62, is that you double-check your mirrors, then you signal, slow down – braking gently if necessary – and drop down the gears, just as you do for turning left (except that you use your right indicator this time!).

However, it's best to begin everything a little earlier than you would if you were turning left, perhaps 50 metres earlier. Start to reduce speed from **A**, as much as 300 metres out, dropping to about 25 mph before taking 3rd at **B**, roughly 175 metres from the junction.

This gives you extra time and space in which to concentrate on correct positioning, which is trickier when turning right. You need, here, to ease out from quite considerably early on, across towards what will be your final right turn position, so that you are fully lined up with it, comfortably before you reach the GIVE WAY lines. (By then, the righthand side of your car should be fractionally inside, and parallel to, the centre line of your minor road at its end. Visualise that line if none is painted.)

Beginning to ease out early makes sure that anyone behind

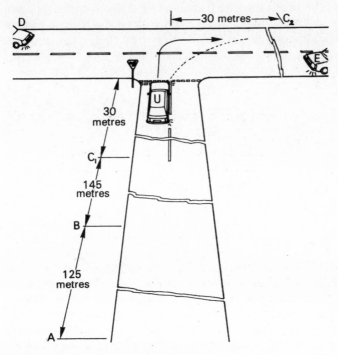

Fig 62 Right turn onto a major road.

203

you, if he is driving a bit too close for comfort, swiftly realises you are going to be turning right. This is especially important if you have a choice of two marked lanes at the end or, indeed, *whenever* there is room there for more than one vehicle to pull up alongside another. Since ''another'' vehicle could be a bike or motorbike, a heightened awareness of the necessity for good rear observation, *before* you signal or start to take up your right-turn position, is essential!

Once you are running just inside the centre line, which you should aim to be doing by C_1, in fig. 62, stick to that. Avoid wandering back to your left. (You could bump someone already moving up there!)

During your remaining approach, two possibilities must be weighed up, so that one of them can be acted upon accordingly:

1. If you can now see that you are going to have to stop – Here, in fig. 62, because of **D** and **E** you will clearly need to STOP. In this situation there is no necessity to drop right down to 2nd gear. Pull up in 3rd. Having stopped, it is, as is emphasised throughout this book in so far as junctions or proximity to pedestrians are concerned, safest to apply your handbrake and come out of gear (into neutral); patience may now be necessary, until the major road is clear, or about to be clear, both ways. (Were there to be a STOP sign and line, instead of the GIVE WAY lines in fig. 62, the choice would have been made for you; in that case you must, anyway, **STOP**, as the Law demands, and as has already been made plain.)

In making your final, visual checks, next, you will need to take into consideration all that I have to say under *The Eyes Have It*, just a few paragraphs further on below. However, I will deal with the overall procedures first.

Once traffic clears from your right (and remains clear), and there is, or soon will be, a safe gap from your left, select 1st gear and bring your clutch pedal up to the biting point. Do this so that you are ready to release your handbrake and tail in to that gap – using your (by now) well-executed **Smooth Start**, together with ample acceleration to make sure you get away cleanly, without fail. If not ready, you will miss opportunities. Provided the gap 'arrives' OK, and no stray pedestrian poses concern, GO. But be ready, should traffic reappear from your right before this, to put your clutch pedal back down, and wait once more. If waiting is now prolonged, come out of gear pro tem as noted above. Prepare again directly traffic flow allows.

   2. *If you can now see a stop is much less likely to be needed –* As you reach C_1, if open vision thus far confirms the junction is likely to remain clear far enough both ways to rule out risk from traffic **either way**, *no matter how fast*; and no unruly pedestrians or other snags exist to weigh up, then get down into 2nd gear by C_1, still about 30 metres out. Keep slowing down, ready to stop for any unforeseen reason but thus geared to make your turn in control without any unnecessary stop.

   Provided nothing now intervenes demanding a stop, you make your turn without further ado. You will have achieved an ideal turn (that is, in the absence of other traffic) – holding no one up; placing nobody at risk. If something unexpected crops up, your carefully controlled approach should mean you can easily STOP at the GIVE WAY line; wait; then act as in *1.,* above.

The Eyes Have It
Right turns demand the same rigorous *Looking Right and Left* attention to detail I gave in that section ten pages ago. Don't just look; *focus*. If there is anything coming, to be seen, let the eyes have it! Remember especially the cheeky rider who may swoop up alongside on your right; you don't want to knock him off. Joining to go left, or right, or crossing, any major road (though looking both ways no less stringently beforehand and whilst you emerge), train your final look – *at the moment of setting off* – to be always in the direction which *has the least-good view*. Once you conclude all is clear then, if your view right is masked, say by a thick hedge, whilst you have a much greater clear view left, be looking *right* as you start off. Thus, you will be the first to know if a speeding maniac appears there at the critical second!

   You can react safely, instantly: your decision – to stop before much out (or even reverse quickly if no one is behind), or to keep going smartly, will depend just how far forward you are, as well as on evasive action he may take. Never dream out, looking the wrong way. There lies the deadly, side-impact shock. . . . And LISTEN. Open your window(s). You can hear (motorised) traffic well before you can see it. That sound can save life; but its absence *does not protect **from you*** the [silent] cyclist, the soft shoe artist, the [literally] laid back, arm-propelled tricyclist, or the electrically powered wheelchair or scooter.

The latter three, so low to the ground, get too easily hidden. (They are, incidentally, desperately vulnerable on blind bends in country lanes with high banks or hedges, come upon as they often are, with complete surprise.) Near urban junctions choked by illegal, kerbside parking obstructing everyone's sight lines, they can be even more at risk – concealed by boots, bonnets or even backs of door mirrors. Your critical awareness of this, remote as the possibility might seem, must never dim.

At such a tricky junction, look past behind the dangerously parked vehicles and listen – long enough to observe all that's possible – *before* edging forward abreast of them to where you can see more and others can begin to see you, so as to make doing that as safe as you can. Give them time to note your presence. If there is but one prior point from which you can see the most, make sure you use it in this way. Do not rely solely, as some would advise, on what you may try to guess perhaps from reflections across the road in windows, etc. Nor dare you assume certainty from looking through parked cars at window level; smears, dirt, sunshine or rain can still fool you.

Use the steering wheels to observe the human blind spot. *All eyes have it.* Close **right** eye. Look at the wheel on the **right**. Hold this picture about a foot distant and straight ahead of **left** eye. Move the book in line gently toward or away from you. The wheel will pass, hidden, through a wide arc. Hence the necessity for the sweeping looks I advocate – never the casual glance – at all junctions.

Correct "Line" When Turning Right

Don't cut the turn (dotted line, fig. 62). Follow the continuously-arrowed path. Add speed smoothly, to get away safely. Again, watch your mirrors straightaway. Check your signal cancels. Aim to be up to 3rd gear by C_2. Other people can still spike a good turn! Car **E** may overrun his left turn and encroach your side. Car **D** could cut across your nose before you reach the line.

The latter fault is common; be prepared.

In either event you may be forced to brake sharply, stop, or even move in to your left. That third option would be a last resort, precluded if your mirrors warned of someone already moving up on your inside.

(Such a person, if preparing to turn left, would be perfectly correct if there was room. Indeed, your proper positioning helps him to do so, and this is sensible because, as a right-turner into the major road, you might well need to wait longer – longer than he would have to before being able to turn left into it.)

Anticipation here has to come to your rescue. Watch for the possibility of an **E** type, rushing in to the turn; hold back, and don't ease out towards the centre line, until you are sure he will make it without endangering you. Remember, he could skid, too. For a potential **D** type, similarly, hold back from the GIVE WAY or STOP line, until you see how badly he tries to cut the corner. These menaces illustrate the necessity for starting to look both ways *well before* you reach the line(s) with the major road.

Another possibility to anticipate, if the end of your road is narrow, is that of a lorry trying to turn in, and needing extra space so to do. Be prepared to hold back and help lorries. They're tough to drive and crunchy if they hit you!

Car **D**, in fig. 62, can fool you another way as well. If he gives no signal and appears to be going straight on, you may be preparing to tail in behind him, everything else being clear. Just as you start to move out, he swings right and takes off your front wing! Don't be hasty; watch him! It takes two (mistakes) to tango . . .

RIGHT TURN *OFF* A MAJOR ROAD

Study fig. 63. Double-check your mirrors before signalling with your right indicator. Then, if safe, **U** ease out gradually, beginning 350 metres or more from the turn, to a position running just to the left of the road centre line by C_1, 250 metres from it.

Your object is to be in this crown-of-the-road position *before*, or almost before, you need to start to slow down. Once there, you can change down to 3rd gear and, if necessary,

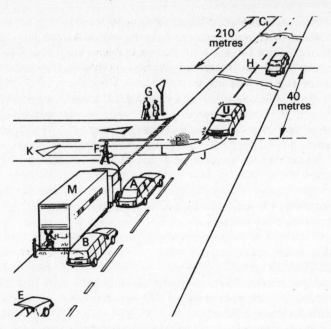

Fig 63 Right turn off a major road.

brake a little, as you carefully judge the speed of your arrival at the turn.

Hold that crown-of-the-road position. It tells everyone what you are doing. It lets those behind, who are going straight on, begin to filter past to your left as soon as they have room; *otherwise, they know they must slow or even stop if needs be, while you get clear.*

If your mirrors are telling you someone is pressing on your tail, start signalling earlier; that should forewarn him not to pass. However, if someone still forces his way past you, you may need to let him go first, and even give up trying to turn, if necessary, rather than have an accident. Thankfully, such dangerous driving would be rare for you to meet.

You must be in 2nd gear by **H**, in fig. 63 (around 40 metres from the turn), speed down to little more than a running pace. All the time, so far, you should have been assessing the oncoming traffic (and taking account of anyone wanting to emerge to his right from the minor road, even though he should wait for you). This assessment is in order to judge (a) whether there may be a safe gap in any oncoming stream, through which for you – keeping in 2nd gear – to turn without a stop when you reach the junction (perhaps with a bit of skilful timing and, maybe, an **Almost Stopping ... But Not Quite** routine added – see page 47); or, (b) whether you will have to stop where I have shown **U** in fig. 63, and then wait there until you can go safely, using a **Smooth Start** in 1st gear.

Remember the *general priority*, noted at the start of this chapter; that traffic **A, B** and **E**, because it is going forward on its own side of the road, takes precedence. As you will be turning across their path, it will be up to you to GIVE WAY, and wait if necessary.

If there is a safe gap, make your turn without stopping, confidently, but at no more than a fast walk. Unless you are turning into an immediately steep, uphill road (in which case you will need to take 1st on the move, as explained on page 141), 2nd gear will supply ample power – always provided that you don't teeter to a halt just before committing yourself. Make sure you get into 1st if there is any danger of that.

If you are in *any* doubt that you will be able to cross the path of the nearest oncomer without him having to blink, touch his brakes or make any evasive move, **Stop**. Stop with your front bumper just short of an imaginary line, one which is an extension of the centre line of the side road. (I have put the line in, in Fig. 63.) Next, apply your handbrake, go into neutral, etc., as per normal routine.

Make sure that your right indicator is still flashing.

Then, *anticipating* the next safe gap for turning, take 1st gear shortly before the last oncoming vehicle passes you by. Go the instant you can, but not without sneaking a glance over your right shoulder – in case someone on two wheels has crept up outside of you. You would have to let him go first. Remember to give resolute (though not ferocious) acceleration before, as and after you release the clutch, to be certain the car will take you safely to **K**, out of danger.

Wait for a gap long enough for you to cross at a mile-an-hour. You go more smartly when the time comes but *need that safety margin* in case the engine "coughs" on you, a pedestrian from **F** or **G** – to whom you MUST GIVE WAY – wanders into **K**, or anything unforeseen causes you to have to stop at **L**, straddling the oncomer's path. I hope you won't ignore this advice until you have a fright or an accident. If you ever did have the misfortune to find yourself stuck on the way round, anyone coming, like **A**, needs a fighting chance to pull up in time. So, never risk cutting things too fine. Make sure he would always have it.

The correct "*line*" (long wide arrow) is the same, whether you stop or not. You start turning only as the nose of your car passes that imaginary line, *not before*. Never cut through **P**.

In fig. 63, I show the correct stopping position, waiting for cars **A**, **B** and **E** to pass. Never creep to **J** while waiting for **E**. So doing prevents a clean turn. When you go, enter the minor road well in to your own side and at your normal distance out, as shown. Capture the new view in your mirrors, as you accelerate promptly up to an appropriate speed for whatever conditions you now find in the minor road. Check that your right indicator has cancelled.

In fig. 63, I have had to shrink the picture to make it fit. Imagine how much further back **A**, **B** and **E** would have been at various stages as you were lining yourself up from before C_1. During your continuous assessment of whether, or when, there might be a safe gap to turn through without a stop when you reach the turn, you may have been unable to judge, between C_1 and **H**, or even after **H**, the answer to the question of whether you will ultimately arrive in time to turn, before **A** is too near. **A** might confound your calculations by trying to be helpful, and decide (at his own risk) to slow down or stop to let you through!

It is for exactly this sort of reason that you *must always* get down into 2nd gear on your approach. Then you are automatically ready to shift smartly, without a stop, out of danger to **K**, should an opportunity safely so to do unexpectedly present itself.

To be able to reach there at least partly under momentum anyway, rather than having had to make a standing start, tends to be safer; a stall which can leave you stranded half way over is less likely. But you must always – AS EVER – be certain **K** is free for your arrival . . . see below!

Hidden Dangers

Imagine, for a moment, that, in fig. 63, cars **A** and **B** pass by, well before **U** arrive. **E**, having been much further off prior to your arrival, is not coming fast. As it appears **E** could not be inconvenienced, you decide to go on without a stop.

Suddenly, pedestrian **F**, without looking, strides smartly in front of you across the minor road. **U** stop dead at **L**, heart pounding. Before you can move on, you discover why lorry **M** has been so out of order for unloading at the junction. There is a screech of brakes as **E** narrowly manages to pull up without smashing your back wing.

Not only did **M** block the zone of view to the right for drivers who might have come up to exit from the minor road (as well as for drivers like **E** being able to see *them*), he prevented **E** from seeing what was happening in a wide zone in front of you. Luckily, **E** was covering his brake (and clutch) as in fig. 45, very much aware how restricted was his view.

Another hidden danger can be gleaned from fig. 63. Up to and including when stopped awaiting a gap, **U** should *never* start to put on steering lock for the turn itself. If you do, and then get hit from behind, you will be shunted directly into oncoming traffic. Keep your front wheels STRAIGHT until ready to set off.

When your major road is narrower than in fig. 63, a lorry, parked like **M**, can also make it unsafe to move out fully to your crown-of-the-road position. Hold back a little from your prospective stopping position of fig. 63, until you are sure no oncoming driver might swing out to get round **M**, hitting you in the process. None should; but people rush; sun gets in their eyes; very bright daylight reduces the impact of your flashing indicator; or, so keen are they to miss **M** they forget to look ahead – and see you!

A further possibility, when parked vehicles like **M** clutter a road on either or both sides, is for traffic both ways still to manage to pass by each other, using a little extra courtesy as explained on page 166. Drivers simply regard the centre line of the road as having shifted across to the middle of whatever space is available. Back in a narrower version of the major road in fig. 63, **U** would make certain to *wait-to-turn suitably well to the left of the painted centre line*, so as to allow **A**, **B** and **E** room to pass through even though the driver behind **U** would then have to wait for **U** to clear before he could drive on.

RIGHT TURNS AT CROSSROADS

At any crossroads, imagine a pin, like the beflagged post on a golf green, standing vertically at the point where the centre lines of the two roads would, if painted right the way through the junction, cross each other. Whichever direction you are making a right turn from, the *basic rule* is: keep this "flagpole" on your own right. Drive round behind it.

In fig. 64 your path **U** is shown by the continuous-line, fat arrow and those of **A** and **B** by broken-line and dotted ones. You can see that by each of you going round behind the "pin", you will automatically pass the other(s) who are turning right from opposite, offside-to-offside (with your driver's doors adjacent).

This being so, notice that no priority to go first exists as between **U** and **A**. In practice (disregarding all other traffic for the moment) **U** may have to wait a moment at **D** until **A** has moved past alongside him sufficiently for **U** to go on, or, vice-versa (**A** waiting until **U** move forward enough).

Emerging From The Minor Road
Unless a crossroads which you are approaching from the minor road is obviously clear in all directions, it is nearly

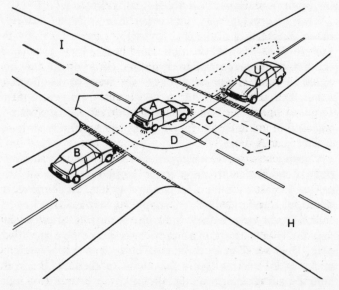

Fig 64 Right turns at crossroads.

always wise, until you have gained considerable experience, to stop at the line, come what may. At STOP signs you must so do anyway by Law, as you already know, but do so at GIVE WAY signs too. This way, you will ensure that you have time to collect your thoughts, as well as making certain that you will be safe to complete your right turn. Traffic driving along the major road always takes precedence.

If – despite his priority – any major-road driver stops, so as to help you (yes, thoughtful kindness still exists!), you must still know you are safe from all the other directions first – as well as making a check for two-wheelers who may attempt to tear past from behind *him* – before you dare move.

When there is someone opposite **U**, *like cars* **A** *or* **B** *in fig. 64, there are further aspects of the basic "round behind the flag-pole" rule to follow:*

To help you plan your own actions, begin by trying to establish which way any such driver is heading. The way he is positioned will probably be your most reliable clue as to his intention. (Thus, for example, you can be reasonably certain what **A** plans here. An arm signal from him would confirm it but that is rare; however, the fact that he is signalling properly, by indicator, does back up this assumption here.)

Lack of *any* type of *signal*, from **B**, may **NOT**, however, mean that he wants to go straight ahead; never take that for granted. Yes, the absence of an indicator signal, from **B**, should, in theory, you might presume, be confirmation but, again, beware! Those very drivers, who leave signals flashing when their use is finished, are the same ones who tend to forget to signal. You can even have a driver who flashes one way before going the other! Keep on your toes!

Erase car **A** from fig. 64, for a moment, just in your mind's eye. Suppose now, when traffic along the major road (from both **H** and **I**) clears, a driver, like **B**, opposite is waiting.

Don't be too hasty. It often happens that, as **U** move, he does too! Don't panic. Either of you can stop easily.

If **B** is – *in fact* – turning right despite his lack of any signal, you both then need go round *behind* the imaginary "flag-pole" and, so, each other. Wait at **D** if you need to, while he gets forward sufficiently for you then to go behind him. Were he to be going straight across after all, incidentally, you must still go round behind the "flag-pole"; that, therefore, likewise *means that you cannot go on until after he clears*. The reason for this is that *he* has priority, as he is driving forwards on his own side of the road – that is to say the minor road – as here extending across the major one. Were **B**, indeed, to pull a stunt like suddenly turning *left* (yes, even from that position!), you are still obliged to cede him priority and wait until you can safely tail in behind. He, regardless how you might view his particular antic here, is merely exiting his own side of the "extended" minor road; whereas you are crossing that half of the "extension" which, in theory at least, is "his".

All the above reminds you of the essential theory.

You stick to it but, beware if **B** starts to cut across in front of you. Be ready to stop and wait at **C** if he does. You can go on, round *behind* your "flag-pole", after he has gone.

You may, however, decide, instead, then to "cross in front" too, depending on all the circumstances. I will come to that in a few more paragraphs' time. *Normally*, unless there is restricted room and/or there are special road markings (either of which result in everybody always crossing in front at that particular junction), then waiting until you can go on round *behind* your "flag-pole" is what you must do.

If there were to be, in fig. 64, more than one driver waiting to come out from opposite **U**, the second and subsequent ones may wait to allow you to cross their "extension" (described above) so as to help avert gridlock. Needless to say, however, they may not! So, be prepared to wait at **D**. You will have to wait until – all other aspects remaining safe so to do – you can go behind them, smartly on, following the continuous-line, fat arrow, as in fig. 64.

As ever, directly you are under way after your turn, move ahead swiftly if you can; check your mirrors straightaway, and that your own signal has now cancelled itself.

Wherever possible, avoid such waiting as at **C** or **D** in fig. 64. Real danger exists from fast, major-road drivers, with their brains in neutral, not expecting that both you and those opposite you may become **STUCK** in the middle. Like the lorry driver in fig. 58, they kid themselves, before they arrive, that their way will be clear. As a result they delay braking until the last second, perhaps too late! Such fools often blare their horns in anger, apparently believing that they have some absolute right to a clear road – a supposed "right" which, despite their general possession of priority by virtue of being on the major road, the law cannot possibly give them. (They should know, too, that the only correct use of the horn is to warn someone of their presence.)

If you do get delayed at **C** or **D**, in fig. 64, then, provided you are established there *long before* any major-road traffic is even in sight, you shouldn't be at risk. You have, arguably, as much "priority" to be there, as they have to come along.

However, if you shoot out, in the teeth of major-road traffic coming, gambling that those opposite won't do the same – *and are delayed at* **C** *or* **D** – you will have mainly yourself to blame if all the others involved turn out not to be sufficiently good enough drivers to protect you from your folly. People *behind you*, for instance, are likely to move up, blocking off any chance of your retreating. Were you to be one of those people behind, I sincerely hope you would have had the forethought not to do any such thing. Would you?

Leaving The Major Road
Double-check your mirrors, then signal, position and slow, as for any **Right Turn** *Off* A Major Road. Wait, if necessary, for a gap in the oncoming traffic. Make your correct, right turn line, by going round behind the imaginary, centre point "flag-pole" of the crossroads that has just been described above. Always sneak that usual glance over your right shoulder (page 209), the one that can save you from trouble on two wheels, last thing before you commit yourself to the turn.

Right-turning, oncoming, major-road traffic should, equally, play by the *basic, "round behind the flag-pole" rule*, and expect (and plan) to pass round, accordingly, offside-to-offside, behind you. If, however, any member of it chooses not so to do, for any reason, including those which will become clear in the next section – *Crossing In Front When Turning Right* – then you will have to be prepared to re-plan your turn on the different basis there explained.

Crossing/turning traffic from the minor roads has to wait for major-road right-turners to clear, before it moves. Should any try to nip across, be willing to stop and prevent an accident. Apply forgiveness. Never abuse your priority status.

Complete your turn swiftly, directly you can. Don't stop in

215

the waiting position (see **U**, in fig. 63) if there is no need. Remember, nonetheless, not to turn your steering wheel until ready to go on round (you might need to make an unforeseen stop after all). Once you are into the turning, accelerate smartly unless there are reasons not so to do; check your mirrors as usual; cancel your indicator, if it has not self-cancelled.

A further complication ensues when there is more than one, oncoming, driver preparing to turn right and, perhaps, you, too, are part of a growing, right-turning queue. Alas for a Learner like **U**, now in fig. 65, traffic has built up before a gap can materialise. If a rotter hoots, as you wait, keep calm. *A hoot only hurts if you let it.*

The position in fig. 65 is probably not dangerous, as **U** are shielded by the other stopped traffic. The difficulty usually resolves simply enough, something like this: **E**, **F** and **G** close up, bumper-to-bumper, and **H** and **I**, sensibly, wait a little back, leaving a gap for **U**, **B**, **C** and **D** to use. Thus the congestion clears. **E**, **F** and **G**, can now make their right turns, once traffic from **Z** has ceased, followed by **H** and **I**. Finally, **M** and **N** are clear to cross provided no more traffic arrives along the major road.

U, before taking the gap left to you by **H** and **I**, dare not go without checking area **K**, as must each of those who follow **U**. **U** must only edge forward, until you can see round **H**. Shoot through, neither thinking nor looking, and you can be in a smash before **U** know it.

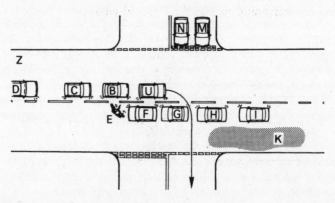

Fig 65 A problem turning right.

Crossing In Front When Turning Right

I have twice referred to this exception – at crossroads – to the *basic "round behind the flag-pole" rule*. Instead of going round behind the "flag-pole" (i.e. offside-to-offside vis-à-vis traffic opposite you), drivers use the alternative of crossing in front, nearside-to-nearside. See fig. 66. Originally, this exception evolved only for crossroads where the weight of traffic trying to turn right, or restricted room, made sticking to the basic rule no longer practical. Nowadays, the road markings at some crossroads (most commonly those with traffic lights) even lay down that, for certain directions at least, right-turners must cross in front at that particular junction. A policeman or traffic warden on point duty may expect it, too; he would give an obvious sign. (Normally, as he will be standing at the centre-point of the crossroads you would pass round behind him.)

When crossing in front, both turning vehicles must go carefully as they pass each other in the shaded area shown in fig. 66. This is particularly vital, lest any vehicle which may be hidden behind the driver opposite – *like motorcycle* **A**, in this drawing, *to which the car must by rights give way* – springs forward. It is *because* of this restricted vision, that the *fundamental "round behind the flag-pole" rule* has to remain your preferred choice – acknowledged in the Highway Code as the safest method.

Other than when road markings enforce crossing in front, you need to assess, at every right turn you make at crossroads, how any driver opposite you is going to handle the situation, and then determine your path and actions in the light of what you see beginning to happen. I would advise you not, as a

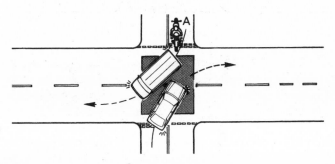

Fig 66 Crossing *in front* when turning right.

Learner, generally to be the first to opt for the exception but, instead, simply be ready to fall in with it straightaway *if it is appropriate* and a driver from opposite is making it obvious that that is the way he wants to adopt.

Remember, you should *not*, normally, *expect* to cross in front, unless road markings demand it or there is so little room that it is a necessity; therefore, be warned, it may *not be appropriate*, despite what a driver opposite may have begun.

If he does start forward, steering to cross in front *inappropriately* (at least in your view), you should either wait, or move out only as far as **C**, fig. 64 (provided you cannot possibly attract danger from either your left or your right), before going on round *behind* the "flag-pole" once you are free so to do.

However, you have to balance the "regimented" discipline of doing that, with the overall situation and any extra hold-up you may cause people behind you. Sometimes, because you will be less exposed to fast, major-road traffic, the better plot will be to accept the situation rapidly and follow suit. Your teacher must be wide-awake to confirm your decisions at first.

Notice that, whilst neither of you ranks ahead of the other in priority when you are *both* crossing in front of each other – any more than when you *both* use the preferred and safer *"round behind the flagpole"* rule – there is real accident potential should you both move out simultaneously, one bent on crossing in front, the other on passing behind. Logically, whichever driver wishes to cross in front must cede priority to the other (because the latter is merely "driving forwards on his own side of the road" – see page 214). Hence my advice above not to rush to cross in front. Choose the method only where road markings dictate or sheer lack of space makes any other way impossible.

Crossing in front may be necessary, too, as you *leave* a major road at a crossroads. Again, you need to assess road markings and sum up whatever an oncoming right-turner may do, as well as the overall situation; then act as befits the circumstances. Major-road traffic speeds heighten risk. Eye-ball ahead repeatedly, lest a blind spot (in your eye; caused by a hidden dip, etc.) conceals anything coming (perhaps on 2 wheels . . .) or masks a sudden "change of plan" – *by a far-too-late positioning or forgot-to-signal oncoming driver, for instance.* Be even more careful about "hidden" traffic which may yet spring from behind your opposite number.

Remember, *YOU must give way to that traffic*. The increased danger may be easier to visualise if you imagine two of the right-turners, in fig. 65, trying to pass in front of each other when someone from **K** or **Z** was belting through, dangerously fast. For such drivers from **K** or **Z** that would be a sin the like of which, I pray, you yourself will never be guilty. Be warned that sinners, nonetheless, are everywhere . . .

GOING STRAIGHT AHEAD

Assume, for the moment, that *you are driving along a major road*. As we saw with fig. 58, you are *not* free to ignore all side roads. At all turnings, either side, and particularly at crossroads, be alert. People *often* pull out carelessly. They may just forget to look, or they may look and not see; perhaps a foot slips off a clutch; or maybe they drink and drive. The reasons are endless.

Always slow down, in readiness, for the remotest chance of trouble. Picking up speed again is easy. The hard thing is stopping when things go wrong.

How much you need to cut your speed – FOR EACH AND EVERY MINOR ROAD TO BE PASSED – depends on your present speed, the width of *your* road, whether there is oncoming traffic, whether someone waits at the end of the side road or, if not, then on how far you can see to be clear down it, on your road surface and the weather, on the space available for avoiding action, and so on. A toot should warn a driver, rider, or someone on foot of your presence if you think that you might not have been seen coming along. Always watch out, when someone waits at or pokes out from a side turning, for anyone else, *hidden on the far side of him*, who may also pull out without seeing you.

MAKE ALLOWANCES! A junction in town, swarming with pedestrians, is different from one with none. Just one pedestrian, if he is standing where he might be vulnerable were you to have to take emergency action, can mean that less than half your original speed is, still, *too much*. Crossroads with vision limited by woods, hedges, long grass, etc., have to be passed more slowly than ones in open, flat countryside.

Where a blind turning joins a narrow country lane on a bend, walking pace – even when you are on the major of the two roads – may be more than enough. OK there will be turnings you may pass without needing to slow down – but never pass one by without giving the matter any thought . . .

Whenever someone does pull out across or onto your path – even with plenty of time – **ASSUME THAT HE WON'T MAKE IT FULLY OUT OF YOUR WAY** *until you can see that he* **HAS** *done*. Slow sufficiently to stop if, ultimately, you have to. Not to, is madness. You don't want to become a joint victim of anything going wrong for him. Equally, if someone ahead already blocks your path when you first see him, perhaps because he is having to wait, **NEVER ASSUME HE WILL BE ABLE TO MOVE CLEAR BEFORE YOU GET THERE**.

A vehicle prematurely sallying forth from a turn to your *right* may cause an oncoming driver suddenly to swing across onto your side . . . What then? Fault hardly stops just with the exiting or the oncoming drivers; not if *you* are coming too fast to take avoiding action.

Another cause for caution is when an oncoming driver may be intending to turn right, into a turn ahead of you on your left. Suppose such a driver – let's say of a lorry – risks shooting right across your bows. You brake enough to miss him, but then you find the driver of a smaller vehicle behind the lorry has committed himself to swing across you as well . . . In driving, minding your own business is rarely enough. You should have noticed that the lorry hadn't been slowing up sufficiently to stop before making his turn. You should have slowed more, and kept covering your brake so as to be ready; in other words, you ought to have been assuming that the unseen risk behind him might be there, too, until you saw it was not.

In stop-start traffic you may notice a driver waiting desperately in a side road to join yours. Where reasonable, be courteous; slow or stop, and let him out. Help by giving by arm, a slowing-down signal. See page 225. This alerts everyone else, too. But don't wave him out. It is for him to decide if it is safe. Stop a little more short than necessary. This helps him to be able to see that no one is trying to pass you and, hopefully, ensures that anyone so silly as to attempt

220

that will, before any such folly, see why you have stopped!

I now consider what you must do when *you want to go straight ahead at a crossroads where you are on the minor road*. As with **Right Turns At Crossroads** (where you are emerging from the minor road), even when the sign only commands that you GIVE WAY, it is better for a Learner to stop in any event.

First and foremost, it gives you the extra time to look all ways properly.

Secondly, it enables you to allow for the unexpected. Slow down, getting down as far as 3rd gear, just as you would for any junction where you intend to stop. Remember all I have said about eyeball work on approach to the line, at the line, *and* as you go across. The examiner will want to see you taking account of what anyone opposite is doing. He is, also, watching to see that no one, from either direction along the major road, will be caused to slow because of your crossing.

You will see over-confident drivers spurt across major roads when traffic coming along them is much too near. They make no allowance for the unforeseen; for example, sudden drive-shaft failure. Never copy. Instead, stay alive, by making it your own, additional, iron-rule **NEVER TO DRIVE ACROSS ANYONE'S SAFE STOPPING DISTANCE**.

Which Queue?

Where two lanes, in which to form queues, are marked at the end of a minor road (or, where there is room on your half of it for two, even though they are not marked), then, if you are going straight across, you can choose either one – unless an arrow on the road reserves it for turning traffic. Subject to there being no one in your mirrors to consider, choose an appropriate lane early, position accordingly, and stick to that. In the absence of other factors the righthand lane is normally best; because, quite often, this allows left-turning traffic to filter away whilst you (or, perhaps, anyone turning right) has to wait. Never straddle two lanes. That's selfish.

No indicator signals are appropriate when going straight on. However, an arm signal may, occasionally, be useful; for that, please see *Arriving At A Major Road*, page 226.

LANE DECISIONS FOR JUNCTIONS

Up to this stage of discussing your practical handling of junctions, I have made but brief mention of *pre*-selecting an appropriate lane. Many wider roads, particularly in towns, have two, or more, lanes each way. Whether or not they are fully-fledged dual carriageways need not concern us here.

On all these multi-laned roads, you must pre-select the appropriate lane (if you are not in it already) long before you reach any junction.

If it is a major road, primary route, you are on, this may not only be necessary if you are to make a turn off; it may, if lane direction signs or arrows so decree, also be a requirement for going straight on.

Lane Discipline applies very much (see pages 136 and 170 to remind yourself) to such (prior) lane changes; so you have to operate a long, long way ahead. Otherwise, you may be thwarted from taking your planned route! Your object must always be to be in an appropriate lane well ahead of the game. If you are turning, that should be comfortably in advance of the point at which you will start to signal for the turn itself. If you have to move lane for going straight ahead, you will need to be similarly well planned.

In my previous section, GOING STRAIGHT AHEAD, I urged you to **SLOW DOWN** for all junctions, no matter how apparently insignificant they might seem at first, properly matching your speed to the specific circumstances in hand. In these multi-laned conditions, you must apply further care still, especially if, when going straight on, you are ''hemmed-in'' to your lane by traffic alongside as you pass through the junction. Make sure you are neither in the process of overtaking, nor, indeed, undertaking (even with due cause, see page 137) as you all pass through it . . . see page 247, too.

If it is a non-primary route, minor road you are on, two lanes each way is less common; however, quite often, such roads are widened out for a fair distance either side of a junction with a major road. Again, be sure to select the correct lane for your intended direction, early; usually, that can be from directly you reach the widened part. Remember, good drivers create lanes if there is room – even when none may be marked.

"HERRING-BONE", AND OTHER
TRAFFIC-SEPARATION LINES

Fig. 67 demonstrates how these, *when enclosed by a broken white line*, create a safe "sanctum" for traffic turning off a major road. All through traffic is channelled to the left of a "herring-boned" area (as seen from one's driving seat). Pairs of large, curved arrows, in the middle of the road as shown in fig. 67, and reached well before the white-painted "sanctum" itself, forewarn all major-road drivers, who are *not* turning, to move into a single file as they pass the junction. This allows anyone, who *is* turning, to move into the sanctum and to be able to wait there safely if necessary; there, he is in full view of but sheltered from fast, through traffic. No one amongst that traffic can be unaware – either that there *is* a junction or, that *he must not now be overtaking*. Traffic exiting from the turning is also able to benefit from the protected, waiting area, if needs be.

Sometimes these "sanctums" are also set out to reflect special priorities for the turning or crossing traffic using them. The position of additional, GIVE WAY, lines, on the safe area itself, within the otherwise blank part, may, for example, indicate at a crossroads layout, that *Crossing In Front* is expected. You need to study some live examples in your area and relate them to the *basic "flag-pole" rules* I gave you earlier. Compare using these "sanctums", too, with the principles of using **THE** *SAFE AREA* **FOR TURNING AND CROSSING** at dual carriageway junctions, described from page 233.

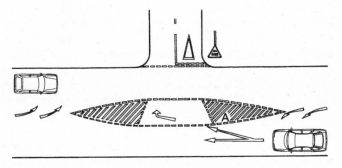

Fig 67   Herring bone traffic-separation lines protecting turners.

223

Technically, because its surrounding-edge line is a broken one, you can drive over the diagonally striped part of a safe "sanctum". Normally, I would *only* so do if I was turning right, off the major road. Then, I might move over a little early, initially using area **A** (as seen in fig. 67) of the hatched area. Doing so can save any following, through traffic from having to slow down unnecessarily, behind you, before you move over. However, you may be best to leave such advanced courtesy until after your Practical Test.

Continuous lines around diagonal, herring-bone stripes or chevrons create a widened, double white line – a very different [kettle of] fish. You find these at brows of hills, etc., and, *because the defining-edge lines are continuous, it is illegal to drive onto this type*, just as it is to drive on the wrong side of any double white line with a continuous line nearest to you.

CROSSING BESPOKE LANES/PAVEMENTS

If you are turning off a main road at a small turning or into a private property, you may need to cross a tram, bus or cycle lane during its "active" hours of operation, or a pavement. The essential thing whether turning right or left is that YOU are always the person obliged to GIVE WAY! Keep your wits about you; such lanes may be *contraflow* ones, so look the correct way. Remember too, the former Highway Code absolute command: **"pavements are for people – not for vehicles"**. Let those on foot pass by, not away.

ARM SIGNALS

Arm *direction* signals are not usually expected to be used on your Practical Test unless perhaps, unluckily, your indicators were to fail. Nevertheless, you may be asked to describe when they can most usefully be employed and to demonstrate how each is given. You also have to be able to recognise those given by others! So I will go into detail.

Neither is the all-important, *slowing-down* arm signal necessarily essential whilst you are driving your examiner around and about; however, it is well worth giving one correctly should an appropriate circumstance for so doing arise during your Practical Test. For one thing, this should reassure him that, on arm signals, you know what you are about.

Appreciate that any arm signal, *alone*, is not always seen. Another road user who is on the wrong side of your car won't see you give it. Nor are those intended to be given only from inside the car universally noticed. Appreciate, equally, however, that your flashing indicators and/or brakelights may scarcely show up in strong sunlight. Then, an arm signal can make a dramatic reinforcement to your electrical one; as also it can in circumstances that are out of the ordinary. Wise drivers, therefore, regard the two separate means of signalling as *complementary* to one another, to be used *in conjunction* whenever an arm signal can add a substantial benefit, rather than to be considered as alternatives.

Please refer to the Highway Code, where you will find that all the arm signals are illustrated. Make your arm signals boldly; there is no place for some undemonstrative, "wet" wave:

Arm Right-Turn Signal
Get three-quarters of your arm *straight* out, at right angles to your car, with hand and closed fingers extended. Face your palm forwards; hold your arm steady.

Arm Left-Turn Signal
Exaggerate this, using a continuous, forwards, circular motion (anti-clockwise), with your elbow bending – rather like an Olympic, crawl swimmer.

Arm Slowing-Down Signal
Give a full metre of down-and-up movement *from your shoulder*, keeping your arm and hand (palm downwards) out straight. Repeat the movement with a steady, heartbeat pace.

Arm Signals **From Inside Car** Mainly To Police, Etc.
If you want these to be seen, make certain that your hand is as close to the windscreen as is practical without risking greasy smudges thereupon. **Note:** though common and often very sensible, it is, officially, incorrect to use these to signal your intention to drivers *behind* you.

ARM SIGNALS TIMING

Never put your arm out of your window at a moment when it could be wiped off!

For the timing of an arm *slowing-down signal*, please refer back to page 149.

For arm *turn* signals, first refresh your memory of *positioning*, and of speed and gear control, at different types of junction – all from the beginning of this chapter. These factors are always similar; so, an arm-signal, timing "system", as now described below, flows conveniently from them.

One Arm Signal Is Enough

Whichever arm signal you may be making, one signal, given long enough to be noticed, should, in combination with your indicators, be enough. There is rarely time for more anyway.

Arriving At A Major Road

If you intend going *straight ahead*, no arm signal is required on your approach. Nor is one necessary if, when you arrive, all is clear and you have no need to stop.

If you do have to stop and wait, then there may, at some stage during that wait, be a need for a *straight-ahead* arm signal **from inside the car**. This would either be for the benefit of someone controlling traffic, or that of someone waiting opposite, or, possibly, unofficially to inform someone, **behind** you, of your intention. You have to judge how valuable it might be. Your teacher can help. The main, practical use of this signal is, probably, that of helping an officer on point duty. Just give it briefly, until you see that he has understood. But always work on the basis that he might *not* have noted your signal (yet) unless you have seen a nod or an acknowledgement.

When you are *turning into* a major road, an arm *turn* signal, should you decide it would make a beneficial addition to your indicators at a particular junction, needs to be given surprisingly well in advance of your arrival. You cannot flap your arm in-and-out of the window and change gear at the same time, because **AT LEAST ONE HAND MUST BE ON THE STEERING WHEEL** *at all times*. Nor do you want to be

226

giving it during the last few metres – just when you should be concentrating on eyeball work.

Therefore, the arm-signal, timing "system" which it is always best to follow, for left or right *turns*, is: add your – once only – *arm* signal as soon as you are down into 3rd gear, before any further gear change may be needed – and within a moment or two after you have put on your indicator signal.

The only time you might repeat an *arm turn* signal would be if you had had a long wait before you could get out into the major road; then it may be useful to repeat it briefly, just before your **Smooth Start**, so that any new arrivals will know where you are going. For a right, repeat *arm* signal – do take care of that arm . . . For a left, repeat *arm* signal, note from the Highway Code that it may be appropriate to give it, this time, **from inside the car**.

Leaving A Major Road

Arm direction signalling for *turning off* a major road can follow a generally similar "system" – giving the signal once, directly you are down to 3rd gear. Here are some further hints.

For a **RIGHT TURN** *OFF A SINGLE CARRIAGEWAY* **MAJOR ROAD**, change down a bit early, so that you can begin it before starting to move out towards the crown-of-the-road; and complete it, too, before you reach that, just-left-of-centre, running position. Firstly, the signal has to come (as ever) *before* you begin your (outward) move; secondly, keeping your arm intact can become tricky once traffic coming in the opposite direction is flashing by close to you! Again, unless you are having to wait for a long time in the middle, any repeat arm signal is here probably unnecessary (never mind chancing your arm . . .).

For **LEFT TURNS** *OFF A DUAL CARRIAGEWAY*, your judgement – of whether someone who is already expecting to pass you might "twist your arm" (albeit inadvertently), if you were to thrust it out in front of him – is rather important! For a **RIGHT TURN** *OFF A DUAL* the same may apply before you can move to the righthand lane. So arm signals hardly suit duals. However, if after that you are likely to need to stop on the dual carriageway itself, blocking the righthand lane temporarily, then an arm right-turn signal can prove to be by far the best way to highlight for those behind this exceptionally tricky plight. Avoid it if you possibly can.

Roundabouts And Traffic Lights
To all intents and purposes you can take it that arm signals and roundabouts are mutually exclusive! You need not even consider giving one. At traffic lights your road's status (major or minor) effectively alternates, just as do the red and green phases. Therefore, any of the timing tips and constraints of this section may need to be applied accordingly.

MORE TRICKY JUNCTIONS

WHEN A LATE SIGNAL IS CORRECT
In fig. 68, **U**, if planning to go left at **Z**, should have been summing up the situation and lining up what will become unmistakable positioning for that turn, from long before **A**. **U** will be wise only to start a left signal *as you pass* **B**. Nevertheless, your careful positioning line, following the broken arrow, and slowing down appropriately for entry to **Z** rather than **Y**, should ensure that drivers **B**, **C** and **D** recognise your intentions correctly. Lorry **D**, correctly positioned ready to go to **Y**, waits as shown until he is sure what **U** are doing! He is particularly careful not to edge forward, prematurely, on what would turn out to be a false premise – i.e. that **U** would be going into **Y**.

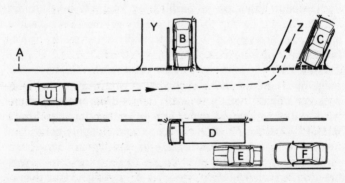

Fig 68 Skilled positioning to back up signals.

MAKE NO ASSUMPTIONS

B, in fig. 68, waiting to come out left, watches your front wheels, so as to confirm, beyond doubt, where **U** are going. He does not presume to know whether your indicator, if it's on, means you are heading for **Y** or intend to turn into **Z**. To move on any such assumption invites catastrophe. Suppose **U** had left it flashing, by mistake, and had no thoughts of turning at all? Suppose **U**, having signalled and lined yourself up to turn into **Y**, then changed your mind, and had, inexcusably and without warning, switched onto a bee-line for **Z**? Only once he saw those wheels turn and **U** physically entering his own road would **B** prepare to go. (Even then, he would wait until **U** were sufficiently into **Y**, to be certain that there could be no one – not even a bicycle – hidden close behind **U** . . .)

Never trust the indicators alone, watch those front wheels.

B, who would probably start as soon as **U** have passed, is very wary that he doesn't then smash into **C**. **C**, hopefully, should have earlier recognised the likelihood that **B** would be able to join the major road before himself and, accordingly, been ready to wait a little longer.

But suppose **C** had arrived in a hurry, too late for **B** to spot his sudden "materialisation", too rushed and too careless properly to assess the overall position? Excited by an apparent chance to tail in neatly behind **F**, **C** might have risked moving out during the split-second or so while **B** was masked by **U**. Bang! Bad boys both, **C** and **B** . . . each for assuming there was nothing hidden behind **U** **at the crucial moment**.

TURNING LEFT AND, ALMOST IMMEDIATELY, RIGHT

In fig. 69, **U** are preparing to get to road **B**. Imagine that **D–E** is chock-a-block both ways with dense, *slow* traffic – more than I can show here. Notice that there are two lanes each way on **D–E**. Wait until both the lanes to your right are clear, and then move smartly. Following the arrowed path, take up an immediate, right-turn "line", changing your indicator signal direction from left to right, straightaway, at **G**, so that every-one can at once see your intention. Be prepared to wait at **C**,

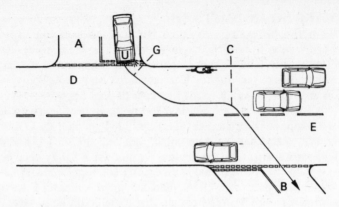

Fig 69 Staggered crossing.

for a gap in approaching traffic, before **U** can complete your turn.

If, initially, the nearest lane to **U** coming from **D** clears, but the outer one is still choked by stop-start traffic, it may be safe – guided by your teacher – to edge out to **G**, change your indicator, and then wait there. Continue to wait there until the second lane clears too, or someone in it stops to let **U** go, before **U** carry on to **C**, etc. Fresh traffic arriving in the nearside lane from **D** should pull up calmly if **U** are still waiting at **G**; however, see also page 215.

TURNING RIGHT AND, ALMOST IMMEDIATELY, LEFT

Normally, **U** must wait for the road to clear *both ways* before **U** commence this, similar, "double" turn. Your "line", this time, will be as per the arrow in fig. 70. **U** change your indicator to the left directly **U** begin to move out.

In "rush-hour" conditions, however, traffic sometimes never seems to clear both ways at once! In this situation, **U** may need to move out, first of all, into position **A** in fig. 70, by now already having switched your right indicator to the left one. **U** can only make this move if a safe opportunity arises. There would have to be an extra long gap in both lanes **E**, or drivers in both of them would have to have courteously stopped for **U**.

You would also have to be certain that none amongst traffic

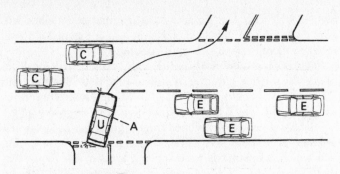

Fig 70   A little courtesy goes a long way.

C will want to turn right into the road U are leaving. U can't just move out into an immediate clash with them, usurping their priority status as drivers along the major road.

Once U are waiting in position A, if any further traffic, such as E, should arrive newly upon the scene, it then has to wait. Hopefully, it will thoughtfully do so well back, so that U can see past the "front row" – just in case some idiot attempts to pass it from further back. From position A, U are ready to go ahead immediately the last of traffic C goes by.

Sometimes, however, a C driver who wants to turn right will come along subsequently; and, with luck, will turn out to be of the sort sufficiently considerate to stop a little short of his normal, right-turn position. This should enable U to get away first, whilst at least partly shielded from further C traffic. Go for that; however, it will be your look-out to make sure that no inside-lane, C traffic could be placed at risk. It may, or may not, politely stop, too. If it does not, U may need to abandon your immediate left turn and continue in the righthand lane until a safe gap comes free for U to move across and resume a normal, lefthand lane, driving position. In so doing, put on speed to match the other traffic, as soon as safely possible; if U dawdle in the righthand lane, no one is going to be amused. You would then have to make your way back to your original route later.

Thus you must be prepared to accept that you will not always find considerate driving all round. To begin with your teacher must advise you closely. You must temper the Highway Code advice not to block any junction, with common sense in all the circumstances. If you find it necessary to move out and wait with your car across the first half of a major-road, only do so when all lanes of traffic in it have stopped for you, or when there is no one in sight coming.

What is *exceedingly dangerous*, and you must NEVER do, is to attempt to edge out little by little, in the hope that someone may stop. You could find yourself to be the cause of a serious smack-up of **C** and **E** traffic in front of your nose; you *could* get off lightly, with just a crunched front, right wing . . .

Later on, you can give a grateful nod to those who help you, one which a Learner is not expected to give; but remember, then, *never to sacrifice concentration and attention* on **LOOKING WHERE YOU ARE GOING**.

HEADLAMP FLASHING AT JUNCTIONS

To add to being polite, by waiting, as was the considerate, right-turning **C** driver above (and in similar junction circumstances), some drivers add a flash or two of their headlamps to encourage you to get on and go. The trouble is that *other, rude*, drivers may flash aggressively and with the *opposite* meaning – namely, that *they* are going to *carry on going*, themselves! So, these flashes are very prone to misinterpretation. They are also, very frequently, taken by the *wrong people* (even, perhaps, by pedestrians), as being *meant for them*.

For everyone's safety, therefore, *never*, yourself, give such a headlamp flash. Never conclude, either, that another driver's headlamp flashing must be for your benefit only. Skin your eyes all round; be guided, instead, by what that driver is DOING; and take account, too, of what other road users may now DO. Consult your Highway Code. You need to know the *correct* Code position on headlamp flashing for your Theory Test. Leave it to others to flout the rules in all their wisdom, if they so wish. Although the Highway Code does not enjoy the full status of Parliamentary Law, you might, as explained therein, find yourself hard-pressed to escape some blame, were an accident to befall anyone as a result of your giving any signal not recognised within the Code. By the way, it is illegal to flash your headlamps to inform oncoming drivers of an active police speed trap behind you.

DUAL CARRIAGEWAY JUNCTIONS

THE *SAFE AREA* FOR TURNING AND CROSSING

The gap through the central reservation, shaded in fig. 71, is the *SAFE AREA*. It is with your car fully encapsulated on here that, if needs be, you wait, sheltered *both ways* from fast-moving traffic.

Increasingly, such gaps on duals are either being closed, if the central reservation is insufficiently wide, or they are being re-designed with the addition of more adequate, deceleration, "mini" slip roads, to improve safety. Many were *black spots* (fatal accident sites) anyway.

TURNS *ONTO* A DUAL CARRIAGEWAY

Leftward joining should be simple. Just be sure to gauge how very quickly traffic from your right may be coming. Make sure that there will be no chance of your engine stalling. Be geared to accelerate purposefully, once you are into the lefthand lane, up to a suitable speed. Drivers (and riders) can appear in your mirrors at lightning speed on duals, so you can rapidly be in danger unless you pick up speed quickly.

However, in the above concentration to your right, never forget pedestrians who may stride off the pavement from your left . . .

If there is an acceleration slip road, even a "mini" one, provided to help you get onto the dual, use it. Depending upon its length, this should enable you to "time it" – so that you can begin accelerating on the slip road, and then tail in, neatly, as you merge out onto the dual, into the space in the flowing traffic which you have pre-selected. Gaps within that traffic, shorter than could otherwise be used from a standing start, can then be used; however, your teacher must guide at first and make sure you get plenty of practice, so that your own good judgement develops soundly.

To time accurately such acceleration on a lengthy slip road, it is essential, before you merge across onto the dual itself, to *glance directly over your right shoulder*, as well as using your mirrors. However, do watch out for anyone who is in front of you and also trying to merge suddenly coming to an unexpected stop! Believe me they *often* do . . . (If *you* make a misjudgement, you yourself will have to stop.)

Depending upon the length and the angle of the slip road, and the speed of traffic on the dual, success depends upon being in 2nd gear (or 3rd, if speed so justifies) as you merge on, so that you have the maximum flexibility of acceleration at your toe. Aim to be neatly within the peak pulling power range (see fig. 4) of the appropriate gear, so that you won't need to change up again until you are safely out onto the dual carriageway.

The "name of the game", with these merges, is to have already reached the same speed as the traffic on the dual, before or as you merge in. Then it should be easy, safe and simple.

If an acceleration slip road is quite long, a switch of your indicator – from left to right – as you start away along it, will be appropriate. Then you must watch to cancel it – if it does not itself so do – once you are onto the dual carriageway.

As a rule, when you are turning left onto a dual carriage-way, if someone opposite you is waiting in the *SAFE AREA* to complete a right turn, they should let you go first. (See page 214.) But remember that they won't always so do and that they are likely to be heading across into the left lane of the dual! Don't let their ignorance lure you into an accident.

When you turn right *onto* a dual, the *basic "flag-pole" rule* (of passing drivers from opposite, offside-to-offside) applies, unless road markings dictate otherwise. Here, that passing occurs, of course, on the *SAFE AREA*. Be very careful about any *Crossing In Front*; see below.

If the *SAFE AREA* for you in the middle is still full – **OR POTENTIALLY FULL** – don't budge from your minor road yet. Wait until there will be room for your entire car length to stop on there in safety. Note that, in fig. 71, so far as **U** are concerned, anyone coming from your left and wanting to turn right, i.e. from **C** – even if he is still on the far side of the dual carriageway and has yet to reach the *SAFE AREA* – takes priority. He is leaving the major road. He is a "wild card", a *potential filler* of the *SAFE AREA*, to be looked out for *before* you consider leaving your minor road.

Sometimes, however, where a deceleration slip road has been created for him to run off the dual itself in greater safety, GIVE WAY lines, as depicted in my fig. 71, theoretically –

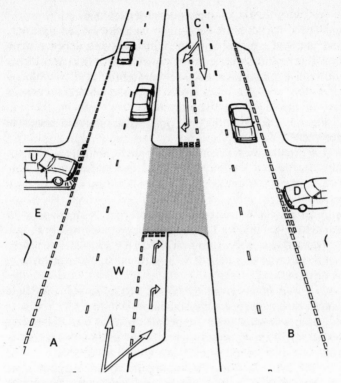

Fig 71 Dual carriageway *SAFE AREA* for turning and crossing.

and legally – then hold him, instead, at the edge of the *SAFE AREA*, while you come out onto it. My own view is never count on that! If he were to move forward at just the wrong moment you'll be in a far more deadly pickle (having to leave your boot sticking out) than he will. So, whilst observing road markings yourself, study more carefully what others actually DO, be they right or wrong!

Suppose **U** are turning right onto dual road **B**, in fig. 71, and dual **A** clears first. Assuming you're OK to get onto the *SAFE AREA* (see above), you can now nip over and wait on the left side of it. You may then still have to wait *after dual* **B** *clears*, while **D** crosses to beside you. Technically, as ever, he expects you to go round behind him on your way to complete your turn – *correctly into the left lane of* **B**.

As with leftward joining, your subsequent **Smooth Start** off the *SAFE AREA* must be equally well disciplined against a stall and you need to accelerate with some gusto once you are into **B**, checking your mirrors immediately, clicking off your indicator if it has not already self-cancelled. Also, as with any right turn, you must be prepared for some nut on two wheels (or, in this case, on four, or more!) to come up on your righthand side from behind, just when you are about to complete your turn. Because of the extra room the *SAFE AREA* often allows, I'm afraid this greedy, selfish and danger- ous stunt becomes *more* likely. Don't get mixed up with him. Let him go. A neat flash-look out of the corner of your right eye at the right moment should spot him coming. (He may – unjustifiably in the circumstances of your being there – be attempting a *Crossing In Front* manoeuvre; see below.)

There is no need to stop on the *SAFE AREA*, at all, if the entire junction and dual **B** is already clear. Just get on with your right turn!

Crossing In Front on the *SAFE AREA*, as you turn right onto a dual carriageway, is another possibility with which to contend, whenever there are people opposite you, themselves potentially wanting to turn right. It may, indeed, be laid down, for that particular junction, by arrows and markings painted on the *SAFE AREA*, that right-turning drivers are required so to do. See page 217. Tackle it as explained there, laced with self-preservation! If there is the slightest doubt about what someone opposite will do when they get onto the *SAFE AREA*, do not head over there yourself yet. The chance of being caught half-way on to it, exposed at your rear to high speed traffic, is too serious to take.

I said, four paragraphs above, that you complete your turn "*correctly into the left lane of* **B**". Sometimes, during heavy traffic, you will see drivers head into the righthand lane instead. They are usually ones who have also *Crossed In Front* on the *SAFE AREA*. Instead of waiting for both lanes from the direc- tion of **C**, fig. 71, to become clear, they just wait for the outside one to be empty (or shielded – see page 231) and scoot into it, accelerating like a scalded cat. Although the growing popularity of this manoeuvre undoubtedly serves to speed up traffic flow at busy times, its safety depends upon a high degree of skill. Leave it to others until you are much older and wiser!

If arriving from **C** yourself, be prepared to have this happen in front of you, ill-executed as it may be. Harness your brake power; react – as urged on page 179 – whether or not you are turning.

Suppose **U** wish to cross the dual to go straight on, towards where **D** comes from in fig. 71. Any of the traps described for turning onto a dual can befall you in double-quick time if you are not maintaining your **Lane Discipline**, *thinking*, and **LOOKING WHERE YOU ARE GOING** – as well as at what may come your way. Extraordinary mistakes can happen at night and in fog. In fig. 71, **U** might turn to **W**, not realising it is the wrong half of a dual carriageway. Signs and layout should prevent such gross errors but be on your guard.

TURNS *OFF* A DUAL CARRIAGEWAY
Lane Discipline is here vital because higher traffic speeds make any sudden moves very risky. If you are going to have to change lanes for your turn (back into the left one or over to a right one), this must be *complete well before* the point where you are anticipating slowing down for the turn itself. It would be rude and dangerous to slow up immediately after overtaking someone, and thoroughly dangerous to so do no sooner than having joined a fast-trafficked, righthand lane. If you cannot achieve such a lane change as a separate, prior operation, it is usually best to abandon the turn. The safety of fast traffic behind – and your own – is at stake.

For leftward leaving, save holding up non-turning followers by slowing up mostly on the slip road, if there is one, using it *from the earliest possible moment*. At the slip's end, just before turning, eyeball the *SAFE AREA* (to your right) if one there be; if someone tries to whip across from there, let him. You may avoid being smashed into. You dare not leave him stuck across the dual – despite the priority, technically, here, being yours.

Fig. 72 shows a right turn *off* a dual. Wait in the forward, far half of the *SAFE AREA*, as shown, leaving room for anyone such as **A**, wanting to turn right, to come out onto it beside you. If the *SAFE AREA* is already occupied or is about so to be, wait near the front of the deceleration ''mini'' slip road, close in, like car **B** is shown here, until you are safe to move

237

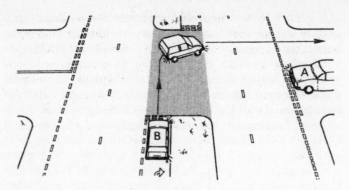

Fig 72 Right turns off dual carriageways.

forward. Do so even if there isn't a GIVE WAY line forcing you to cede precedence to any who need it. If you cannot yet finish your own turn anyway, you should always be prepared to let others through, as in fig. 65.

However, if a deceleration "mini" slip road off to the right – designed for your safety – is *itself* full, or is in danger of so being, or is conspicuous by its absence, you *must* anticipate such a serious snag; if possible, spotting it several hundred metres further ahead even than usual. Then, your extra early signal, *and* slowing down, can forewarn those behind you that you may all be having to stop in the fast lane . . . An arm, right-turn signal may help – see page 227.

Unfortunately, correct positioning in the *SAFE AREA*, as above, can (as ever) encourage idiots from behind to swoop up on your righthand side. They hope to nip ahead, off the *SAFE AREA*, before you move. Whatever you may think of them, the only safe policy and one which can, at least, be viewed from the moral high ground, is to let them. Of much greater importance is to spot them coming . . .

DO UNTO OTHERS . . .

As you drive along a dual carriageway, you can often help anyone, joining into your stream from the left, to come in earlier. Provided always that it is clear behind (and beside) you, simply move out one lane, well in advance of the junction. You move back later. This goodwill gesture enhances your own safety, too, against the chance he might have pulled out without having seen you. The *planned avoidance of danger*, here, combines defensive driving with doing unto other drivers as you would have them do unto you.

Wherever there are junctions along a dual carriageway on which you are driving, YOU must be prepared, as you pass through, for any sudden blockage that may strike as a result of the mistakes or pitfalls I have here described.

Truly, *in these circumstances*, speed kills. Control yours.

TRAFFIC LIGHTS

Study the traffic-light rules in the Highway Code. Go to some busy lights, stand and watch. Notice the *sequence* of the light changes even if you *think* you know. Review the lights from the point of view of pedestrians, too. Think about what those on foot ought to do. Observe what sort of things they DO.

You probably won't have to stay long before you see some drivers "shoot" the lights; that is, cross when they ought to have/be stopped. Either, they will be trying to rush ahead before green appears, or, they will be attempting to keep going and squeeze through after amber has come up. Amongst the two-wheeled fraternity are often found a "hard core" who weave in-and-out of slow traffic, turn "against" red, etc., with apparent impunity. However, to be fair to those *pedal-cyclists* among them, some traffic lights feature an advanced stop line at which those on *pedal-power* are allowed to wait a little ahead, in front of motor vehicles. Some even feature a priveleged waiting position for *buses* up front . . . All these are "streetwise" matters which concern you . . . Your eyes cannot afford to miss a trick, ahead, either side, or in your mirrors.

APPROACHING TRAFFIC LIGHTS
Mirrors, signalling, positioning, and slowing and selecting the right gear, can all be handled at traffic lights in a similar way to the methods used at crossroads, with a few adjustments as below.

Approaching Lights When Intending To Go Straight On
Imagine, in fig. 73, **U** are doing a shade under 30 mph and will be going straight on. Well before you reach the lights your long-range, searching eye (and your prior study/experience) will have told you what colour they are likely to be when you reach them.

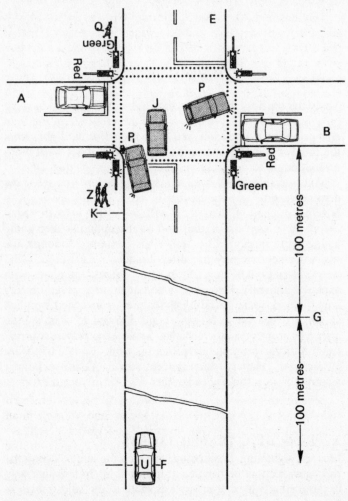

Fig 73 Traffic light timing.

240

For instance, if the lights *change to green* when U are only 200 metres away and with no one between you and the lights – as at fig. 73, F, were you to delete all the shaded cars for the time being – you would normally expect they will stay green until you have passed through them. There should be no need for you to drop below 25 mph.

Mind U, a few lights change again remarkably quickly, so be warned!

You must judge how fast is safe, allowing for the road width and for your stopping ability in such an event as that a pedestrian, like one of those at Z, in fig. 73, or maybe the one at Q, might step into your path. Take 3rd gear around G to give you acceleration "in hand". This will ensure that, even if you do have to slow down a bit more, say, for example, until you are certain Q won't step out, you can then pick up the speed straightaway as you pass the last danger point. Neither that pedestrian at Z nor the one at Q should try to cross in front of U; after all, red will be shining in their direction. But do remember that there are plenty of exceptional pedestrians!

Alternatively, if you can predict or should at least expect the light phase to change to amber and then red, before you reach it, you prepare to stop. Take 3rd gently from around F, then get down to 2nd gear roughly from G, 100 metres before the lights. You are ready to stop but, by being in 2nd, you are also furnished with the pulling power, should the light unexpectedly remain green, to carry on through, keeping up your speed appropriately.

It is correct to continue on amber *only if there is no time to stop safely*. Never go through after red comes up. If amber appears when you have already almost reached K, in fig. 73, you have to take the lesser risk – stopping or going – judging by traffic conditions. (You should already be in the correct gear, if to go on is safer.)

Because the amber phase should cater for any surprises, it follows that it is undisciplined driving to land yourself in an emergency stop for red. The streetwise anticipation given here above is the best way to prevent it. To approach a green traffic light above 35–40 mph – even if it was one the timing (or phasing) of which you knew well and it was in a wide, open space with no other people or vehicles around – would be too fast. The situation can alter too quickly. Hence, although there are lights at which to pass through a little faster may be safe, my descriptions, in this book, range around an approach of 30 mph or slower.

Approaching Lights When Intending To Turn

Return to fig. 73 and imagine, this time, that **U** are *going to turn at the lights*; as they have just changed to green, you anticipate they should remain so for your forthcoming turn. Right or left, there can now be pedestrians to whom you must expect to GIVE WAY. They are, indeed, *likely* to step out to walk across the road **A–B** just as you want to enter it. Take note that traffic along **A–B** has stopped for *them*, as well as for **E–F** traffic. For their direction of walking, the lights are showing *green*. Whereas, instantly **U** begin to turn into **A–B**, you are then moving "against" the red light of **A–B**, albeit properly and legally to make your turn. Therefore **U** must be prepared to stop for them at **P** or **P₁**, only completing your turn once the way is clear or they are making it obvious they would rather wait while you go first. If there is *anyone* in the vicinity on foot, your speed must be down to a mere trickle at the point of turning. **U** are thus ready (as always) to allow them the "red carpet treatment" reserved for kings, should they wish to cross.

Suppose **U** are going to turn right, in fig. 73, and, again, green is likely to continue until well after you arrive. You may well first have to wait at **J** – or a little less far forward if *Crossing In Front* is going to be necessary – before going round "through traffic" from **E**. Either way, if there are pedestrians walking across road **A–B** – *for whom you will have to wait* – do not move to **P** until there is *no* traffic coming from **E**, however far distant, or until what there is is already clearly stopping because the lights are now changing again. Otherwise, during a long, green phase for **E–F**, you can easily find yourself unnecessarily blocking the through traffic.

WAITING AT LIGHTS

As explained under **Traffic Stops**, from page 143, when you are stopped at red traffic lights, you should always use your handbrake and then come out of gear.

You are thus enabled also to relax your legs by releasing

your foot pedals. This fundamental routine, as well as removing any risk to pedestrians, has the further added bonuses of removing brakelight eyestrain for people behind (the glare can be considerable in wet weather or in darkness) and of preventing unnecessary wear within your clutch operating mechanism.

If you are first to arrive at amber or red, *gently* pull right up to the solid, white stop line. Avoid leaving several metres of unnecessary gap between you and the line. That just wastes time for everyone when the lights go green again.

While waiting, keep an eye in your mirrors so you are up-to-date there. Also watch the lights facing the crossing traffic, if you can see them, as well as for when that traffic itself, if any, starts to pull up. That helps you anticipate amber reappearing for your queue, this time with red still there. This red-now-with-amber phase has the same meaning as does solus red: that is **STOP**. It provides notice that green will appear in a moment or two, and this allows you ample time to select 1st gear and prepare for a **Smooth Start**. You are thus ready to go as soon as green comes on.

A word of warning is appropriate here. When you are at the front of the queue, you must never "jump the gun"! Never move before green.

Never assume that green means "go", either. Unless your immediate path is also clear, it doesn't.

Nor may you go at green if, in heavy traffic, there is not yet any space for you to occupy beyond the junction, whether you are going straight on or turning. Stay where you are – even waiting right through to the next green phase if necessary.

Look in the Highway Code and confirm that your understanding of each light colour, or combination, is complete. You will see why, for example, a pedestrian walking across (which can also happen anywhere in the queue, remember) is still king, despite green shining for you! If he is there, don't take 1st until he has passed. And believe me, if you want to avoid accidents, it is still your look-out, before you move on green, that no wheeled-maniac is shooting through across your bows on amber, or even on red!

Whenever you have been waiting for however little time, you must double check each side and behind, before you move on again. Waiting – here – also *includes* moments held up at **P** or P_1, in fig. 73, as described above. This extra check *especially* applies if you are turning – *or even shifting position within your own lane* – and it may well require a rapid glance over your appropriate shoulder first, particularly to make sure you are not going to knock some rider off his mount. Even if it may not strictly be your duty to Give Way, if there is any risk of a bump you are best always to let others move on first. My focus is on two-wheeled pests (the ones who push their luck too far), in this regard, because – although they are not the only ones – they do have a habit of infesting traffic light queues.

Yellow Box Junctions

In fig. 74, I illustrate yellow box junction rules in action at a traffic lights. They are common sense, and *should be applied to all junctions* (as urged in your Highway Code). We shouldn't need millions of litres of yellow paint to tell us not to block junctions – whether they have traffic lights or not. I would love to save the paint to tip over the drivers who do it!

The box junction principle is that, if your exit off a major route junction is blocked, you shouldn't move onto it yet; then you can't easily yourself become a blockage to someone else.

In fig. 74, imagine a queue of traffic ahead of lorry **B. U**, intending to go straight ahead, wait this side of the yellow criss-cross box as shown, even when the light is green, if traffic in or beyond the box has built up and blocked your exit from it. Don't go until you see at least area **C** is clear. But you can move up during green, ready to turn, if you are going to be turning right and only await a gap in oncoming traffic through which so to do (that is, provided the equivalent area **C**, in that road, is clear). However, if drivers from opposite you will also be turning right, be reminded of fig. 66, and the consideration for others that is needed, before any silly rushing forward.

The next snag can happen at other junctions but it seems to be a special favourite at red lights – perhaps because periods of waiting lead us into temptation! A large lorry is waiting at the front but there is room to move up on its left. **Beware!** It could be turning left! It simply needs the extra room so to do. Only last year, I witnessed a brand new small car being squashed beyond recognition against a steel, pedestrian

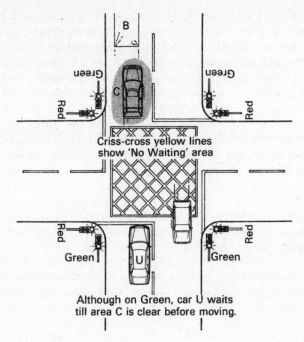

Criss-cross yellow lines
show 'No Waiting' area

Although on Green, car U waits
till area C is clear before moving.

Fig 74 A yellow "box" junction.

protection barrier by (as it happened . . .) a huge demolition
lorry. The deed was done in seconds; long before its driver, in
his noisy cab, woke up to why everyone round him was
hooting, flashing their headlamps, pointing or shouting.

A Little Right Relief

At many lights turning right is made easier. A phasing adjustment allows several right-turners through after all other traffic
stops, before renewing priority for the crossing direction.
Where that hasn't been built in, courtesy and sense have to
suffice.

Arrows On The Road

As shown in fig. 75, enormous white arrows, painted on the
road, often indicate which lane(s) is/are marked out for your
direction. Knowing the road enables you to take a correct lane
early but it is easy to be "on the arrows" before seeing what is

expected. Watch out for an "appropriate traffic lanes" sign (which you can find illustrated in the Highway Code) giving you advance warning of such (a) required lane(s).

Don't panic or swerve if wrong; from what you know of positioning, you should already be in a reasonable place for your intended path, and drivers around should be careful on seeing your L-plates. Check mirrors, then signal. Double-check your mirrors with a swift, backward glance to the relevant side; then move to the correct lane if you can. However, remember, **Lane Discipline** (from page 170) comes first. Unless there is time and a gap to do this, you may need to jettison your intended direction, and take one which the arrow on your lane directs that you *can*, adding a signal if necessary. You can always find your way back en route later. You will thus avoid holding up and annoying following traffic, and you will keep on the right side of the Law, too.

Look at **U** in fig. 75. Assume you intend to go straight on. If not already in lane by **A**, 400 metres out, then, allowing for traffic behind and perhaps beside you, ease to the middle or

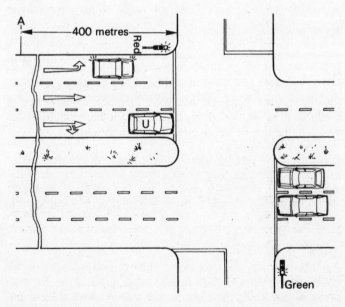

Fig 75 Arrows on the road.

right lane immediately you can do so safely. Always signal the lane change. As, in this instance, you will not be turning, cancel that indicator immediately its purpose is over. Here, you are correct in either of these lanes for going straight on, as both have an ahead arrow.

Your choice will, naturally, depend on what lane you were in to start with. It may also depend on whether the middle lane is relatively full and/or on whether anyone ahead may be turning right. However, do remember that, in traffic queues, you are not allowed to chop and change purely selfishly (see page 172).

TRAFFIC LIGHT SNAGLETS

On a multi-lane carriageway it is sometimes difficult to avoid passing through a traffic-lighted junction almost exactly alongside another vehicle. This can reduce your vision to that side dramatically. Try to time things so that you retain that view by being just ahead, or else drop sufficiently back to be well sheltered from that quarter. Remember that the sight-lines of the driver(s) you are alongside must be considered, too (see page 222). The Highway Code rule never to be overtaking at *any* road junction is, here, difficult to square with the realities of traffic conditions as you will find they exist. In the forefront of your mind, nonetheless, you must hold to the necessity of upholding it. You must do your best to apply its essence, as you pass through such traffic lights, in a manner consistent with the degree of danger and with the width of carriageway available to all parties. Being alongside another vehicle at that time may be inevitable; overhauling it ought never to be.

Banned Routes, Obligatory Routes

A great many traffic lights combine with other signs giving orders: no entry, no left (or right) turn, no U-turn, ahead only, turn left (or right), are common examples. Look out for them. They must be obeyed. They are often, though not always, mounted on the traffic light post itself.

Green Filter Arrows

These allow traffic heading in a particular direction to go, while red stops all other traffic or, perhaps, a separate filter also allows traffic to flow elsewhere. They may apply to left, right or, sometimes, to straight-ahead traffic. For example, see fig. 76. If a green filter lights for your lane, *go* where it points, *even if you have made a mistake*. You cannot simply obstruct correctly positioned followers. **Beware** though! Walkers, hidden by traffic waiting at red, may choose just that moment to stride across your filter lane!

If Red Reappears Before You Get Clear
At traffic lights, although you may have, quite correctly, moved forward ready to turn right, a chance to complete your turn, sometimes, does not offer itself until after the lights have again turned amber (from green). Fortunately, there is then usually time before red comes on (see fig. 65; this time imagining there are traffic lights), for **U**, **B**, **E**, **F** and **G** to take 1st gear and turn, and this is what you would do.

C, in fig. 65, not yet up to where the stop line of those lights would be, waits, as do **H** and **I**. If there is sufficient empty space behind them, **H** and **I** could drop back, if necessary, to help the others get clear. **M** and **N** – possibly (in extremis) throughout the whole of the next green phase in their favour – would have little choice before they could cross through the junction but to wait for all this to happen. (To be stuck at the front and have to miss a whole green phase, without moving, is not uncommon at some traffic lights at busy times.)

In circumstances such as these, it would be bad luck if, were you still to be stuck in the middle of the junction when the lights turned against you, a crossing, speed merchant, either

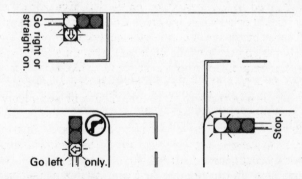

Fig 76 A green filter arrow.

248

shot off on amber (+ red) or was so discourteous as not to give you, an **L**-driver, a little extra time. If it happens, stop; wait (were you to be hit, whilst stationary, it ought not to be judged your fault); allow more-experienced drivers to circumnavigate you until the position opens. *Remember*, every red light has a green lining! Then, your teacher can guide you as to whether to go on, keep waiting until the lights change again, or back up – whatever is appropriate.

ONE-WAYS

One-way traffic tends to move faster and (to some extent) to crowd the lefthand lane. Perhaps drivers feel more comfortable sticking to their normal side. Nevertheless, you need to learn to use any designated lane, or to select the most appropriate lane which is free for your direction, whichever side either of these might be, or to choose a middle lane when that makes sense. When you are in a righthand lane, other drivers, joining your one-way from a street on that side, may not appreciate that it is a one-way they are joining. They may well be looking the WRONG WAY as they arrive to enter. Watch out for those dangerous types who seem automatically to stick their bonnet out a bit, too – before looking! Slow; consider a toot; above all, never fail to *react*, so that you could stop in the event of such a driver making a mistake.

You need to become used to having traffic – especially two-wheeled traffic – pass you on the left, right, or even on *both* sides at once, when you are in a one-way street or system. You must overcome, too, the strangeness of yourself legiti-mately passing other traffic on its left from time to time. And you must be prepared to make a right turn, like **U** are going to in fig. 77 – from the extreme righthand lane – not from the usual, crown-of-the-road, position. You will see plenty of sleepy drivers fall into that trap!

The key thing, if you ever have a doubt about what to do next, is to *keep to the lane you are in*. Slow down; stop, if necessary; but keep in lane whilst you work things out. Only change lane after having checked your mirrors and signalled, and when you have double-checked behind, by a flash-look over the relevant shoulder, to confirm that your move is safe.

Never wander. Never – except when crossing from one to another – straddle two lanes. You will find that most drivers do stay in lane well; and that they hold a steady course even where no lanes are marked. If you miss a lane change prior to a turning you want to take, go on until you can find another turning off, one for which you can move into lane in time. Take that turn and find your way back to your original choice of road afterwards. Never hold up a busy one-way; they are ONLY put in place to *ease* congestion and *stimulate* traffic-flow!

MERGING INTO LANE

In fig. 77, **U** want to turn right. Limitations of scale in my picture mean I must ask you to imagine that **U**, **B** and **C** are much less near to the end of the one-way than can be illustrated. Count the artist's break in the one-way as a good 75 metres; indeed, more would be better, unless unusual circumstances made earlier lane changing impracticable.

What happens at **A** and **D**, where – taking their respective paths – the different parties potentially could collide, will depend on the timing and, quite often, on the degree of give-and-take shown by those concerned. As explained under

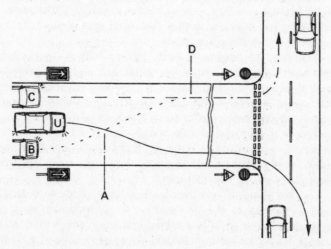

Fig 77 A one-way scrap?

Lane Discipline on page 171, the driver who is already in lane for his intended direction will normally take priority; the driver requiring to merge into that lane will, if necessary, GIVE WAY. Thus at **D**, driver **B** will wait for **C**, unless he can go ahead easily without **C** having to slow down.

Before that, what happens to **B** at **A**? U and **B** *both* want to change lanes in opposite directions, essentially at the *same time*! Here, both of you are, correctly, signalling already. As **U** have your nose ahead of **B**, he may let **U** go; *but don't count on it*. If he looks like cutting ahead, avoid a "battle". Scrapes and higher insurance premiums are the usual results. Guilt may be impossible to prove and, besides, your Practical Test examiner would take a poor view of an aggressive candidate.

The thing to do, once you discover that you are *both* needing to change lane, is to take a lower gear while **U** assess what **B** will do. Then, as soon as he slows, if he does, you can – provided that you still have sufficient distance, that there are no two-wheelers squeezing up between the two of you AND that *any traffic ahead isn't unpredictably grinding to a halt* – accelerate so as to nip in front without delay. If **U** have to slow up and cross over behind **B** instead, the lower gear makes that easy too. But remember that, by then, your mirrors may be telling you to wait for more traffic from behind **B** first . . .

Very often, in a one-way street, a chance arises to change lane long before you might need, finally, to have completed it.

Grab it. Avoid the possibility of any hold-up later. On the other hand, don't panic about changing lane and insist on trying to do it far too early; if your turning off the one-way is still half-a-mile away, that can cause an unnecessary delay, too. Stay in the lane you are in and keep your eyes "skinned". An opportunity to merge over safely will, as you all flow along, almost certainly arise in good time, encouraged by your signalling extra early.

As you merge towards either edge of a one-way, be particularly careful about roads entering from that side. People arriving to join the one-way *often* fail to look beyond the lane nearest to themselves. They don't expect you to be coming across from a lane further away . . . In the opposite situation make sure you don't make that same error!

Occasionally, you will come across a much wider one-way than depicted in fig. 77; one which arrives (in three or four lanes) at another multi-lane major road or dual carriageway, as the stem of a T; that other main road, itself, also having, say, two or three lanes each way. There would probably be a traffic light to control the extra volumes of traffic you would expect to find converging at such a spot.

In this type of place, left or right exits from the one-way are often made from two (or more) lanes, all moving ahead side by side when the lights turn in their favour. These drivers enter the appropriate lanes of their new road still parallel and alongside each other, at least for the time being. Therefore, you may *not need* to get to the lefthand-most (or righthand-most) lane in advance of such a junction. You can make your turn in a next-door lane and review in which lane you want to continue, later, after joining your new road. This double-laned entry to another big road allows much more traffic to exit the one-way at each change of the lights.

It is worth noting, here, that such double-laned turning sometimes takes place at wide, ordinary, two-way traffic lights, and also, quite often, where two dual carriageways meet in a T or where traffic lights guard the entry slip road of a motorway. Be on the look out for it.

U, in fig. 78, are having to cross the one-way street to reach road **B**. Imagine that heavy traffic in the one-way is, here, at a near-standstill, though individual lanes do, from time to time, open up and move. You have to wait for a sufficient gap to

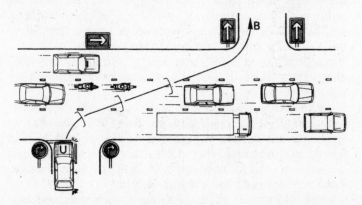

Fig 78   Crossing a one-way street in stages.

252

come free in the nearest lane, or for someone to wait for you, so that you can then move part-way out, switching to your left indicator as you so do. From there, your line should be more or less direct, as arrowed but, because of the traffic, the remainder of the operation is almost certain to have to be a stop-go affair, rather as the breaks in the arrowed path show. It depends on how traffic in each further lane which you need to tackle is flowing, on its speed, and on how easily you can merge across. Although drivers will often wait for you, you must avoid forcing anyone who is already moving up and closing a gap, to have to brake or slow; you could be failed for being insufficiently careful. In your haste to go when someone does wait, never forget to look forward **WHERE YOU ARE GOING**. Vehicles there may still be STOPPED!

AN L-DRIVER'S NIGHTMARE?
Look at fig. 79. This is not really a nightmare but it is well worth studying a big, city junction like this one, if you can,

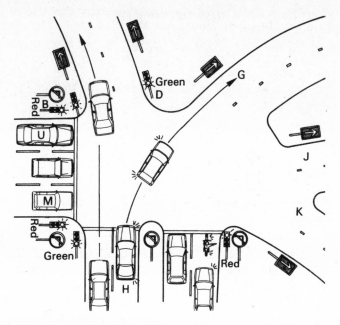

Fig 79   A L-driver's nightmare?

253

either on foot or as a passenger. You will gain useful insight for the day you arrive at one at the wheel. **U**, whilst waiting at red, must be careful to watch your traffic light **B**, and not, say, **D**, by mistake, because that activates the crossing traffic from **H**. It is easy to cause an accident by starting to move on the wrong lights.

If **U** are going to **K**, you ought to have been where **M** is but, though wrongly positioned, you may still, when green appears, be lucky and, after a thorough, direct look behind, be able to ease across (with a signal and great care), a little later – *always provided* that: (a) you have been able to confirm that there is, by then, no one behind you; (b) that there is no one else coming through who is correctly laned for roads **G** or **J**; and (c) that the lights have not, now, changed again! Otherwise, as you cannot abruptly turn sharp left without a signal either, you will have to move on at green and go to **G** or, perhaps, to **J**, if that can be done safely; and, into the bargain, you will have to accept that having to do that is your just penalty for being in the wrong lane.

ROUNDABOUTS

Roundabouts are clockwise, one-way systems devised to smooth the safe interchange of traffic from several roads at once. At the majority of them, there is more than one lane on each approach/exit road, and there are several lanes around the roundabout, too. **Lane Discipline** is therefore of paramount importance and, mostly, my descriptions concern these bigger roundabouts. However, the roundabout rules themselves apply equally to huge roundabouts, such as those betwixt dual carriageways, as they do to smaller roundabouts and, likewise, to MINI-roundabouts which (apart from their entirely different advance warning signs – as shown in the Highway Code) are just smaller ones still.

ROUNDABOUTS' SYSTEM
The first and principal rule of all* roundabouts is that, when you reach the broken line across your entry point, you *must GIVE WAY to ANY traffic from your right*. *Exceptions to this rule exist at a tiny minority of roundabouts; however, any different priority is always specifically marked out on the roadway.

Arrival

On approach take 3rd gear and, soon thereafter, 2nd, as you slow down sufficiently, so that you are fully prepared either to GIVE WAY should the circumstances – or any sudden change in them – so demand, or to move on purposefully, if you are clear so to do. (At a vast, empty roundabout, you might consider that 3rd gear would be sufficiently powerful to make both your entry and your exit safely. You would have to be sure, before using 3rd rather than 2nd, that there was neither any potential need for a further change down, nor any likelihood of having to stop at all, anywhere on the roundabout.)

Double-check your mirrors, *well* beforehand, so that you can indicate for and safely carry out a lane change, *SEPARATELY*; to be completed, if that is going to be necessary for the direction you require to take, *comfortably before you arrive*. You need to reach the roundabout in this correct lane, to be selected as described next. If no lanes are marked, *position your car on the road* along similar lines, so that you do not hog space others could be using. Think in lanes!

1) For the first exit left:
Use the lefthand lane, indicating left.

2) For an exit that is more straight on than it is to the right, **DO NOT** – other than, *briefly*, if necessary for changing lane beforehand – **SIGNAL YET**:
Use either the lefthand or the righthand lane – in that order of preference – taking account of the weight of traffic approaching with you, or already on the roundabout. With more than two approach lanes, here choose between a lefthand or a middle one, on the same basis.

3) For an exit that is more to the right than it is straight on, or for returning whence you came:
Use the righthand-most lane, signalling right.

During your final approach to the GIVE WAY line, by now down to 2nd gear and moving at no more than a brisk, walking pace, weigh up whether or not you will need to GIVE WAY to anyone from your right. If the answer is yes, pull up gently at the line. If you are clear to go on, go (that is why the power and flexibility of 2nd gear is so necessary); lose no (unnecessary) time; but lose no care, either – see *Entry* a few paragraphs hence.

Note well that, if someone is in front of you, you must also anticipate whether *he* will stop *anyway*, even if all is clear! Lots of drivers do just that, despite the very purpose of a roundabout being for drivers to keep going – if they reasonably can – so as to optimise the multi-directional traffic flow. No matter how daft he may be, you don't want to biff in the boot whoever is ahead, just because *you* may be distracted (by looking for traffic coming around the roundabout) from looking in front **WHERE YOU ARE GOING** ...

There may be pedestrians wandering across the neck of your entry road – *especially if traffic in another lane next to you has stopped*. Look out specifically for them. Hold dear their lives.

Should you reach the GIVE WAY line in an incorrect lane for your intended direction, think fast! What you do next may depend on how much traffic there is. You must not be inconsiderate and hold up other roundabout users because of your error – either those behind you to start with, or ones that would be messed up were you to bungle sorting yourself out on the way round. Therefore, be prepared to accept, straightaway, the ultimate "penalty" of your having to switch to a route correctly reached from the lane in which you have found yourself. If, however, at some point before duly exiting along that route, an opportunity arises safely to continue round the full circle instead, you may be able to solve your problem that way. Your teacher needs to be wide awake!

Entry

To reach **A**, in fig. 80, **U** have to consider car **B**. Unless you can clear across **B**'s route sufficiently ahead of him in time and space so that he could not possibly be inconvenienced, **U** must GIVE WAY to **B**. It certainly looks as if you would have to here! If **U** wait for **B**, you still cannot then go, without first double-checking on **C**, who, in fig. 80, has already begun his left indicator. Make sure that his front wheels confirm his route. I'm afraid that all too many drivers DO, just when you

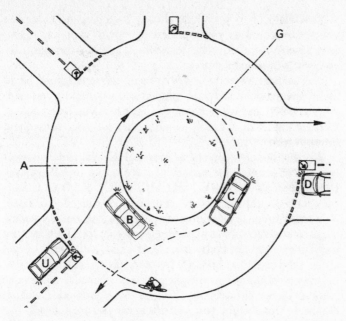

Fig 80 Roundabout priorities.

are not looking, change their minds! Once you have confirmation that **C**'s signal is *bona fide*, you may have time in which to go on, whilst you are shielded from **D** by **C** himself; but, possibly not – if **D** is quick off the mark . . .

Cars **B**, **C** and **D** are not all that need concern you here, as I hope, before now, you will have noticed. Your eyes must sweep *all* the tarmac to your right. Move your head about; you need to allow both for the blind spots, of which we all have one physically in each eye, and for the roof-pillar blind spots, etc., which, inevitably, will be somewhere in front of your eyes.

What about that pedal cyclist, in fig. 80 – to whom you must GIVE WAY – who is spinning around the outside edge of the roundabout, quite properly encouraged so to do by the Highway Code? (He may even be in a properly marked cycle lane that runs parallel, next to that edge.) *He will be crushed if your neck or your eyes are lazy.* (He ought to have warned **U**, with a brief, righthand signal by the stage I have shown him, but few bother, I can promise you!) What about motorcycle riders,

257

to your right or to your left, already sweeping up alongside you from behind as you are slowing down? You saw *them*, didn't you? As ever, yield to riders. They are exceptionally vulnerable at roundabouts.

If all is clear for you to carry on, onto the roundabout, being in 2nd gear should, as I have emphasised, now allow you so to do positively, and without risk of stalling. If you have to stop, then 1st gear will normally be necessary for your subsequent **Smooth Start**.

Whether or not you have had to wait, **NEVER** allow yourself to get over-excited the instant you see a gap to tail on into. **LOOK FIRST WHERE YOU ARE ABOUT TO GO**. Traffic, there, could have just stopped, right in front of your nose! You must, I repeat, double-check pavements as well for pedestrians, particularly for any crossing from your left. That does not mean they may not come from your right, too! Don't forget either (as I make no apology for also having said before) all manner of riders (to your right or left); especially those ones who specialise in creeping ''out of the woodwork'' and up alongside from behind you, particularly if you are delayed.

Only go, once satisfied there can be no danger from any quarter or to any other party. Remember, none for whom you should be GIVING WAY ought to be caused to slow down because of you. If what you thought would be your gap for which to aim vanishes (as, so often, such gaps seem to do!), be critically aware of the need then to reassess *afresh*, ALL ROUND.

Going Round
Continue to think in lanes! Stay strictly in lane round the roundabout, *even if painted lane-divisions are non-existent*.

1) For the first exit left:
Keep to the lefthand, outer, roundabout lane.

2) For straight-on exits:
Circumnavigate in the lane you chose on *Arrival* and *Entry*. That is what other roundabout users and your examiner will expect. (Should you, exceptionally, decide you really must change lane as you head round, make sure – as with *any* lane-change – that (a) you give ample warning, (b) you GIVE

WAY to anyone already in the lane to which you want to move, and that (c) you will neither place others at risk nor hold up anyone else.)

3) For a righthand exit:
Keep to the righthand-most lane throughout.

Exiting
1) A first-left exit should cause few problems:

However, caution must remain your watchword, as at *all* exit/entry points. There may well be pedestrians milling around the pavements at the neck of the entry/exit or, maybe, even squeezing their way through gaps in traffic queuing either to enter or leave the roundabout, for any one of whom you must be prepared to allow safe passage (see page 189).

Always take a prior glance across your left shoulder before moving off the roundabout lane itself. You are looking for that perimeter-spinning cyclist (see above), for whom, if you are to avoid knocking him off into the gutter, you are likely to have to allow the freedom to pedal on through.

Enter your new road in its left lane if there are several. Accelerate promptly unless traffic prevents you. Watch your mirrors at once; fast drivers/riders frequently choose this often safe opportunity to overtake. Check that your indicator cancels.

2(a) For straight-on exits *when you are in the lefthand-most roundabout lane*:

Begin signalling left (you have not yet signalled your *direction* at all, remember), as you are about to pass the entry point last before your exit – in time for anyone waiting/ arriving there, to see it come on. Continue as in 1) above.

Look out! *Before* you even reach that *previous* exit/entry – especially on a large-scale roundabout – someone from a middle or a righthand lane may swoop across, in front of your nose, heading for it! Seeing you in the lefthand lane he could, mistakenly, expect you to be taking it too.

In a bump, fault might be hard to apportion, although he should have noticed that you were *not*, yet, signalling left.

Against that, should you have given way to that driver, as he has come (basically) from your right (on a roundabout) or,

259

should he have waited for you, before such an apparently shameless attempt to barge across your lane?

In my opinion it would be the former; at least, unless only the rear half of your car was damaged, thus demonstrating that you were clearly well ahead in the first place. The Highway Code, indeed, stipulates that you show consideration for exactly the likes of him. That advice, take note, being exactly in line with the first rule of all roundabouts – GIVE WAY to ANY traffic from your right.

2(b) For straight-on exits *when you are in a middle or a righthand lane*:

You face the opposite dilemma. Begin your signalling left at much the same stage, or perhaps a fraction earlier – but not so soon that anyone could imagine that you were actually taking the previous exit.

Although circumstances might be such that it could be convincingly argued you had priority – as just examined above – you must, now, be prepared to allow anyone who is alongside, or nearly so, in a lane to the left of yours, either to enter the new road first, or, indeed, as *remarkably often happens*, to swing on round the roundabout to a later exit!

The alternative plot – of cutting across his bows to your exit, on the basis that it's up to him to give way anyway – only leads to bumps and huge expense, even if you do win any legal argument later; and it's just not "worth the candle". Only go on if you are certain from his actions that he will wait for you so to do.

Such a driver could have popped out from the previous exit itself, or may have zoomed round from somewhere further behind you. Don't swerve about; just slow – continuing in your original lane for the time being – or pulling up, calmly, if necessary, until you are free to move across and access your exit. (Never *reverse*, if you have gone too far; just circle the whole roundabout and try again.)

Where your exit road has several lanes on your side, you can choose to join any of them; however, in your learning days, it is generally best to use the lefthand lane as your preferred option. Note, however, that ample lanes and space of this sort *may* enable you to join it at the same time as (and parallel to) someone on your left (or vice versa). Only do so, provided *you are certain* that the other driver *is* going in the same direction as you and that he cannot be compromised by your action. If you were the one in an outer lane, you would need to decide quite shortly thereafter whether now to overtake him, or to fall in behind (see **Keeping To Your Lane**, page 136).

Again, look to your mirrors and your indicator cancellation as soon as you are into your new road. Pick up speed promptly, unless a traffic jam or good reason is stopping you.

3) For a righthand exit:
Hug the roundabout-island edge until you are in line to leave – when **U** reach **G** in fig. 80. At that stage, or maybe a fraction earlier, as has been explained, you switch your right-hand indicator (which, you will recall, should have been on all the time) to signalling left. Continue from here onward just as described from 2(b) above.

ROUNDABOUT SNAGS
Traffic frequently grinds to a halt (or even stops suddenly) on a roundabout; so, your eyes must be, systematically, "every-where". (Significant causes of such blockages are the dilemmas of **Lane Discipline**, as detailed in 2(a) and 2(b) above, and vacant minds – for which see six paragraphs on, below.)

On approach to *any* roundabout you must cast your searching eye mainly to the right and to the front but, never forget, in your mirrors, too; then, as you progress round the roundabout, you must, also without fail, keep flashing them ahead, right the way round (and on, into the exit you want); all of this being punctuated with direct glances to the left and across your shoulders, as required, so as to cover other entries/exits prior to your exit, and your mirrors' blind spots too.

At any stage whatever, if you have a single doubt about another driver's/rider's destination in relation to where you intend to drive, hold back. Stay where you are, slow up or stop, accordingly. See where that individual *does go*, first. Drivers of little brain change their minds and/or wing round and off roundabouts very fast. You may not see them often but good judgement of just how very quickly such antics can place you in jeopardy will, I can assure you from my experience of Learners, take much longer to acquire than you expect.

If on Practical Test you re-routed yourself – unable to merge over to the lane you needed – your examiner shouldn't fail you; however, he might do so for any stupid or panic actions that revealed plain inexperience. So get plenty roundabout practice.

Remember that your good roundabout positioning and your correct speed will, almost by themselves, tell others where you are going. *Make sure they are telling the right story.*

Extra busy roundabouts have traffic lights' control full time or at peak hours. White destination arrows may adorn the lanes on the approaches and going round. Beyond the entry lights may be more sets of lights before you take your exit. Normal traffic-light rules apply when the lights are in use. Arguably, by alternating the priority between those entering and those on the roundabout, they assist traffic coming in, and the phasing ought to help clearing through to your exit but this doesn't happen if drivers are silly. See next paragraph! Obey all the roundabout lane selection and discipline rules above, whether or not the lights are working: they apply identically except insofar as the lights take over who has priority. Remember them especially if ever simultaneously passing through green lights and changing lanes on the roundabout itself or en route to your exit. Obey destination arrows, too. To assist traffic flow, they may dictate another lane for your route than one you would have picked. To avoid accusations of careless driving, be sure only to make your exit from that lane and, once in it, do not exit elsewhere!

Treat every roundabout as if it were a yellow box junction (see page 244). If your route *out* of a roundabout is blocked, that really is no excuse for sitting, mind vacant, strangling an earlier entry (or exit) point; especially when other drivers (including those who may come along before you are able to get clear) could, perfectly easily, make their way to or from different (open) exits, if only you had left them room.

Several roundabouts (or mini-roundabouts) sometimes interrelate and work in conjunction with one another. GIVE WAY to traffic from your right as you transfer across between them. Look beyond the nearest one for traffic coming, as it does, suddenly from an unexpected quarter; some drivers swirl through these multiple-roundabouts fast! These layouts often include points where traffic already *on one of the roundabouts* has to GIVE WAY to traffic *entering* that roundabout from another one. (Yes, this *is* the reverse of the first rule of roundabouts – page 254!) GIVE WAY lines across the roundabout lanes will be clearly marked. Be alert!

Huge one-way systems round buildings or whole blocks often equate to vast roundabouts. Combine roundabout principles with those of ONE-WAYS as appropriate.

Horse riders *should* keep to the outside perimeter and, like cyclists if they do it, give a righthand signal if they intend to ride *past* any exit. Some hope! I suggest always giving the animal a wide berth and precedence if ever the rider needs it.

Beware of big lorries! They often cannot avoid straddling roundabout lanes, or even pulling right across your path before they can negotiate their route at all. That means you can be crushed. (See also page 244.) Why argue?!

Mini-Roundabout Snaglets
Imagine going straight on at a mini-roundabout while someone from the opposite direction, giving no signal, appears to be of the same mind. Without warning, he swings round across in front of you to turn right! You get a real fright once it dawns *you* were meant to **Give Way**. Assume nothing until you see *from his front wheels* that he will be going straight – especially if he is going slowly enough to be able, instead, to give you a sudden turn! Tight space may mean some of your wheels have to mount the mini mound itself. That's OK but mustn't excuse cutting brazenly, needlessly across. Stay alert as above for lorries or extra long vehicles which have no such option . . .

UNMARKED CROSSROADS
NB: *No Vehicular Priority In Any Direction*

Mainly found in residential and country districts. When snow conceals all road markings you may need to treat affected junctions as unmarked too – especially ones lacking signposts (see page 88). The life-preserving rule, from whichever direction you may have arrived, whether or not your road appears to have a higher status, is to stop, or be prepared to GIVE WAY *to all, unless they clearly stop for you*. If it is blind in any direction, listen, and hoot, if necessary, too, before you go. Remember to be looking, as you set off, in that direction from which danger could spring its nastiest surprise.

In fig. 81. **U** must watch that vanman **K**, suddenly appearing at the edge of your sight-line, perhaps thinking of other things, doesn't just sail out, without seeing **U**. With the buildings, and being in a van with poor side vision, his view is restricted. *YOU*, therefore, must slow more than otherwise you might, lest **K** really does dream on out.

K is in danger again if he, mistakenly, presumes **F** (who intends going down the main road) wants his road. Gaily

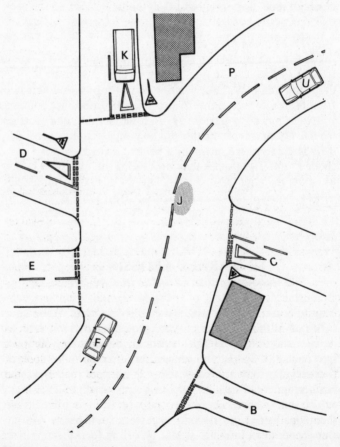

Fig 81 A multiple crossroads.

roaring out, he and **F** would, quite probably, *crash!*

If **K** wanted to go right to **D**, he would go to **J**, when safe, making, from there, a proper right turn when clear. *He must not cut straight over.* If he wanted road **E**, he would, to make his intention 100% clear, delay signalling until after **J**. **U** should signal normally for **K**'s road but, in each instance, choose the correct moment to begin signalling for either **D** or **E**. When your signal can so easily be misinterpreted, the key issue becomes to position correctly and carefully adjust speed to make it obvious to all which turn you intend to take.

Were someone to be coming out from **D**, to go left, along the major road, he would signal left whilst still within the neck of **D**; he would cancel his signal at the instant of setting off, and steer directly towards **P**, so that, were **K** still to be awaiting his opportunity to emerge, **K** could hardly misinterpret this plan. The driver from **D** would still keep an eye, however, lest **K** did misunderstand!

EYE CONTACT

At any junction never be fooled by the naive idea that apparent eye contact with anyone else on the road justifies believing you have both instantly read each other's mind. Misunderstandings *do* happen, even with gestures or nods.

Neither must you assume, because a driver, rider or walker has looked your way and seems to be waiting or preparing to give way, that he *has* seen you. He may have looked (even in his mirrors . . .) eyes wide asleep, brain dead – as we all do sometimes. Still less presume that *he will do* what you would do in his circumstances. Anyone can make a mistake. (Suppose your presumption of what he correctly should do is plain wrong!)

The safest thing to do about direct eye contact is to treat it as but one human (i.e. fallible) factor in confirming your own right course of action. Pay far greater attention to his look of "urgency" if any, position, speed, chances of error, the weather and road conditions, likely actions of others about, and so on. Above all – especially where you may have [theoretical] priority – position yourself intelligently and get your speed down to match risk.

7

Tricky Conditions

BAD WEATHER

FOG AND *SERIOUSLY REDUCED* VISIBILITY

As a Learner, avoid pea-soup fog. When qualified, do the same. The finest drivers can get enmeshed in terrible accidents, knocked on from behind, smashed across from the side, or whatever, through no fault of their own. Fog tires your eyes and brain fast and seems to fool them, too. So, why risk being out in it? Consider a hotel – if you are far from home. If you must drive, my advice, right or wrong, is stay off the fast-trafficked duals and bigger roads, the ones prone to attract multiple smashes. Phone home too; that takes the stress out of any worry that your relatives may be alarmed by your lateness.

IN FOG CONTAIN YOUR SPEED WITHIN THAT FROM WHICH YOU CAN STOP IN LESS DISTANCE THAN YOU CAN STILL SEE IS CLEAR – FROM MOMENT TO MOMENT.

See, and be seen! In fog – when visibility is *seriously reduced* – the law requires you to have both sidelights and headlights **on**.

Seriously Reduced Visibility, you will find, is decreed by your Highway Code as being when vision has dropped down to 100 metres or less. No difference between daylight and darkness is, however, stipulated: presumably – because the same *seriously reduced* definition applies to when you may choose, *in addition to headlights*, to switch on front and/or rear foglamps – it follows that at night 100 metre visibility means *with* the aid of headlights and, if any, moonlight and/or street lighting.

Be that as it may, I mention it because the legality of driving at night in a properly lit, 30 mph, built-up area using sidelights only (which personally I oppose doing anyway) is plainly overruled whenever visibility is seriously reduced.

The necessity for headlights in my view, extends well beyond fog. In particular, I would include in broad daylight (never minding in darkness) such times as when there are threatening squally patches, cloudbursts, teeming rain, unusually excessive spray, and hail or snowfall.

When severe, these are all – while they last – very definite, headlamps-on, daytime conditions if you seriously want to be seen. Whilst such conditions turn drastic, as, frequently, they do, if only for a brief period, you will, naturally, want your front and/or rear fog lamp(s) on, too, unless you have none.

As in fog itself the law limits use of either front or rear fog lights to when vision is *seriously reduced* (100 metres or less). If you don't want to be, quite rightly, stopped by the police and accused of driving without due care and attention, or worse, you simply **MUST** remember to switch off *all* bespoke fog lamps, directly their need has passed, *day* or *night*. They are piercing, dazzling lights, especially at night and, when used unnecessarily, cause dangerous eye-fatigue to others. Get to grips with their switches and what the dashboard reminder lights look like. Don't join the thousands of sleepyheads who fail to turn them off directly conditions of *seriously reduced* vision have abated. They are breaking the law!

In fog, you are nearly always best to keep your headlamps on dipped beam. High beam produces a back-glare off the misty droplets, and restricts vision rather than helps. Be sure your windscreen does not start off, or become, steamed up inside, by running your demister at full, *hot* blast. Keep a clean cloth handy for an emergency wipe. In damp fog use windscreen wipers frequently – continuously if necessary. There can be no excuse for making matters worse with either a fugged up or a fogged up windscreen! Take a moment to clean all your lights and reflectors, too.

Maximum, sane speed, in dense fog, may be walking pace or less. Satisfy your conscience that your speed is safe. Glance often at your speedometer so you know what it is! It takes will-power not to be tempted to "hang on to his back lights" and try to keep up with the man who whizzes past too fast. He may have superb eyes, or even lights; more likely, however, is that he is one of those "born every minute". Being mesmerised into undisciplined driving, in this way, ends in countless crashes. If you are reduced to next-to-no-speed at all, following the pavement edge or, in the country, an edge line or the verge, using whichever is there as your guide, so be it. Range your eyes ahead, around – and up for traffic lights. Otherwise, over-concentrating on the kerb could find you past a GIVE WAY line, or an amber or red traffic light, before your brain registers.

Whatever else you do don't be tempted to follow a centre line . . . like the fool coming the other way!

Wherever you might cross the path of other traffic (or vice-versa and regardless of whose priority it may be) at roundabouts, crossroads, when turning right etc., you may be wise to stop, keep your brake-lights on, listen out through your open window, and perhaps even sound your horn before moving on.

Patchy fog can mean *real trouble*, especially at night. It is even more frightening if driving fast but, unfortunately, it is on the very roads through open, low country, where speed tends to be higher, that infrequent patches are most common. If caught unawares, slow right, right down at once. Get your headlamps/fog lights/rear fog lamps *on*, fast. **NEVER** speed on, hoping that you will pass rapidly through this patch at least. (It might turn out to be just you that passes – rapidly elsewhere!) Once you know there is fog in the air, drive slower, much slower. When you see the fog clamping down again ahead, slacken speed to a safe level *straightaway*. To risk panic stations, by running into a wall of fog too fast, is madness. When, later, you go on motorways – after your Practical Test – remember that "motorway madness" *is* just that.

FIRST SPITS OF RAIN, HAIL, SNOW, ETC.

Wipers, used on too dry a screen, can scratch it and ruin your wiper blades, as gritty dust and dirt is swept back and forth. Worse than that, your vision can be "wiped out" as grease and dirt spread into an opaque, blinding film, before your very eyes! Sometimes, switching your wipers off again, for a moment, lets that "grease" evaporate, offering you temporary respite.

Always look at the road, NOT smears on your screen.

Be prepared:

(a) *Before* you switch on your wipers, slow down ready for reduced vision. Choose a lull in traffic/danger which will last at least until you can see clearly again. Wherever possible, take the opportunity for that first switch on at traffic lights or similar halts.

(b) Let appreciable wetness build up before you switch on, and use your windscreen washer from the outset to clear dirt and insects quickly. (Top it up weekly at least, not just with water but with a cleanser which should help to clean away dust and grime.)

(c) Deploy your intermittent wiper setting so that, between wipes, raindrops can accumulate again, ready the better to wash the screen at each wipe. On some models the wipe-frequency can be adjusted to great advantage.

(d) Activate your demisting heater fan full blast and your electrically heated rear window, from the outset of rain or snowfall, until you have any misting-up under control; but keep a clean cloth handy and stop and use it if you have to.

(e) Make sure you have clean, effective wiper blades, with a clean windscreen, and a clean bonnet too. (Muck from there quickly makes its way up across the screen.)

(f) Always have de-icer additive in your washer reservoir in winter. Otherwise, in any sudden Arctic conditions you risk instant, wide-screen, icing over, blinding your view completely.

Maximum heat demister blast, fan-boosted onto your inside windscreen, also becomes essential in this degree of cold *before* you dare operate your wipers, and certainly before you risk using the windscreen washer. Your inner screen must be warm first and you must then keep it warm.

(g) Carry a plastic scraper for emergencies. Humble it may be, but it is still the most effective tool for removing windscreen ice, and it never runs out! (Snow or ice must be cleared from all windows, wing mirrors, lighting units, number plates and, not least, your shoes, before commencing your journey.)

(h) Transform wiper blade power by renewal before each winter, or at least once every 10,000 miles. Keep a sponge handy to wipe the blades clear of grease etc., whenever needed – with a little fluid help squirted from your washer reservoir. This may be necessary at every stop on a filthy night on a motorway. Boost your lightpower too, with a clean of all your lights at every rest stop, particularly in winter when salt off the roads can quickly make you wonder if your headlamps are even on. This takes mere seconds; *no more than it takes to knock down someone you might not otherwise see.*

NIGHT DRIVING

As an advanced Learner, you are almost sure to want to gain some (later stage) practice at night, even though your Practical Test will be in daylight. There is no better way to consolidate your Theory understanding of night driving, either; so, although I don't recommend you to go out in the dark on day one, I do suggest that you have, say, 10%, or more, of your practical tuition after dark, if you can, once your teacher feels you are ready for it.

I remind you of the former, general Highway Code instruction to use your headlamps not just 'at night' (as it now says) but from within the half an hour *after* sunset and, similarly, right through darkness, until the last half hour *before* dawn.

From the tick of lighting-up time (given in daily newspapers) until the following sunrise, it is illegal to drive (or to park, except where regulations, which you must study in your Highway Code, allow it) without sidelights on.

Your headlamps *must* be added shortly thereafter, as just explained; unless within a 30 mph speed limit in a built-up area and NOT including urban motorways, there are street-lamps alight at less than 185 metres apart.

Sidelights, naturally, remain obligatory on the move, however well the road is lit but, frankly, in my view, this exception and lamp-post density test is somewhat of a theoretical technicality because most drivers nowadays realise how essential headlamps are if you are to be seen, and the days when car electrics/batteries could not cope with all the demands upon them are long gone.

The fact is that in lighted town and city streets (where, thankfully, only a few – mostly ancient – drivers still seem to delight in the legality of switching them off) *having your headlamps on saves pedestrians.*

They also alert people leaving side streets; those who take a quick look and pull out; who should not [do that] but do. In their, too hasty, glance, these drivers miss mere sidelights, especially if their attention is drawn, instead, to a vehicle correctly *using headlamps*; that is, one further behind what, on sidelights alone, might as well for all the difference they make, be a completely blacked-out vehicle when thus "eclipsed".

So, as recommended in the Highway Code, have both your sidelights and headlamps on during all official lighting-up times – wherever. Use them in tunnels, too, even those which are well lit. This way you will be seen, as well as able yourself to see. By all means switch them off if you are stuck in gridlock or, perhaps, on wet nights while stopped awaiting your turn at junctions; this cuts glare for the driver ahead and is especially helpful as he reaches the front of the queue but always switch them on again *before* you move on.

A dim-dip headlamp setting is featured on many cars. The Highway Code recommends its use as an alternative to dipped headlights at such times as well as on dull days. I prefer full, dipped headlights but with dim-dip you can choose. However, remember that for *Seriously Reduced* Visibility (day or night), full, dipped headlamps are obligatory. Dim-dips will not do.

WHICH BEAM?
In **STAGE ONE**, Chapter 2, you should have learnt to find and use the headlamp on/off switch and the dipswitch, by touch and feel. Did you also spot the (usually) blue dashboard warning light which, when your headlamps are on, tells you whether or not they are on High Beam, penetrating their furthest? You must recognise that warning light before you can drive safely at night, so that you can be certain that you are on dipped beam whenever necessary, and vice versa.

1) Whenever you are following, or catching up with, another motor vehicle, your headlamps must remain *dipped*.

This should prevent dazzling its driver via his mirrors. If you feel that even your dipped headlamps are causing him difficulty, drop further back. When traffic is moving on well, the forward pool of light cast by your headlamps, on dip, makes a good

271

minimum following distance anyway; one which keeps the cut-off level of that intense light-fall well below his rear window.

If you are dazzled from behind, you can use the anti-dazzle position of your interior mirror. Beware, however, that the mirror then distorts and reduces what you can see, giving the impression vehicles are further behind than, in reality, they are. I prefer, instead, to offset my interior mirror a little and retain a truer picture. Avoid letting your eyes become transfixed by such dazzle and, if ever you cannot stave off being blinded from behind, slow right down, until your eyes readjust.

2) Always dip before turning at junctions.

3) With nothing going in your direction ahead of you, High Beam is *essential to see properly*. However, it MUST ONLY be used when there are no oncoming road users who might be dazzled or discomforted. That includes the humble bicycle and, sometimes, even pedestrians.

4) *Whenever someone is coming the other way – dip*, but make sure you return to High Beam immediately you pass by each other, provided no one else now approaches.

In busy, town streets you may only rarely be able to use High Beam, for obvious reasons. But don't let that make you lazy once you hit side streets or leave the suburbs! It is when driving through the countryside that the use of High Beam most comes into its own. Use it whenever you can. Try not to dip again, until just *before* the headlamps of a first oncoming vehicle themselves appear in the distance. You will quickly learn to judge – from the growing strength of his light beams – exactly the right moment. As you come up to the brow of a hill, or the onset of a bend, you can normally see these beams, extending ever closer, for quite a while beforehand. Were either of you to dip too early, all the advantages to the other, of becoming aware of, and being able roughly to gauge the speed of approach of, your opposite number, early, are lost.

Remember to apply exactly the same rules above on dual carriageways and, after your Practical Test pass, on motorways. It is just as much your duty to protect oncoming traffic on the *opposite* side of such trunk routes from being dazzled by your lights as it is anywhere else.

Outside urban areas, safe night driving depends very much upon all this proper use of the headlamp dipswitch – *by everyone*. Traffic streams, otherwise, build up rapidly behind slower drivers at night. The many lazy (or perhaps fearful) ones, unable or unwilling to use High Beam, invariably head such 'everlasting' streams, as they meander along on permanently dipped beam. This selfishness particularly irks faster drivers on single carriageway, country main roads. Time and again, they miss safe overtaking opportunities because their long-range vision can extend only the length of that permanently dipped beam on the vehicle ahead. Their resulting impatience – equally inexcusable as it may be – often leads to dangerous risks being taken. On dual carriageways and motorways, overtaking drivers are, similarly, tempted to 'blast past', risking insufficient clear forward vision until they can put up their own High Beam.

5) So, always help yourself to visual safety, as in 3) above, by using High Beam whenever your road is clear ahead. Doing so, as here explained, will also ensure that you never frustrate anyone behind who wishes to overtake you. Dip directly anyone passing you has taken the lead. Remain dipped, at least until he has moved ahead well beyond the range of your High Beam, before you, yourself, revert to using it, if that continues to be appropriate.

SPEED IN THE DARK
AT NIGHT, CONTAIN YOUR SPEED SO THAT YOU CAN STOP WITHIN THE DISTANCE YOUR HEADLAMPS SHOW TO BE CLEAR – **ALWAYS**.

Maximum safe speeds, on High Beam, will be slower than in the day and, on dipped beam, considerably slower.

If dazzled by oncoming traffic, YOU *must* slow or stop until *you* can see. Never risk shut eyes or panic steering, or blame others; *you* are responsible for your driving. Reduce dazzle by concentrating mainly upon seeing your own side of the road properly. Where there is a white, continuous edge line this can help you stay on track. Never gaze, "hypnotised", directly at oncoming headlights; that prevents you from seeing pedestrians, cyclists or obstructions on your own side. Look *where you are going*, **NOT** at those lights.

If an approaching driver has forgotten to dip, an early, *brief*, single up-flash of your lights may remind him; it may be to his benefit, too, if he then dips, saving dazzle for others behind you. Deliberately to cause him dazzle or discomfort, however, is *illegal* and dangerous.

Be aware that glistening, wet roads worsen dazzle both in bright sunlight (when you may need sun glasses and/or visor rapidly to hand) but perhaps more in darkness when less reflective clothing and surfaces may also remain hidden, deflected from your view until too late. Rain itself substantially blurs night vision too. Make allowances.

NIGHT TIPS

Imagine yourself driving through the countryside at night, using High Beam, and there being no one else about at all. In such circumstances, dipping your lights down and back up in a couple of "flashes" can be used to help announce your imminent arrival at hazards – for example, approaching a bend, a junction with a minor road, a hump-back bridge or a hill top. *In the momentary seconds you are dipped, you see approaching light beams more easily. Back on High Beam, others, yet out of sight of you, see yours*; the quick contrast, as you dip and un-dip, itself drawing their attention, too. However, take care not to dazzle anyone already waiting at the mouth of a minor, side road, waiting only for you to pass by. Dip, and remain dipped, for their benefit. On a sharp lefthand bend, having "flashed" in this way, you may need to use dipped beam going round, to avoid any chance of dazzling a surprise oncomer. By contrast, on a fierce righthand bend, it may be safe to round it on High Beam, provided you are ready to dip at once, if necessary; the direction of your light beams will be such that they won't dazzle an oncomer at first sight, anyway. If ever you are in doubt whether you should take a bend on High Beam, give potential oncomers the benefit of that doubt; dip. Slow down more, too; you must match your speed to the instant reduction of the distance now ahead of you that is still being effectively flooded by your lights.

It is crazy and illegal to drive with just one headlamp. Oncomers can mistake you for a motorcycle, until it is too late!

There's little point, either, in lighting up dirt on the outside of your headlamps! The answer to this problem is on page 270.

Never reverse at night unless you must, and never further than is essential. If you do, get out and look first. Seek an assistant to guide you if possible. Though the Highway Code contains no specific reference to reversing in the dark, you may find it useful to put on your hazard warning lamps briefly. This helps you to see, as may flicking your brakelights on intermittently with a light touch on your brake pedal. Both tips improve the poor vision most automatic reversing lights give and, importantly, are likely to help alert someone suddenly coming on the scene as to what you are doing.

If you need to wait at the kerbside for a few moments in the dark, be sure your sidelights are on but your headlamps are off. Headlamps blazing on a parked vehicle at night somehow penetrate extra fiercely, even when dipped, and are a serious danger to other traffic. At night, whether you are waiting or parking, you must always face your car in the same direction as the traffic flow on your own side of the road.

Downward beam adjustment for heavy loads that otherwise push your light beams alarmingly skyward is very important. You may have a cockpit control knob or a garage can oblige.

'CALAMITIES'

BURST TYRES, PUNCTURES, STEERING

With a puncture you usually get warnings, e.g. heavy steering (although loss of power assistance would also cause this), bumpier ride, wandering, general worsening unbalance. If you suspect something, or firm (or light) braking makes you swerve, check ALL your tyres. Pay attention to shudder or vibration at any wheel. You may just need to have it re-balanced. But beware of any tyre carcass degeneration with bulging inner/outer walls or slabs of tread about to be thrown off.

A burst (blow-out) is rare. Provided you avoid hitting kerbs at speed, you may never have one. If you do, you may hear the bang or hiss or, if you have hit some fallen object, expect it, but possibly your first warning will be a sudden "chattering", bumping noise and/or a feeling that the car wants to veer. *Act*: *never panic*. Grip your steering more firmly. Keep straight, unless you have to steer to get past immediate danger.

Aim to slow and stop with no braking or the gentlest possible braking space allows, to avoid further unbalancing your car. Should it swerve anyway, or circumstances allow you no choice, you may have to battle with your steering and/or brake harder to avoid hitting anything or going over a precipice! Once your speed is right down, signal left and pull in – *off the road* if possible. If unable to avoid temporarily obstructing traffic, use your hazard warning flashers. A red warning triangle also displayed, well to the left on your own side and at least 45 metres behind you on an ordinary road, may be essential. They are inexpensive; never drive without one.

Place it further back if traffic arriving might not see you in time. Notice that the Highway Code forbids their deployment on any motorway *lane* – where even trying to do so is too dangerous – but that they can help protect you when on the hard shoulder, if placed at the left and suitably far back.

Before changing the wheel consider your life. Relentlessly passing traffic may make calling expert help your safest bet.

SUDDEN POWER LOSS

Your engine splutters and conks out. Perhaps your accelerator snaps, or a drive shaft fails. Maybe you are out of fuel. Directly you realise you are grinding to a halt, get your clutch pedal down. This should enable you to coast a little further and, mirrors permitting, if you are quick enough, even to get the car off the road into a safe position. Failing that your starter may help you exit danger. See **Stalling** shortly. (Note: wise drivers *never* travel on a nearly empty tank . . .)

WINDSCREEN SHATTERS

Stop as quickly as safety allows. If the opportunity exists so to do, try to get off the road, before some idiot hits you. My advice, then, is to telephone and have a screen specialist come out and replace it immediately. To attempt to travel on, vision distorted by cracks, or peering through a crazed screen which might suddenly cave in, is asking for big trouble. You will probably have seen drivers who try to carry on whilst looking through a bashed-out hole. They endanger others and risk fine particles of glass whisked into their eyes . . .

STALLING

Stop and hold the car on your footbrake; bring on your handbrake at once and return to *neutral*. Re-start quickly (remember your engine start routine – page 33), so you can then move yourself out of danger. Make sure you are in the right gear this time, if that has been the problem. If your engine refuses to start and you are about to be hit, then, as a

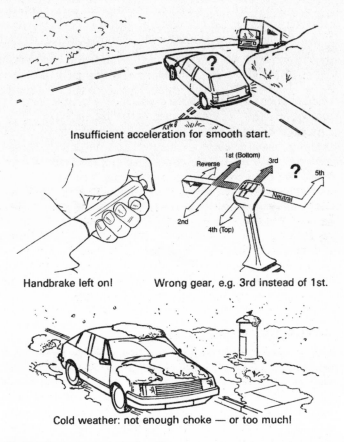

Insufficient acceleration for smooth start.

Handbrake left on!   Wrong gear, e.g. 3rd instead of 1st.

Cold weather: not enough choke — or too much!

Fig 82 Common causes of stalling.

"life-saver" – for example, to get your car off a level crossing – move on the starter, in gear. The strength of the battery and starter motor should easily take you to safety, off the road if possible. Use 2nd or 3rd gear (or reverse if appropriate), clutch up. Unfortunately, with automatic transmission you cannot employ this last resort.

Stalling is one cause of many grave accidents at junctions. Avoid being a victim. Vouchsafe always to remember what figs. 58 and 82 have here emphasised.

BREAKDOWN

If you break down on a fast-trafficked road, don't just sit there! Activate your hazard warning lights at once. Drive your car on its starter, as explained under **Stalling**, above, if that will take it safely off the carriageway or else, on, into a less vulnerable stopping place. Failing that, summon help to push it there, if at all possible. Then follow the breakdown and/or accident, Highway Code, advice you should have learned so thoroughly when you were immersed in Chapter 3, page 91!

An open boot-lid, with a back-seat squab or a spare wheel leaned up against your back bumper, is a universally recognised sign to warn people coming up from behind of your trouble. An open bonnet alerts people from ahead. Other than on a motorway always deploy a red warning triangle (correctly positioned) and/or cones, as well, if you can (see page 276).

BRAKE FAILURE

Don't freeze. Pump your brake pedal on/off/on several times; then continue to hold it down really hard. Either action may restore partial braking: few brakes fail totally at once. "Crash" down your gears, harnessing engine braking. Add firmly held handbrake. The latter won't help much but it's worth having and works best once you are nearly stopped. Warn everyone, with flashing headlamps and/or rapid-fire – long beep, long beep – horn. Look for any safe escape route. Miss all you can, rather than hit soft, human flesh, another vehicle head-on, or anything hard, like concrete or a big tree. If that means leaving the road *before* your speed could run away on a steep descent, or as a last resort, grip your steering tight as you go for it.

FAST DRIVING

Driving too fast for your personal ability to cope safely creates emergencies and leads to terrible frights. Skids, crashes and death or tragic injury for innocent people are the inevitable results, whether or not you kill yourself.

Nevertheless, driving reasonably fast, hitting the best average speeds, genuinely within your honestly assessed capabilities, can, particularly if it tends to raise your concentration and attention, hone your skill and make you a safer driver.

The first necessity is the *self discipline* constantly to match speed to conditions, never exceeding the maximum speed for safety, *even when that is under walking speed*. The hallmark of the **SAFE**, fast driver – and it's no paradox – is actually his *slowness*, his almost obsessional slowness in potential danger, where others rush on, without thought. You may not "see him for dust" otherwise, but that is one of the key features that consistently marks him out from the fast fool.

The second prerequisite is skill, built on experience. Until you have *several hundred thousand* miles at the wheel behind you, don't even consider faster driving. Please believe me: you are still a babe in know-how.

The third indispensable requirement is fitness. This must include first-class eyesight, hearing and speed of reactions. Lack of stress is vital, too. Never argue with passengers and still less on a mobile phone. Never allow irritability, tiredness, annoyance, illness or temporary discomfort (e.g. hunger, cold, needing a lavatory, etc.) to influence your driving. A bereavement or any major personal loss or catastrophe can, at the time or for several days, upset your driving very considerably. Never drive whilst your mind may be temporarily unstable.

Finally, you must be willing to accept restricting yourself according to the quality of your car. Tremendous extra stresses and strains affect a car driven fast. A car built for speed – a precision machine, also maintained regardless of cost – is quite different from many, so-called, sports cars, or the ageing, family banger. Forget any fantasy that your car can match a brand new Ferrari – unless it happens to be one! In that event, your obligation to drive it at a level of skill and responsibility fitting for the make will, I hope, always take precedence over any desire for undue or illegal bursts of speed.

SKIDS

Skids always arise from *lack of anticipation*. Drivers go recklessly fast when space for manoeuvre is tight and, even worse, when road-surface conditions are also tricky – gambling that no emergency will ever happen. Of course, one day, one will.

Skidding is the predominant factor in single vehicle crashes. This supports the view that inexperience and ignorance play the biggest part; the ignorance, unsurprisingly, going hand-in-hand with excessive speed and failure to anticipate. In truth, skids are much, much easier to avoid than to correct. Skid recovery is an art, *not a dependable science*.

A few exclusive cars have computerised traction control and other roadholding devices. However, space precludes their discussion here. Much more important is that we all grasp the viciousness of skids as they affect the majority of vehicles.

Locked Brakes
"Locking", first mentioned in Chapter 2, describes when one or more road wheels *stop turning*, momentum (weight x speed) thereafter taking the vehicle along with that (or those) wheel(s) sliding.

With locked front wheels, caused by continuous excessively harsh braking, steering control evaporates. There may be a loss of sideways control at the back, too, when your rear wheels slide. On wet surfaces your stopping distances also increase beyond recognition, because your brakes lock up so much more easily. You slide, instead!

Cut dry-road speeds by at least 15% for wet roads. Double or even treble your *THINKING* time, *braking* gap if you seriously want an accident-free life.

Anti-lock braking systems (ABS) largely eliminate the brake locking problem. See pages 129 and 294. However, they may only reduce overall stopping distances, even for the most skilled driver, by very little; so cut those speeds!

Under heavy braking, a huge transfer of the impact of the weight of your vehicle suddenly bears down on its front wheels. You see the nose dive. It's not surprising, therefore, that the hold against the road, exerted by the tread "footprints" of each front tyre, has a limit which will be beaten eventually. A locked-wheel slide *is certain to take over, if you continue to brake hard enough*. Less obvious, perhaps, is that, because weight is also *lifted, off* the back wheels, by the braking, they will usually be first ones to lock.

The added momentum which results from going *downhill* will cause this tyre adhesion to be broken *dramatically* sooner. On the turn (e.g. for a corner), additional (wheels') rolling resistance and sideways weight re-distribution further exacerbate your problems.

Aquaplaning

On wet roads (any that are more than just damp), traction (road grip) gradually lessens as speed rises, until your tyres, instead of gripping, are sculling on a film of water. As a water skier will skim the surface at speed but sink when he stops, so it is with vehicles. We call this phenomenon "aquaplaning".

Photographic evidence proves that, with rear-wheel drive, a *front* wheel stops revolving as it aquaplanes, and that this effect sets in from as low as 65–70 mph – a critical speed, and one severely reduced where road drainage is poor or if your tyres are balding. (Judge the quality of a road surface by comparing the amount of spray being thrown up by other vehicles. Much less is thrown up from surfaces with good water-dispersal.)

With front-wheel drive (and four-wheel drive) you can, by contrast – though it won't always happen – instead get *front* wheel wheelspin, the onset of this being even at 60 mph or less.

Either way, steering control vanishes from aquaplaning front wheels – here, with your front wheels physically separated from any chance of early retrieval.

You sense the onset of aquaplaning through your steering. Lift off your accelerator instantly but don't brake. Grip your steering straight, so that you won't be wrenched round when your front wheels re-contact the road. Don't keep repeating the experience! 'Skimming' along at the 'edge' of control is madness.

On a good tyre, the tread absorbs surface water, then squelches it out behind and away to the sides. The road contact area of tread is only about the size of the sole of a big gum-boot; however, it works its wet weather "magic", by the revolving of the wheel bringing a constant, fresh supply of "thirsty" tread, with which it mops up the loose surface water. This it stores within its "footprint" during the fraction of a second before that leaves the tarmac again, as it continually "processes" and ejects it. Thus it is that bald tyres, which can no longer do this job, are illegal.

Aquaplaning **DOESN'T ONLY REQUIRE SOME MASS OF SHEETED WATER TO HAPPEN**. It will hit you on *any* wet road if you drive too fast. With luck you may hold a straight course. But you have had it if you need to turn . . . The slightest puff of wind or other change to the precarious overall balance of your aquaplaning car, can, I must also warn, throw you at the mercy of the gods. Prevent such terrifying dangers, by keeping your speed on wet roads *below* 65–70 mph, and well below when sheets of storm water are about.

Locked-Brake Aquaplaning

On drenched roads, locked brakes also rob your treads of the processing mechanism – explained earlier, above – for clearing away excess water. This is perhaps the deadliest yet least understood aspect of aquaplaning. Your wheels not only slide; they aquaplane, until again allowed to rotate! They can "ski" down to 10 mph, or less, unless released. Until you get your foot off your brake, that mass of surface water, now a "torrent" because it can't get away, works like a continuous "wedge" in front of each wheel. All this water lifts those wheels affected into aquaplaning and exponentially escalates your apparently helpless, unsteerable, unstoppable, onward trajectory. Even ABS brakes may not cope well in these conditions.

SKIDS WHEN BRAKING HARD
The Mechanics

Over-worn tyres court death. Replace them. Keep your best treads on the front wheels. They provide around 80% of your braking effort, 100% of your steering and, with front-wheel or four-wheel drive, motive power too.

Replace worn shock absorbers. They are there to dampen the up-and-down reactions of your springs at bumps. Skidding is encouraged by such wallowing, and this will be accentuated on any road made uneven, for example, by subsidence.

Slow punctures, at the *back* as well as the front, can cause a lurch sideways, instantly you apply your brakes. Suspect them if you notice heavier or wandering steering.

Wrongly adjusted brakes or oil contaminating any of their linings (usually from leaking hydraulic seals) may have equally drastic effects, the more violently so, the faster your original speed and the harder you apply them. Have your teacher test them on dry, empty road, first from slow and then from higher speeds. Brakes which appear normal from 30 mph can mask a fault lethal from 70 mph. So, he must test with caution. Observing this will give you a feel for what good brakes *should* do. When you have your full licence continue occasional testing yourself, so that you always spot falling brake efficiency straightaway. Do this when you have an extra load, too, so that you can visualise the *vastly* longer stopping distances needed, and the increased possibility of losing control.

Any brake warning light coming on or any loss of brake performance demands immediate investigation. Air can enter brake hydraulic fluid. Its effect is to make pushing your brake pedal feel spongy instead of firm as normal. Should pumping the pedal improve things, you can be pretty sure air *is* getting in. This can happen if all the brake pads/linings are low and the fluid reservoir level falls below the minimum level, or you may have some faulty seals somewhere in your hydraulics.

For all these reasons and because brake wear differs with every driver, brakes really MUST have regular maintenance.

Braking Technique
In the quickest stop, your road wheels at no time lock but you are braking to the point of locking throughout. Your tyre grip depends on the uninterrupted supply of fresh tread maintained by keeping your wheels rolling. Directly a wheel locks, a tiny footpad of tread abruptly finds itself scraping along the tarmac which, if it is dry, will leave a trail of skid rubber. On a wet road, lubricated by the water, it will, instead, simply slide or, worse, you may suffer *locked-brake aquaplaning* (see above).

Consistently to apply the exact maximum pedal pressure that will not quite lock any wheel demands practised skill

283

(notably absent amongst those of the tailgating mentality) or ABS computer-controlled braking. (If you have ABS read from page 294 in conjunction with my description on page 129 but also make sure you understand what follows below.) If you do not have ABS, here is the exercise I promised on page 128. It will equip you to recognise locking brakes and to ingrain that skill – with the correct reactions to them – now in live practice, as distinct from theory.

You need a *wide, quiet road, with no traffic.* Remind yourself of the basic theory from page 280. Then do some trials, combining with that theory my more explicit instructions below. *Work on a dry day first,* before trying on a wet day – preferably at the same place so that you discover the dramatic difference a little water can make . . . Each time, your teacher should demonstrate before you try – to focus you on what to expect in the prevailing road and weather conditions.

Without ever exceeding 20 mph, practise fastest possible stops. More speed too early could be dangerous. Keep well away from the edge; look out in your mirrors; abandon your test stop if traffic appears from any direction. Treat each attempt like an emergency. Hit your footbrake fast. Squeeze hard – to the point where a wheel locks – instantly easing a fraction when this happens – to unlock. Equally instantaneously (for a locked wheel frees up that fast), squeeze again with resolute pressure to the lock point, ready to ease – only ease, note – before restoring the same firm pressure directly it unlocks again.

By repetition you strive towards the ideal that stops you fastest – holding your brakes on the point of locking throughout. Progressively harder pedal pressures (which come naturally!) become possible as your speed drops.

For these ''emergency'' stops your car should halt in a reasonably straight line. (The amount of sliding and how quickly you stop will depend on how adept you become at working your brake off and back on at every hint of a wheel locking. Your skill will be tested harder when you come to wet roads.) Slight loss of steering direction or of sideways control at the back is allowable but any serious loss, provided your steering was straight, signals a *mechanical defect* that needs looking into at once.

Practise at every lesson, until you can confidently minimise your stopping distances, wet or dry; and, though always keeping comfortably within your capability, from gradually higher starting speeds.

Add in some *downhill* stretches and see, for yourself, how massive is the extra distance you need when going downhill. Try *uphill* too; you will find, conversely, how the hill, then, helps you stop.

How To Handle A "Real Life", Unexpected Braking Skid

Let go your brakes and steer as straight as possible, instantly. (Turned steering, remember, encourages brake locking. It also promotes getting your car into a spin.) *Resume braking at once*. Use the method just described, until you regain control.

During a desperate stop from any very high speed, *there is always danger of slewing round into a spin* – EVEN ON A DRY ROAD.

Once destabilised, there is a dramatic abruptness with which you can find yourself spinning more, going backwards, or crashed. This will happen particularly if, in panic, you lock your back wheels and 'freeze' on the pedal. They want to lock first, you will recall, because all the vehicle weight is thrown forward, lightening their load. (Conversely, the increased downward pressure at the front tends to improve grip there – at least in the early stages of excessive, unrelieved, harsh braking.)

Once locked into a slide at high speed those back wheels will quickly drift sideways if any centrifugal force is at hand. Somehow, it always is! You can practically guarantee that, if you are braking so hard that your back wheels lock *and* you are too slow releasing them, you will spin at least 180°.

Backsliding, if it begins to happen, whichever way, must be counteracted very swiftly: a) steer *into* the skid – left if the back slides left, right if backsliding right; and b) simultaneously, be sure that you ease your brakes enough briefly to unlock those back wheels. (You won't, if it has temporarily vanished, recover your steering control, either, unless you do.)

You should, thereby, be able to stop the back sliding, and then at once resume your former heavy braking, if appropriate; always, remember, steering as straight as possible.

Too Late! You Are In A Spin

Stay with it! Most spins subside within 180°, and the vehicle rolls on backwards. Getting the steering straight helps this. Quick wits, in putting the brakes on once running back, may save you from smashing something solid unnecessarily. Having come to rest, move out of danger if possible, or set your handbrake, switch off your ignition and abandon ship – with care – and then comfort passengers away from danger. Don't sit and be hit!

Don't Follow The Crowd!

The mind of the *thinking* driver is continually planning away subconsciously! Immersed in any high-speed flow of traffic, he will be giving thought to the danger that might be posed by an amateur, braking, up ahead, were that stream suddenly to have to slow rapidly. He knows that, were such braking to develop into a spin, his own *THINKING* time, *braking* gap would have to have *already* expanded. Otherwise he might be left with no escape from all the "flying" metal that could swiftly come his way.

This is because he knows, too, that, if the first, amateur driver happens to wallop into those closest by himself, the incident may then rapidly escalate, as others, *driving too close anyway*, follow suit . . .

Traffic Grime

Whenever it first rains, an accumulation of traffic-created dust, oil, flecks of tyre rubber etc., becomes absorbed into an invisible, greasy film. This can make black ice (see below) seem friendly! Traffic lights, roundabouts and sharp corners seem to be very susceptible (justifying the cost of non-skid surfacing at many junctions which, though not perfect, has saved untold accidents). Only prolonged heavy rain clears the slipperiness. Damp patches appearing on dry roads are real traps because you tend to come on them fast. Diesel spillages take first prize!

Your chances of stopping quickly, or *even slowly* sometimes, in such treacherous conditions, are often similar to those of retrieving a soap tablet from a foaming bubble bath! Feather-light braking still locks your wheels. Fortunately, if aware that conditions may be ripe for such a slithery patch, you can conduct a gentle test; or else a feeling of lightness in your steering or a slight, 'tail waggle' skid may warn you. *Accept that warning as a major alert.*

Foreign Bodies On The Surface

Your tyres grip gravel, loose chippings, wet leaves, mud, etc., but these themselves then slide over the road; your first experience of this may be your last! Likewise, shiny surfaces like cobbles, white lines, yellow box lines or tram tracks can fool you – and, when they are wet, "take you (all the way) to the cleaners"! (On a motorcycle a single wet drain cover can be all it needs to spur you in that direction.) In very hot, sunny weather, patches of tar may glisten and soften, turning alarmingly skiddy; on cheaply maintained, minor roads this can affect the whole surface and become very dangerous. You often get advance warning from a "sticky", ticking noise that sets up and emanates from your tyres.

Black (Invisible) Ice ... The Surprise Killer

Take the hint if you see lorry or other professional drivers going slowly, or motorcyclists putting their feet out, or if ice is forming on parked cars. Much over 10-15 mph on black ice is extremely risky; usually you must be going *slower*.

Even in the icy blasts of winter, in city conurbations the weight of traffic, and gritting and salting (another good "clue"), usually keep important roads passable. Overnight frost quickly melts. However, scientists tell us that the watery residue remains skiddier – because of the salt content – than pure wet. The city driver is, nonetheless, thus largely insulated from extreme cold conditions. A generation of so-called drivers has grown up who "haven't a clue" in snow or ice. At the start of any cold snap you see them strewn about, impaled upon bollards or each other, etc., their combined incompetence turning whole districts into grid-locked traffic jams.

How then, do you detect black ice? A wintry hue in the weather, and the forecast, begin the alert. The most significant clue is usually in the speed of any temperature drop, rather than in the mean temperature itself. A sudden drop below freezing, which follows earlier melting or rainfall, can freeze water before it can disperse or evaporate from the pores in the road surface. Or, you can have "freezing rain". The wet road looks its normal, shiny self. In reality it's a skating rink!

You can usually distinguish mere wetness from black ice in one of three ways: *By ear* . . . through a slightly open window you can, at modest speed, hear the characteristic hiss of tyres on a wet surface. On ice all is quiet, deathly silent. Be cagey – because sometimes, even with the hiss, the ice has not melted right through to the road. You are running on water but it is still on top of ice! *By tyre-watching* . . . once the ice is melting substantially you can see, on a vehicle in front, tell-tale spray thrown up behind its wheels, particularly on sunny, frosty days. *By testing* . . . check doubtful surfaces by judicious but *gentle* test braking. Choose safe places where you cannot get into a bump – including one from behind! Maintain eternal vigilance on changing road surfaces. Treat suspect ones with enormous respect. Always slash speed until a test confirms it can safely be increased. If gradual icing is likely, test wherever your suspicions are aroused. You must know your road surface!

Again, front-end lightness or tail waggle, like the camera, cannot lie! Nor can instantly locking brakes. React to any of these at once. Slacken speed to 10 mph or less *as soon as you possibly can* but: don't jam on your brakes and skid to kingdom come! Keep really slow until sure you have a better surface.

Beware: 1), the unbeaten track – for example, met when turning across the middle of a road; 2), shaded patches yet unmelted; and 3), stretches particularly exposed to biting wind. All harbour ice. When driving out of town on a winter's morning there may be no sign of ice in the suburbs but, when you reach open country, you can discover that, whereas everybody else is fully aware of the ice, you are the only one who has not spotted it! It may only surprise you the once . . .

On widespread black ice, vehicles can become unstoppable, and just slide wherever wind, slope or road camber (see page 290) take them. In case you meet this, admittedly rare, circumstance, I must warn you that *10 TIMES* your normal *THINKING* time, *braking* gap still may not be enough.

On thin (or thick) ice, dismiss conventional notions of stopping distances. Work on trial and error, testing and re-testing, so that you are 100% aware of your stopping ability (or lack thereof) at all times. Otherwise, a 200 metre skid is by no means impossible, and it could all be yours!

Note: Wise Learners, having absorbed this section and the next one, will want to avoid driving on snow and/or ice, until after passing their Practical Test. (Indeed, the Highway Code suggests avoiding non-essential journeys in snow.) With that much more experience will be time enough to get behind the wheel in arctic weather. Then, if/when opportunity knocks, try not to miss it! For there is no substitute for again seeking permission to use some *deserted*, flat ground, for example, a large *empty* private car park at a week-end, when snow blankets in. There (with, if you are sensible, your teacher back beside you) you can discover in safety the limits of your car and your skill. A minute or two skidding around in the snow may scare you rigid. A few sessions of a couple of hours, or more, getting stuck, getting out again, spinning right round or sliding the odd 50 metres helplessly out of control, all from well under 15 mph, *may teach you more than the whole of this book*. It is best to have a couple of mates along too, to share the experience (and some of the pushing!).

If severe wintry weather drops in before you are ready, a good teacher can "show you the ropes"; but do observe them from the (comparative) safety of the passenger seat, until such time as you have your own, full licence and a good measure of personal experience.

Snow Or Snow With Ice On Top

If snow is likely, always carry additional warm clothing, and have a full tank of petrol – just in case you are stuck in your car for a long time and need to have the engine running to keep warm and alive. Be prepared. You might be forced to leave the car in a safe position and walk to safety.

On fresh or falling, settling snow, 15 mph is probably enough. Twenty miles per hour is often *much* more than enough. Where snow gets packed down and ice forms on top of it, you need to be back *under* 10 mph, and testing . . . "Locking" can occur instantly on braking. It can even happen to the front wheels when all you do is try to alter course!

Pick your track onto virgin snow wherever you can. Even if you can only get one side of your car off the beaten track, the overall grip/traction which you can obtain should be improved. Although, when you brake, your wheels may lock nearly as quickly as on the more icy parts, at a sensible and very slow speed, the snow-plough effect, as they each have to push a quickly-mounting pile of snow, should help to stop you.

For stopping on snow – fresh or packed down – use gentle braking. If your brakes lock on the touch then, instead, work your way smoothly down the gears until you can grind to a halt in 1st, using engine compression control. (Try to avoid skid-inducing jerks each time you let in the clutch in a lower gear.)

Approaching a downhill slope, drop speed to almost nothing and get into low gear *before* you arrive. (For a steep downhill, 1st gear may be necessary.) Thus you avoid risky gear changing mid slope. Other than in impassable conditions, you should be fairly safe to venture down, only letting speed rise little by little, and holding back as soon as you sense it may be getting too high. Were you ever to lose control downhill you might even have to take to the edge or jump the verge – pedestrians permitting – as your main hope; but the important thing is not to get into such dire straits in the first place . . . You may worry that the car will stick through lack of speed. Don't (worry)! That is a damn sight safer than losing control. I will deal with keeping going, shortly, when I come to wheelspin slides. Meanwhile . . .

Adverse Camber – *a lethal multiplier on snow*
See fig. 83. All roads have an inbuilt camber. Their surface is generally curved in a slightly convex fashion; the road centre-line being constructed higher than the edges. If you could take a sectional view across at right angles to the road, you would see

Fig 83 Adverse camber.

290

why, in foul weather, rain-water will always drain away from the middle and towards the gutters. On well-engineered roads this cambering effect is re-designed at sharper bends, so that both sides of the centre-line slope the same way – into the inner angle of the corner. The revised camber tends to help a car cornering too fast on the outside of the bend, to stay on the road. Where the engineers haven't cambered a road properly in this way at a bend, then what is known as *adverse* camber, far from helping, acts as a positive hindrance to vehicles sticking on the road – much exacerbated when the surface is wet. In Area **A** of the badly built road in fig. 83, the camber is distinctly adverse.

On snow or ice you must make use of road camber when it is in your favour and become critically aware of when it is not; even a bumble-bee's wingspan on to the wrong camber can throw you into an accident skid – perhaps instead of a harmless slide into the nearside grass verge. Whereas the slope of an adverse camber applies a lethal multiplier to the effects of centrifugal force and/or downhill momentum/gravity, helpful camber counteracts these forces. Your problem is to learn, in safety, how to relate your driving to the camber. Fundamental to achieving that is correct cornering technique, coming next.

Brake Not On The Corner . . .
WHEN YOU APPROACH ANY CORNER, ALL NECESSARY BRAKING MUST BE COMPLETE BEFORE YOU REACH IT.

"*Slow* in *fast* out" at corners is an old racing-driving motto. "*Slow* in *drive* out" (not so fast) should be yours *whatever the weather conditions*. Otherwise, you will soon discover that skids (when braking too hard and too late) are no fun on corners – even in the dry!

If you brake, or are still braking, once you begin to turn, like **U** have been doing in fig. 83, and your wheels slide (which, as explained earlier, is more likely anyway when your steering wheels are not straight), several forces instantly gang up against you as well. Centrifugal force tries to whirl you out off the bend. Momentum wants to take you straight on. Any adverse camber will, as discussed, speed you on your skidding way. Downhill, the potential dangers inherent in all these factors are, never forget, hugely increased.

291

If **U** arrive at the apex of a bend at a speed well over the top, as in fig. 83, the chances are that **U** will skid straight on, if once **U** slide, whatever corrections **U** try to make. Even if **U** get your foot eased off your brake quickly enough to kill the initial straight-on skid and regain steering control, **U** may still be in trouble from the above unholy trio of forces, further round the corner, by then in the clutches of a deadly All-Four-Wheel skid – for which I can only offer scant help (see from page 298).

Therefore "*Slow* in" is crucial. But why "*drive* out"? Because your renewed, forward traction, then helps to take you where you want to go. It counters the nose-dive of braking and redistributes the weight more evenly between the four wheels as you go round.

You should begin re-accelerating lightly from a little *prior to the apex* of the corner, all slowing or braking (as stated above) having been completed well before that.

When you take a bend correctly, you can feel the car perky and squat on the road, instead of lolling over towards the two outside wheels, as will happen if you arrive too fast, and precariously close to overcooking it.

So, the "*drive* out" technique is as vital an element of safe cornering as is the "*Slow* in" routine. It is the *combination* of the two that should keep you well-balanced and safe throughout every corner. To have the one without the other, though better than nothing, can never be half so good.

In the context of avoiding skidding, therefore, I reiterate that you must complete all braking before a turn or a bend. In the course of *normal, smooth, safe driving*, however, your objective should be always to time your approach so that *such braking is hardly required anyway*.

That's what good driving is all about.

You have to relate your reduction of speed to the sharpness of the corner. That reduction must be sufficient in all the circumstances of wet, snow, adverse camber, available vision, being downhill or whatever, to enable you then to "*drive* (through and) out", with only a light touch on your accelerator until you are again on the straight, safely on your way.

Never *over*-accelerate on the way round the bend; otherwise that is, indeed, where you will be presumed to have gone! Doing so could cause a nasty over-acceleration skid, about which see on a few pages.

If the bend is sufficiently sharp to dictate a speed slow enough for 3rd or 2nd gear, get down to that gear well before you arrive. It is important not to have to change gear in mid bend. Being in the right gear from beforehand enables you to take a bend properly, STEADILY, under very gentle but constant power, and then pick up your former speed, without delay, directly you come out of it.

Get down those gears *smoothly*, using the changing down refinement of my page 152. On a treacherous surface, a bad match of engine revs to road speed, as you changed, could be, were you to be close to the limit of adhesion, all it needs to make your driving wheels lock, which – at the least – will trigger a temporary skid, until speed drops.

Last Resorts

In extreme danger (through ill-judged, late braking) you may, to save life, have to give your steering priority over your braking. Remember: while your front wheels are "locked", you *cannot steer*. Only in the moments your foot is eased off the brake will you have a chance so to do. (However, if you have Anti-lock Brakes, you may manage to achieve both at once. I will return to ABS in a moment.)

Faced with having to save a human life or, perhaps, immediately to avoid certain self-destruction, steer for *the least dangerous course*. Choose a glancing blow against a wall rather than a direct hit on a telegraph pole or a head-on smash. Alternatively, in extremis, you might have to mount a kerb, provided no people could be placed at risk. Forced over an edge to avert a disaster, hold your steering wheel tightly as you steer across it at a reasonably sharp, not a shallow, angle, or you may risk bouncing off, back into danger, and perhaps having a greater chance of being overturned. Your wheels and tyres may be ruined but, with luck, you will be safe.

In fig. 83, **U** should have braked *harder earlier*, while on the preceding straight. At this late stage, far too far out in the road, **U** would need to brake gingerly, if at all, so that if the grip of your tyres were, with luck, to be strong enough, you would still get round without upsetting your balance. However, if you knew in your heart, bones and water that you weren't going to make it, and **B** appeared, you might well need to choose the honourable sacrifice of going – deliberately – through the hedge at **G**, rather than having a head-on smash a split-second later. That might depend on what evasive action **B** was taking (that is, if he was sufficiently wide-awake to react).

In Chapter 5 (page 129) I wrote how ABS brakes should take over the unlocking of your brakes so that skidding is almost eliminated. I must now warn you, however, that ABS may be no better at very low speeds on *snow*, *ice* or *mud* (or gravel or wet leaves) than an ordinary brake. Indeed, on some models the ABS computer can (and should) be switched off while you dance the very slow-speed slither. It can also suffer with *Locked-Brake Aquaplaning* (page 282) or may succumb caught by a diesel spillage.

Those apart, emergency braking is transformed in almost all other conditions. Nevertheless, it needs plenty practice of straight "emergency" stops with your teacher, beginning from slow speeds, on both dry and wet roads. No wheel should lock, however harsh your braking, even on wet. Provided you brake consistently hard, each stop will be the quickest possible. The added, life-preserving bonus with ABS is that you can also steer almost normally – because of the fact that the front wheels virtually cannot slide and lose their grip. Being able to steer to avert danger as you brake may one day save your own or another life so it deserves a lot of attention and practice.

If you have these brakes, try and get additional emergency stop practice somewhere safe, away from all traffic, where you can deliberately add steering, gauging how much is possible in modest increments. A large, empty, wet expanse of tarmac is ideal. Cardboard boxes, as suggested in Chapter 2, stood two up, are invaluable here, too, because you have to learn to look where you want to steer – that is, towards empty tarmac *beside* the object and not at the object itself – if you are to succeed in missing it. This is the best way to learn "live" the extra skills steered-braking demands, ready for that ultimate emergency.

OVER-ACCELERATION "WHEELSPIN" SKIDS
This exercise gives first-hand experience of wheelspin. With your teacher, find a long, gravelled drive; one where you can obtain permission, there is no danger, and you can sweep the stones back afterwards. Or look for an already muddy edge to

a playing field, again, with permission!

Do a standing start in 1st gear, using rather fierce acceleration as you let the clutch up fully and quite sharply. Your
driving wheels should spin at first. You stop that at once by
cutting your acceleration. *Don't touch your clutch pedal.*
There is no need. The wheelspin ends the instant you cut the
power. You should immediately regain control of the steering,
too, if that was lost. Likewise, loss of any sideways control at
rear driving wheels, if you have them, will be scotched. You
can immediately restore (much less) power, and drive on
calmly (almost) as if nothing had happened. You won't need
many tries before you can cope adequately with take-off
wheelspin; not that it should occur more than very rarely on
the road, other than in deep-frozen weather. That is the time to
be on your guard. Snow, ice or mud can make some get-away
wheelspin of the driving wheels inevitable. Then, minimising
acceleration is the main antidote. Also, use the highest gear
that will just pull, without your engine stalling.

The game is to get this right *first time* or your wheels very
quickly dig in. Keep your front wheels straight or you make it
harder. A better game in these conditions, wherever you can
play it, is not to stop in the first place where you might get
stuck! On these surfaces, employ ultra-acute anticipation to
avoid complete stops on uphills or against camber; park facing
downhill; whenever possible, use your own fresh tracks in
which to stop.

Spinning a wheel or wheels violently in an effort to move
off usually fails. It also wears tyre treads away almost as fast
as it melts the ice or snow or spatters mud in all directions.
Much smarter, if stuck and you have tried all the tricks helpful
bystanders love to urge – like "rocking" forwards and backwards at very low revs and in (hopefully) bigger and bigger
sweeps – is to turn off your engine, select neutral, leave your
handbrake off and simply have your vehicle pushed out with
their help. It works!

On a snow-, ice-, or mud-bound get-away, continuing slow
progress, or driving wheels which skid sideways, each prove
wheelspin is still in charge! Directly you ease your acceleration (just enough will do) steering control and traction should
return – just as you should have discovered for yourself in my
wheelspin exercise, above. Once you are under way, get up

your gears as high as you can as soon as you can but *without excess speed*. (See figs. 4 and 16; your engine can still pull in top gear, down to 10 mph on level ground.) This way you minimise the chance of catching another dose of wheelspin.

Uphills On Snow Or Off The Beaten Track
Tackle short climbs with a cautious build-up of speed (after waiting for any drivers ahead of you to clear), so as to keep going and complete them in the highest possible gear. Longer ascents need the gear that will get you right to the top and beyond from the bottom – even if that is a gear lower than you might otherwise have chosen initially. If you try to change gear half-way up, wheelspin may well defeat further progress directly you engage it. (If you do have to change down, do so with confidence, quickly, matching your subsequent accelerator position to your road speed in the new gear with utmost precision.)

Snow usually restricts available road width. Always be prepared to wait at the bottom of a snowbound incline until no one coming down could be remotely endangered by your attempt to go up. Then you can keep out from the gutter, rather than risk being gravitated towards it if the camber is steep; however, your tyre treads bite better into fresh snow, so you must balance this against the possible advantage of choosing virgin snow nearer the edge.

Wheelspin On Everyday Manoeuvres
An outbreak of wheelspin when going at a good speed tests the strongest nerves! No road surface is immune from it, though wet (and more slippery) surfaces clearly demand heightened respect. For example, inadvertent use of an automatic transmission kickdown can precipitate excess power wheelspin, if it occurs whilst you are cornering near to the limit of adhesion on a slippery, wet road.

Any harsh acceleration, even while cornering in no worse than damp conditions, can provoke wheelspin. If you are crazy enough to over-accelerate into a *downhill* bend, the consequences are likely to be dramatically worse . . . Your best preventative is anticipation. So watch all suspect, skiddy surfaces.

Wet roads often portend a somewhat sneaky risk, simply because one wet surface can be very much more slippery than another. Take no chances. If in doubt, go slower – until you can try a *gentle* brake test on a straight section of the road, traffic all around permitting.

On sheet ice, the most feather-light acceleration, even in top gear, can provoke wheelspin. Momentum may at first conceal that it is happening. Never waggle your right toes on ice!

High speed, incidentally, in the context of an icy road, can be anything from walking pace upwards . . .

The expression "hang the back out" rather neatly describes just such a wheelspin skid, in this instance with rear-wheel drive; this skid provides a chilling foretaste of a full spin. It invariably results from excessively punchy acceleration being clapped on, mid corner or bend. The back wheels break away and snake out of line in a most alarming manner – sometimes greatly assisted by bad camber, such as seen in fig. 83. With front-wheel drive, the front end may behave similarly, though usually less violently.

Bald or soggy tyres, lopsided loading, tired shock absorbers, or a wheel running on something extra slippery like a patch of diesel spill or even just a stretch of uneven road, can promote wheelspin. So can aquaplaning of a driven front wheel! Watch not to be caught napping. Attend to mechanical defects.

To kill excess power wheelspin which catches you unawares at immoderate speed, you must slash your acceleration instantaneously – though, as with the take-off wheelspin exercise of a few pages back, *not completely* – sufficient only to stop the wheelspin. The same applies to front-, rear- or four-wheel drive. (To cut it more, during the tightest part of a corner, say, could so unbalance your car that you create a much more serious, All-Four-Wheel, skid – for which, see further below.)

Simultaneously you must steer *into* any sideways skid which may have begun. Steer the same way that your vehicle is sliding. With rear-wheel drive this is more vital – to prevent the car spinning right round, which it has started to do. With front- or four-wheel drive, to straighten your steering, rather than switching it further into opposite lock, is usually enough.

The instant you regain stability, steer again for where you want to go, and *gently* increase acceleration to "set" your vehicle back on course. Fractional acceleration – applied with great sensitivity – is essential to your initial recovery from such a skid.

ALL-FOUR-WHEEL SKIDS

These are too deadly to suggest any exercise to give you experience. I urge you to study this section closely. Then, on the road, you should be well prepared to anticipate and avoid such serious skids. They happen suddenly and develop even quicker. You can be off the road before you can say "woof"!

"Gripped" by an All-Four-Wheel skid, directional adhesion vanishes. You fly off your steered trajectory with all the finality of a stone leased from a sling-shot. Abruptly, you are at the mercy of centrifugal force and momentum. The skid is sometimes described as a 4-Wheel Drift; all wheels, although apparently still rolling, float off course – AWOL. The trigger may be an uncorrected over-acceleration or harsh braking skid, or aquaplaning, in which events you will probably be half expecting it. More often, however, an All-Four-Wheel skid strikes with the surprise of a thunderbolt. You were going too fast. You have misread the conditions . . . Such inattention can snatch control from you as easily at 60 mph on wet as at 17 mph on sheet ice.

You can be ditched off a dead straight road *by excess speed alone*. I saw one lady going 40 mph (while others kept under 15 mph) hit black ice. Zap! Round she went, spinning off, looking surprised. A young man, belting up a wet motorway, hit storm water. He was lucky to finish up the grass bank and alive.

At silly speeds on the edge of control it only wants a bump, a gust of wind, a touch of aquaplaning or some similar free offer, to take you out of this world!

As with all skids – aquaplaning, mechanical defects, excess or unbalanced loading, an uneven road, or surface imperfections caused by things such as water, ice, **Traffic Grime**, **Foreign Bodies On The Surface**, **Adverse Camber**, and also just the fact of being on a downhill slope, can each play a significant part in All-Four-Wheel skids, too – usually just when the factor that matters has escaped your attention! Go back a few pages if you want to refresh your understanding of any of these.

Cornering Too Fast

Nature limits the speed at which a particular vehicle can negotiate a specific corner. Slight bends can be taken faster than tight bends but your safety always hinges on whether your tyres can maintain their sideways grip. Driver skill has its bearing but nature will always win if that skill or the vehicle's design capability is exceeded. One problem of the huge advances seen in vehicle construction is that the point of breakaway, in terms of speed, is nowadays generally so high that inexperienced drivers, gradually taking their corners ever-faster, begin to believe an All-Four-Wheel skid will never happen to them.

Until finally . . .

With rising speed, *straight on momentum* (weight x speed) and centrifugal force together increasingly oppose steering effort. When speed gets too high relative to steering applied, tyre grip must, ultimately, succumb under their combined onslaught. If your worst fears are realised and All-Four-Wheels go at once, you skid (more or less) straight on.

And Now, The Weather
Our weather is unjustly blamed for many a "surprise" All-Four-Wheel skid. Ignorance, as you might expect, is the true culprit.

You must take high winds seriously. Wind normally only affects a car on its own above 50 mph or so. Whereas, in a severe gale, any high-sided vehicle, and cars towing large trailers, may easily get turned on their sides. The latter, along with articulated lorries, may jack-knife, too. When hurricane/gale warning bulletins are broadcast, take notice! If you must still drive, keep well out of the way of all wind-vulnerable vehicles. Bicycles and motorcycles are especially prone to being blown off course, even in quite moderate winds.

The effect, on a solus car, of an exceptional gust in a high wind, is most dramatic on wet roads. You can be slid, bodily, as if shoved rudely by an unseen hand, several metres across your lane. Watch out, whenever you (or anyone near you – especially if he is on two wheels) emerge(s) past a windbreak such as a dual carriageway bridge or a belt of trees, or if you have been shielded by a big lorry or two which you have been overtaking. You must hold your steering wheel firmly, in order to guard against violent wind, from wherever the source . . .

Flash-floods can leave undrained, surface water, pooled or

rippling across the road for several hours. Country lanes, where drainage tends to be poor, are very susceptible to this problem. Hitting such a broad, and possibly quite deep, sheet of water can produce *instant* deadly *aquaplaning* (see page 281) – even at *below* typical aquaplaning speeds. Make sure you are gripping your steering wheel firmly. Hitting one really fast and on *only one side of the car*, can so violently unbalance you, as well, that the wrench itself triggers off a spin. (Then you need razor-sharp reactions: see page 303.)

If, luckily, you do not spin but were, instead, to "sink" back to the road unevenly (as this aquaplaning subsided), that, too, could shoot you off in practically any direction you like to name – especially if you allowed your steering wheels to "land" on the turn . . . Nor would you want to slam your brakes on in panic and "bounce" your front wheels off the water, Dambusters' bombing style, leading into a *Locked-Brake aquaplaning* skid (as described on page 282).

Excessive speed in the wet or in *any* other slippery conditions *can* alone lead to an All-Four-Wheel skid. The most ferocious "other" ones are probably black (unseen) ice and widespread oil spills, where such loss of control can be so unexpected. At least on snow and most other obviously dodgy surfaces, you should already have speed right down and ought to have been anticipating trouble.

My Strongest Advice – *On Preventing All-Four-Wheel Skids*
Constantly weigh-up changing road surface factors. Ignore any minor braking or over-acceleration skid, or a feeling of lightness in your steering, at your peril. At corners, always use the "*Slow* in, *drive* out" technique which I gave you under **Brake Not On The Corner** . . . earlier (page 291).

NEVER DRIVE AT A SPEED FROM WHICH YOU CANNOT, IN THE PREVAILING ROAD CONDITIONS, STOP – WITHOUT SKIDDING – WITHIN THE DISTANCE YOU CAN SEE IS CLEAR. As you encounter blind bends, dips or brows of hills . . . *think* what this means. *Never* arrive at *any* of these at a speed from which you cannot survive an emergency on the way round, in and out, or over, respectively. *Nothing can substitute for slowing sufficiently before these death traps.*

Avoid jerky steering during cornering. Close to the limit of adhesion, that could trigger a skid. Make your steering habit, instead, gentle and progressive and your speed commensurate. The adding on of small steering movements, little by little – as you progress, steadily within the bounds of sensible speed, round a long and tightening bend – will help you retain the feel of how well your car is balanced; by contrast, sharp, excessive movements, that then have to be corrected back, are asking for trouble – especially if you are over-egging your speed.

I can promise you that, if you habitually corner too fast for conditions, especially downhill ones, you are certain to compromise your steering, sooner rather than later. The day will come when the ugly trio I talked of earlier – centrifugal force, momentum and adverse camber – will combine to slam you off the road in short order, with plenty of slither but no dither . . .

Having focused, thus far, almost exclusively on bad road conditions, it would be wrong if I did not warn you in no uncertain terms that – with downright excessive speed – the same thing will, ultimately, happen with precisely the same degree of finality, in the dry, too. Your car will appear to slide, bodily, off the far side of the corner, because the initial steering force you applied will have first turned it partly sideways.

When you overtake, you are often exposed on the "wrong" camber. If you suddenly have to pull back, this adverse camber can prove to be the "last straw" that sets off a skid where, otherwise, there might be none. Think about the possible consequences of the camber *before* committing yourself to pass; not when it is all too late! Often, you must cancel an overtake on a wet day that might have been perfectly safe in the dry; or you must accept, for example, the need to hold back from a downhill pass, one where the addition of adverse camber would stack the odds too highly against you in the event of any unexpected problem.

When you see a fool cornering towards you too fast, watch the camber. Will it whisk him on, into you, if he skids? A correct forecast can save your life if it enables you to keep out of his way!

At lefthand bends, it can pay to keep well in, so as to take the most possible advantage of the favourable camber. In an

301

unpredictable slide, for example on black ice, even an extra quarter of a metre, combined with a bit of helpful camber, can be your saviour. Lacking that extra margin, and perhaps also starting to be gripped by adverse camber, might, instead, spell doom on the very same frozen-over bend. Back in fig. 83, if U had been closer to your edge, U might, despite your late braking, still have managed to escape the various disastrous consequences I there described. On righthanders, however, you should never presume to cut corners to gain a camber advantage. Slow up, much more, instead.

Experienced, faster drivers, always maximise their safety margins against skids, especially at corners, roundabouts and wherever else they can keep camber working for them, rather than against them. On roundabouts, for example, they hug the roundabout edge on the way round (when traffic permits), and then enter their exit road tucked in well to the left, provided pedestrians are not standing footloose anywhere too near to that kerbside.

Understeer And Oversteer

In an All-Four-Wheel skid, it is your front wheels that usually lose their sideways grip first; the rears then join in so fast as makes no difference, turning the skid directly into the full, 4-Wheel Drift.

A purely *front-wheel* skid (which quite often happens) may be regarded simply as a dangerously close cousin of the 4-Wheel Drift; a first step over the edge, as it were; one, however, out of which extrication in one piece is perhaps a little more likely – though probably only for the quick-witted.

The reason why the front wheels are, by a small though usually comfortable margin, normally the first to slide off your steered line when being cornered at excessive speed, is that your car has what is known as *understeer*, built in. The overall balance of the car is designed to uphold this characteristic because it is safer than its opposite number, *oversteer*. An oversteering car would invariably break away at the rear wheels first. That has been proven to be a much more vicious and unstable state of affairs; for the simple reason that rear-end breakaway, coming first, tends, even at quite moderate speed, to be irrecoverable.

A *front-wheel* skid, on the other hand, as you will see shortly, has at least some small hope of redemption, as also does a 4-Wheel Drift where, as just noted, the rear wheels break away *only after* the front ones.

Do not interfere with your car's recommended tyre pressures; you could transform an understeering car into an oversteering one . . .

What To Do When A 4-Wheel Drift Strikes

React fast! Keep your wits. Never yield to panic. If the skid escalates into a spin you will need the advice on page 286. But the immediate thing, if there is room, and time, is that you must steer *into* any *front-wheel* or All-Four-Wheel skid.

Steer like lightning, towards where the *front* is disappearing. Once/if the rear also goes, you may have to steer further into the skid to try to counteract that, too. You have to be just as quick, or quicker, to straighten up again, the instant steering control comes back; otherwise, you will go where you have steered (which is what you are trying *not* to do!)

You must hope that you will win this steering battle, and that your skid will subside whilst you neither brake nor violently decelerate. (You will probably have to hold just a merest touch on your accelerator, in order to propel the car – hopefully – towards where you want it to go. Nil acceleration or, worse, braking, in the midst of this delicate balancing act, can only play you into the hands of that ugly trio, already twice mentioned above.)

And, you must pray this will all be accomplished in time for you to regain control and avoid a smash.

However, you must, as ever, remember that, rather than attempting to save your own skin, the decent thing, in the particular circumstances, may be to "bow out" through a "welcoming" hedge rather than have a head-on crash. Hopefully such points of honour will flash on-screen in your brain at the time . . .

8

Motorways

Learners are not allowed to drive on motorways. However, your Theory Test will include motorway knowledge. One thing you must know is *who else* may not use them. Study the main motorway section of the Highway Code, and also the motorway-specific points to be found under Breakdowns And Accidents and Road Works, together with understanding all signs and road markings applicable to these roads. Make sure you can recognise and obey all motorway electronic signals, for example; that you know what speed limits apply to different types of vehicle on them and which vehicles *may not use* certain outside lanes; that you understand what is and is not, legally, allowed on different parts of a motorway in relation both to driving and to *non-emergency* stopping of *any* kind, and so on. Motorways are also mentioned in several other parts of the Code; prick up your eyes and see if you can spot them!

When you are going to make a long, motorway journey, confirm firstly that your engine oil and coolant levels are satisfactory. These, incidentally, ought to be checked weekly or at least every 1,000 miles. Overheating or seizure, which can happen easily at continuous high speeds if levels are low, is *very* expensive; so watch your oil pressure gauge while you are driving, too, if your car happens to have one. And waste no time checking up, if your oil warning light comes on. Secondly, check before you start that you will not run out of fuel. When you drive fast you burn fuel quicker. If ever the next fuel stop is signed as probably being too far ahead, turn off; never risk running out. Check your tyre pressures and treads before you go. Slightly higher tyre pressures are usually recommended for motorway speeds. (Some car makers suggest stronger quality tyres too; look into this if extensive fast trips are planned, especially if you will be heavily loaded.) Thirdly, make sure you know the junction number at which you will want to leave the motorway, *before getting on to it.* You cannot map-read while driving! The numbers are posted in a small square box on all motorway-related direction signs.

Filthy spray, ejected to the offside of large lorries on motorways, can, as you begin to overhaul them, blot out forward vision in seconds, even by day. Be prepared: see page 269. Get your headlights on; you want the lorry driver to be able to see you coming!

JOINING MOTORWAYS

As you join a motorway, you merge with left-lane traffic exactly as outlined for **Turns** *Onto* **A Dual Carriageway**, on page 233, except that the scale is much bigger; you can expect a much longer acceleration slip road because you will, almost certainly, need to accelerate with much greater whoomph, to match your speed to that of left-lane traffic, before you can merge safely into a sufficient gap within it. (**Note:** Sometimes, your slip road lane may flow on to the motorway to become a new left-lane. Easier, you might expect, but watch out for drivers in another slip road lane already merging out into this new left-lane further ahead of you, as well as for drivers already on the motorway now wanting to join you in this left-hand lane.)

Watch a standard acceleration slip road from a motorway bridge one day. Stay for a good while. Observe how many snags can affect the merging on process. Notice how quite a few, smarter, left-lane motorway drivers move out to the next lane on their right, if safe so to do, before reaching the ingress point where new traffic comes in. (See also **Do Unto Others . . .**, page 238.)

In heavier traffic, when this may not be possible, you are usually best to keep a steady speed. That helps the joining driver(s) to make correct decisions. Nonetheless, you must still keep an eye on every joiner who might not have seen you, or who may make a genuine misjudgement.

If there is one who clearly *is not* intending to Give Way to you in the process of his merging in – despite his obligation so to do – you may need to slow down quite sharply, so that he can get out in front of you before he runs out of acceleration slip road! Alternatively, your best plan here may be to speed up quite early on, thus making it 100% clear to him that he will need to come in somewhere behind you. Only consider this option if you are certain you can pull clear ahead with ease and you are not, at the time, being overtaken.

Look out! When you are joining thick motorway traffic, there may be a strong possibility of a motorway middle-lane driver – to whom YOU would have to GIVE WAY – returning to the lefthand lane at the very same moment that you are about to merge out into it. The most likely time to be caught out on this is when you are poised to nip out ahead of a steady stream of vehicles coming along; for example, this might be one which is headed by a lorry – in front of which you know you have ample acceleration to forge ahead. Because of the narrow sight-lines which you have, that lorry can easily conceal such a middle-lane driver until too late ... Hence mirrors are not enough for these merges. You need a physical look across your right shoulder, to make sure, just in case you will have to hold off making your merge.

Once onto the motorway, wait a while to get used to the higher speeds, before changing lane. Remember that steady driving is the order of the day (or night), keeping well within your capabilities and those of your vehicle, and speed limits. In darkness or poor light, assessment of all that may be happening around you is more difficult. Make extra allowances. Remember headlamps are obligatory at night, whether a motorway is superbly lit or not.

LOOKING FAR ENOUGH AHEAD *AND* BEHIND
I am convinced that one principal cause of motorway accidents is the general failure of drivers to look – and focus – far enough ahead as well as more immediately in front of them. Yes, it *is* a *general* failure.

Lift your eyes to the horizon.

Is traffic up in front, *there*, moving? Is its progress steadily the same in all lanes? Is *all* the traffic moving well, right the way up, betwixt you and there? If that even flow has broken at any point, you should be on the alert, *already* slowing down. Or, if traffic starts bunching, anywhere between you and that

306

horizon, *fall back* likewise, straightaway. Once drivers ahead begin closing-up together, or braking, take the red alert (from their brake-lights) seriously.

Double or treble your immediate *THINKING* time, *braking gap* – NOW! Nothing is easier than catching up again. Except being caught out, unable to brake or stop quickly enough . . .

To see ahead properly and therefore consistently to know the answers to the questions above, you must have, *as well*, a considerably longer gap when behind a lorry than if following a car. (This also allows the lorry driver a better chance of seeing that you exist . . .)

On a straight stretch of motorway (where those next in front of you are more likely themselves to block your view ahead of them), you also need substantially longer following distances than where a motorway flows in a giant curve and thus allows you to see much better past the vehicles closest ahead.

Taking the long view notwithstanding, you must still keep an eye on the man you are first behind; he may run out of fuel, swallow a wasp, suffer a heart attack or have some other, unpredictable crisis, resulting in his vehicle plunging about unexpectedly. And, yes, you must also be watching as best you can, individually, the next half-a-dozen or so vehicles ahead of him, however they may be spread out between all the lanes.

Above all, then, because of the high general speeds, comes watching *that flow*, or lack of it, that is running up to 30, or 60, vehicles ahead, or however many vehicles there may be out there in front, just as far as the eye can see.

At 70 mph, it is those drivers who correctly foresee trouble *that far ahead*, who survive, and help everyone round them to survive, too. At night, and in pelting rain and spray, they are the ones who make our motorways continue to be as wonderfully safe per passenger mile as they are. Whether you drive that fast or not, join their good looks.

A prerequisite of looking far enough **BEHIND**, before changing lane *to your left or to your right* on a motorway, is looking **FOR LONG ENOUGH**. Only my **Mirrors, Mirrors, Mirrors** drivestyle of page 126 can suffice.

Before signalling or moving out to overtake, remember that some drivers exceed the national speed limit by a hefty margin. Ahead of perhaps deciding that you can go before a car

307

a long way back can catch you up, give extra mirror moments, accurately to assess that driver's speed relative to yours.

A nifty glance out of the corner of your eye, back across your right shoulder, should prevent being caught unawares by any driver already committed to passing you. Often, such a driver can be hidden from your mirrors; either because he is already too close or, perhaps, because he has already been skulking there for some time (and, maybe, even some *miles*); or, remember, because he is here returning from a lane further out altogether.

That some such drivers all too frequently "sit", just outside and behind you, for considerable distances on motorways with, apparently, no intention of passing, is wrong. As is made plain from page 136, they should move in behind you, or pass. (In fairness, their progress, completing the latter, is often baulked by being part of a stream of traffic, all of which is overhauling your lane, but so doing only very gradually.)

If you are sure that sitting there for no good reason is what someone, whose speed is no more than yours, is up to, and you wish to overtake whatever is *ahead of you*, you can be faced with the need to "merge", carefully, out ahead of the miscreant. The way to do so is in much the same manner as you merge onto a motorway to begin with. Make sure you signal ample warning and that there is plenty of room. Just as you should not cut in unnecessarily close, after overtaking, you must here avoid cutting out right in front of his nose.

Sometimes, when you are overtaking in the outside lane of a motorway, a driver will come up behind, also in that lane, and maintain his right indicator flashing although he cannot, yet, pass. This is just a way to let you know he would like to pass once you can move over; it's a more polite, unofficial, alternative to a headlamp flash, telling you he is there, only possible because, of course, motorways have no turns to the right directly off the carriageway itself.

MOTORWAY RULES

Essentially, there is no difference between the rules of driving conduct on motorways and those for all other multi-lane dual carriageway roads. You will find all of them fully detailed by looking under **Keeping To Your Lane**, page 136, under **Lane**

Discipline, page 170, and in **Dual Carriageway Overtaking**, page 185. Please refresh your memory on all those sections, prior to your first **M**-way drive – that very day! Secrets of safe driving explained in them apply with re-doubled force on motorways. Mostly higher speeds dictate forward planning even further ahead than on ordinary roads.

SLOWING, STOPPING, LEAVING MOTORWAYS

On motorways even long-experienced drivers can lose all sense of speed if driving fast too long. 70 mph begins to feel like 30 mph. If overtired, dropping to 30 mph can then feel like going backwards! If it happens **STOP DRIVING directly you can.**

Tiredness kills. Hallucination is deadly. Slowing down and moving onto your exit slip road after many miles driven fast, double-check on your speedometer that you really are getting down to an appropriate pace. This saves awful scares. Never drive fast hour-after-hour. Keep sufficient fresh air coming in. Take a minimum ten-minute break and walk-about at least every two hours. If you ever come over drowsy before you can leave a motorway, note that resting on the hard shoulder is illegal. I can only suggest you slow down and keep in the lefthand lane. Open your window, sing, whistle, wriggle, etc., as you go on – but don't let these affect your driving. Pull off at the next exit. Then stop at the first safe place to recover. If rest and recuperative measures still don't revive you and no one else can drive instead, abandon the journey and get some sleep.

Most motorways (and many trunk duals) have a cemented, knobbly, continuous, single white line defining both outside edges of each carriageway. These form an extra, visual aid useful in fog or on mucky nights but their main value at all times is to startle drivers who stray onto them, with sudden noise and rough running instantly fed through their wheels. If you ever do this unintentionally, accept the error as an **extreme wake-up call**. You have probably dozed off in a micro-sleep or a micro-lapse of concentration. Rest is already OVERDUE.

Police cameras have captured devastating film of accident chaos caused by drivers *illegally* reversing back having missed an exit. Should you miss yours, go to the next; it's rarely far.

Beware exits! Eyeball far ahead to confirm each and every slip road hasn't blocked up, with the queue spilling over or about to – bringing the lefthand motorway lane to a halt. This can spread like dominoes falling, into the outer lanes, too, as dangerous drivers either swing out to avoid the queue or even stop in lane 2 in an attempt to queue-barge to leave at the exit.

If traffic in your motorway lane is having to stop, flash your brakelights on to give swift warning to all behind. If it is a sudden stop – especially just after a curve, where the stopped traffic is yet hidden from those behind – add your four-way hazard warning lamps. Keep them on during the final stages of your stop and until your mirrors confirm that everyone behind is *OK for stopping*. It makes sense, here, to pull up with a couple of extra car lengths in hand. Then you have room to move forward if the first subsequent arrival clearly won't be able to stop. This may save you from a bump. In a "concertina" smash from further behind, at least you may avoid being punched forward so far as to hit the innocent party ahead of you. Once it's safe, close up the gap.

M-WAY ACCIDENTS, BREAKDOWNS, ROADWORKS

Look back to Chapter 3 from page 92 to take in afresh your priorities and legal obligations in the event of any accident. Review your Highway Code in respect of motorway rules and those for breakdowns and accidents on them. Accident or breakdown, always shift your vehicle to well back on the hard shoulder directly circumstances allow, unless this is dangerous or impossible. See also pages 275-278. To use a motorway emergency phone never even consider crossing a slip road or the carriageways; go on foot via the back edge of the hard shoulder on your side – where numbered, arrowed posts mark the way to the next one. If using a mobile phone, *first* check the nearest post number so you can give the exact location.

If involved at any accident or breakdown on a motorway all uninjured parties, you included, should be enormously safer (weather and warmth permitting) shepherded *beyond* the hard shoulder to the relative safety of land well away from further accident, fire or explosion risk. Let no one loiter on the tarmac, least of all beside the central reservation. However, it can be unsafe to exit your car unless traffic on adjacent lanes has stopped or you can all step directly onto the hard shoulder from a nearside door. Warn passengers, children especially – who must be kept under control. Don't let animals loose; keep them in the car if you can. Notice how even simple repairs, like changing a wheel, are prohibited on the hard shoulder. Burgeoning traffic has made the hard shoulder a dangerous place to abide, especially at night. Notice how recovery drivers always pull up well clear of a broken down one and invariably turn their steering wheels hard over towards the verge. Statistics prove their wisdom! Follow suit!

I believe casual sighting of a vehicle on the hard shoulder way ahead – too far away to note it is STOPPED – may lead sleepy drivers to think there is another lane on the left. By the time they have drifted inwards, still without focusing on the facts, it's already too late . . . Or have they idiotically tailgated a lorry for miles and suddenly chosen to pull off for an emergency or [illegally] otherwise?

Rejoining the motorway from the hard shoulder treat it as a slip road to pick up a safe merging-on speed. Switch off hazard warning lights. Give a righthand indicator signal. Remember to cancel it afterwards.

Shed loads are hugely dangerous on motorways. Check often that a roof-rack or other carrying system remains secure. Knots must not slip and your fixings must be capable of containing your baggage against momentum in an emergency stop, centrifugal force on corners at speed, and so on. Loads must never project beyond the outline of your vehicle to an extent that could cause danger to others. Do not stop to pick up a fallen object. Phone the police as soon as practicable (see above). Do the same if you see another driver's load about to fall and you believe the driver may be unaware.

Roadworks' signs have, in the Highway Code, a section of their own which especially features the sort found on motorways. Study the precise meanings. Approaching lane closures, re-lane yourself in good time. Whatever other drivers may do, observe the – legally binding – speed limits attached to motorway roadworks, maintain *longer* gaps than usual and avoid switching lanes. It is a chilling fact that, on motorway roadworks' contraflows, twice the normal rate of accidents is statistically proven; and yet drivers in the adjacent, narrow lanes, routinely continue speeding on in opposite directions, apparently – or so it seems – in blissful ignorance. Bright, light green (almost yellow) studs are used to re-define edges and lanes at motorway roadworks. Look for them next time you have the opportunity. Make a mental note of how these look by day and how they show up at night. Then, if you ever chance upon them in fog or bad visibility, you will know instantly that roadworks are at hand. For the same reason you must be clear in your mind, too, about the colour code of motorway (and major dual carriageway) "cats'-eyes" studs. Check the relevant Highway Code rule on reflective road studs as it calls them, now. Has this opened *your* eyes?

Learn the various electronic lane control signals in your Highway Code. Notice how alike the "Change Lane" (to your left) and the "Leave motorway at next Exit" ones are.

Pairs of red lights flashing alternately each side of a square box usually have a steady, large red **X** in the box as well but *not always*. If mounted at the side of the carriageway or on the central reservation **everyone Must Stop when they flash**.

If flashing on a gantry above individual lanes you **Must Not** pass them in those lanes; change to a free lane well ahead of the sign. Be sensible, though; these are rarely used and, if you do have to stop, make it very gently, using hazard warning lights initially. Others close around may be loath to stop while traffic hurtles on in adjacent free lanes. They hope to switch lane soon after the sign instead.

A slip road shut by the red lights forces you to the next exit.

Paired yellow flashing lights above and below the box, with a word, symbol or speed-limit number enclosed therein, likewise command you to respond accordingly before you reach them. Again, you will be wise to expect some drivers not to react until after the sign is passed. (After "End", or as you pass a national speed limit sign, always regain normal cruising speed.)

Huge signs with a white arrow slanting downward on a circular, bright blue background, meaning "keep left" (right if pointing that way – "either side" if two arrows), are often mounted on a yellow background on the back of a motorway roadworks vehicle. Giant yellow lights at each corner of this rear panel flash brightly to stand out from way back. The wagon may be stopped to protect men working in front of it or it may move slowly forward as work progresses. The idea saves closing off lanes completely for repairs. Use care if you need to change lane in advance of reaching the vehicle; slow right down to keep workmen safe. Pass as instructed. Stay in lane until fully clear of the work area.

PRACTICAL
DRIVING TEST
9
On The Day

A few weeks before your Practical Test ask your teacher to run you a mock test. He can ✔ or ✗ below, whether you are up to scratch. Concentrate further lessons putting weaknesses right.

EYESIGHT CHECK...☐
COCKPIT DRILL / ENGINE START ROUTINE...............☐
CONTROL SMOOTHLY: ACCELERATOR, CLUTCH,
GEARS, FOOTBRAKE, HANDBRAKE, STEERING........☐
MOVE AWAY SAFELY – UNDER CONTROL................☐
EMERGENCY STOP – PROMPTLY IN CONTROL.........☐
REVERSE TO LEFT OR RIGHT................................☐
TURN IN ROAD (THREE POINT TURN).....................☐
REVERSE PARKING..☐
SMOOTH START UPHILL..☐
MIRRORS **M-S-M** ROUTINE WELL BEFORE:
SIGNALLING / CHANGING DIRECTION **OR** SPEED....☐
RESPOND TO: SIGNS / LIGHTS / ROAD MARKINGS..☐
GIVE SIGNALS APPROPRIATELY.............................☐
RESPOND TO SIGNALS FROM: OTHER
ROAD USERS / TRAFFIC CONTROLLERS....................☐
USE SPEED APPROPRIATE TO: ROAD SURFACE /
WEATHER / TRAFFIC DENSITY / SPEED LIMITS........☐
MAINTAIN SAFE FOLLOWING DISTANCES.................☐
MAKE REASONABLE SAFE PROGRESS WITHIN
TRAFFIC AND AVOID UNDUE HESITATION...............☐
TACKLE ALL TYPES OF JUNCTION SAFELY:
CORRECT POSITIONING, LANE DISCIPLINE,
EFFECTIVE OBSERVATION AND GOOD CONTROL...☐
JUDGMENT: OVERTAKING, MEETING ONCOMING,
OR CROSSING, OTHER TRAFFIC.............................☐

POSITIONING AND LANE DISCIPLINE:
ON DIFFERENT TYPES OF CARRIAGEWAY ....☐
SAFE CLEARANCE PASSING OBSTRUCTIONS ....☐
COURTESY, CONSIDERATION, CARE – AT ALL
PEDESTRIAN AND CYCLE CROSSINGS ....☐
SELECT SAFE POSITIONS PULLING UP AT KERB ......☐
LOOK AHEAD WHILE OPERATING: LIGHTS,
INDICATORS, WIPERS, HEATER OR DEMISTER ....☐
THINK AHEAD: PREDICT HOW OTHER ROAD USERS'
ACTIONS MAY AFFECT YOU / PLAN / REACT IN
GOOD TIME..☐

Your Practical Test lasts about 40 minutes so that the examiner
can see you cope with a good cross-section of different traffic
situations. He will conduct the Test with clear instructions but
he won't gossip as this can distract. He will ask you to explain,
or show how to do, a couple of frequent maintenance/safety
routines. You can open the bonnet and point. They include
checks/top-ups of engine oil and coolant, brake fluid, screen
washer bottle and tyre pressures, and tyre inspection for faults/
minimum tread. You need to be able to spot a fault in your
brakes, handbrake or steering/power steering and able to confirm indicators, lights and horn all work – the last tested on the
move to make sounding it legal. Such faults may trigger a
dashboard warning display but see also my pages 22, 28, 33,
35, 47, 89, 91/2, 275, and 282-4. Products to use/pressures to
maintain are in your car handbook. Learn quickest, here, by
doing all the checks yourself, guided by someone experienced.

Your car must have **L** plates and current tax disc displayed,
plenty of fuel and be 100% roadworthy, tyres up. As driver, you
take legal responsibility for keeping all windows, mirrors,
lights, reflectors, number plates (and their lamps) reasonably
clean. There must be no malfunction of brakes, major or minor
controls, engine or steering; your handbrake needs easily to
hold the car on steep hills within its normal range of movement;
a non-standard spare wheel must not be used; seat belts must
function properly – remember to fasten same!

Should your examiner find any of the above amiss, he can
stop your Test – just as he can if you drive dangerously. He
requires for his use an extra, interior, "instructor" driving
mirror and prefers to find a built-in head restraint for him. No

baggage is allowed, although you can bring your teacher (gagged . . .) or a non-instructor interpreter by pre-arrangement.

Take to your Test:

1) Your photocard *and* counterpart provisional licence (or valid equivalent and separate photo-identity – page 16)
2) Practical Test appointment notice
3) Theory Test pass certificate
4) Driver's Record and declaration if completed (page 16).

You may like also to carry your insurance certificate as you will be asked to sign a declaration that you are fully covered. If the car is on loan make sure its insurance is valid for you. Wear your glasses or contact lenses if needed. Dress warmly. We react better warm. Your window, unless electric, may be best open, ready for a helpful arm slowing down signal. In fog/ice/snow your Test may be postponed. Confirm it before going.

Drive to your TEST. This gives on-the-day-confidence even if, on the way, things go a little wrong; not to do so is more likely to destroy that confidence. Check beforehand how long it will take to reach the Test centre, allowing for typical traffic at the time you need to go. You want 5 – 10 minutes in hand. Running late won't help you stay calm! Once there, do announce yourself to whoever may be in charge; there may have been a cancellation enabling you to go straightaway.

You need not worry about exam nerves. Your examiner has seen them all before! He is well-trained to spot the difference between bad nerves and bad driving, and won't penalize ordinary "butterflies". If you make, or think you made, some minor error, put it behind you at once. You are allowed up to 15 small faults within a pass. Only a serious or actually dangerous fault committed means he must fail you.

Your Test Pass certificate, combined with your two-part provisional licence, allows you to drive unaccompanied straightaway. Apply for your full licence at once. Legally, you have two years to do so but, if you forget, it's back to **L** plates!

Enjoy your driving always in such a way that others can equally enjoy theirs. Think of yourself at the wheel as part of a team on the road. Every player wants to get home safe; so we must all drive only with the consideration, patience, courtesy and skill which will bring that about. That means you, too!

Index

318